Politics and Rhetoric

Rhetoric is the art of speech and persuasion, the study of argument and, in Classical times, an essential component in the education of the citizen. For rhetoricians, politics is a skill to be performed and not merely observed. Yet in modern democracies we often suspect political speech of malign intent and remain uncertain how properly to interpret and evaluate it. Public arguments are easily dismissed as 'mere rhetoric' rather than engaged critically, with citizens encouraged to be passive consumers of a media spectacle rather than active participants in a political dialogue.

This volume provides a clear and instructive introduction to the skills of the rhetorical arts. It surveys critically the place of rhetoric in contemporary public life and assesses its virtues as a tool of political theory. Questions about power and identity in the practices of speech and communication remain central to the rhetorical tradition: how are we persuaded and can we trust that we are not being manipulated? Only a grasp of the techniques of rhetoric and an understanding of how they orient us towards common situations, argues the author, can guide us in answering these perennial questions.

Politics and Rhetoric draws together in a comprehensive and highly accessible way relevant ideas from discourse analysis, classical rhetoric updated to a modern setting, relevant issues in contemporary political theory, and numerous carefully chosen examples from current politics. It will be essential reading for all students of Politics and Political Communications.

James Martin is Professor of Politics and Co-Director of the Centre for the Study of Global Media and Democracy at Goldsmiths, University of London.

Politics and Rhetoric
A critical introduction

James Martin

LONDON AND NEW YORK

First published 2014
by Routledge
2 Park Square, Milton Park, Abingdon, Oxon OX14 4RN

and by Routledge
711 Third Avenue, New York, NY 10017

Routledge is an imprint of the Taylor & Francis Group, an informa business

© 2014 James Martin

The right of James Martin to be identified as author of this work has been asserted by him in accordance with the Copyright, Designs and Patent Act 1988.

All rights reserved. No part of this book may be reprinted or reproduced or utilised in any form or by any electronic, mechanical, or other means, now known or hereafter invented, including photocopying and recording, or in any information storage or retrieval system, without permission in writing from the publishers.

Trademark notice: Product or corporate names may be trademarks or registered trademarks, and are used only for identification and explanation without intent to infringe.

British Library Cataloguing in Publication Data
A catalogue record for this book is available from the British Library.

Library of Congress Cataloging in Publication Data
A catalog record for this book has been requested.

ISBN: 978-0-415-70667-4 (hbk)
ISBN: 978-0-415-70671-1 (pbk)
ISBN: 978-1-315-88689-3 (ebk)

Typeset in Times New Roman
by Sunrise Setting Ltd, Paignton, UK

For Jacob

Contents

List of tables ix
Acknowledgements x

1 The power of persuasion 1

What is rhetoric? 2
Politics, power and the political 3
Situating rhetoric in time and space 7
Chapter outline 12
Summary 14

2 The truth of rhetoric 15

The sophists and the origins of rhetoric 16
Plato's critique of rhetoric 18
Aristotle and the republican tradition 21
Hobbes, Rousseau and modern sovereignty 26
Summary 31

3 The rhetorical citizen 33

Citizenship, ancient and modern 34
The politics of representation 38
Contemporary political philosophy and rhetoric 43
Summary 50

4 Techniques I: discovery and arrangement 51

The occasions of speech 52
The issue 55
The discovery of the argument 57
Arrangement 65
Summary 70

5 Techniques II: style and delivery — 71

Style 72
Figures of speech 75
Delivery 83
Summary 87

6 Rhetorical political analysis — 88

Political science, ideas and interpretation 89
Rhetorical situations and political strategies 94
Structure, agency and rhetorical intervention 97
Analysing rhetoric: a method and an example 99
Summary 106

7 Democracy, rhetoric and the emotions — 107

Deliberative democracy 108
The affective unconscious: neuroscience and psychoanalysis 113
Affective strategies and emotional orientation 120
A rhetorical democracy? 124
Summary 125

8 Media rhetoric: speaking for the public — 127

Mediating the public domain 128
Public sphere, marketing or showbusiness? 131
Media rhetoric: the example of TV news 137
Counterpublic rhetoric 143
Summary 146

9 Embodied speech: rhetoric and the politics of gender — 148

Situating gender 149
Feminism and rhetoric 154
Gender and the nation 160
Summary 166

Afterword — 167

Bibliography — 170
Index — 184

Tables

4.1	The five canons of rhetoric	52
4.2	The genres of speech	53
4.3	Status theory	57
4.4	The three types of appeal	58
4.5	The parts of speech	66

Acknowledgements

This book took a little longer to complete than I had originally expected. I am very grateful to my editors at Routledge – Craig Fowlie and Nicola Parkin – for their generous patience. I am thankful also to those who have made me think about the various dimensions of speech and persuasion: my mother, Helen, for introducing me to a life of political argument, and my sister, Kate, for demonstrating the importance of style; Susan, Esmé, Luis and Jacob, for supplying dialogue, debate and disagreement; and the following, for reading or hearing parts of the text and passing on much needed wisdom: Judi Atkins (who read the whole thing and kindly provided copious, helpful notes), Soraia Almeida, Giuseppe Ballacci, Alan Finlayson, Terrell Carver, Derek Hampson, Dai Moon, Saul Newman, Nick Turnbull and Graeme Wise. I owe much to all the students on my rhetoric courses at Goldsmiths, where most of the ideas were first tried out, and to participants of various conferences and seminars, including the UK Political Studies Association and its Rhetoric and Politics Specialist Group, the ECPR, the Manchester Workshops in Political Theory, seminars at Goldsmiths (with the Centre for the Study of Global Media and Democracy) and the Universities of Leicester, Nottingham, Swansea and Westminster. Of course, in spite of all the intelligent advice offered by many, responsibility for what follows remains my own. An earlier version of Chapter 6 has appeared in *Political Studies* and I would like to express my thanks to the journal's editors for permission to republish it here.

1 The power of persuasion

It is difficult to imagine politics without persuasion. By its very nature politics requires choices to be formulated, options to be weighed and decisions to be made. Often the uncertainty or ambiguity of the world forces us to confront a plurality of contrasting perceptions of our situation and opposed views of how to act. At such moments – moments of dramatic crisis, perhaps, but also in the more routine, day-to-day choices – people need to be persuaded in order to proceed with any degree of confidence. If everything was certain and clear, if nothing were open to chance, it would be a world without choices, a strangely unhuman world devoid of the anxieties such choices generate. However attractive that sounds to you, it would be, nonetheless, a world without politics.

Persuasion is integral to politics because politics involves making judgements in contexts of uncertainty about what to do. To persuade in such contexts involves transforming, primarily by means of argument, a variety of possible options into a unified judgement, perhaps even a decision. There are many ways to persuade, no doubt, and threatening violence is one of the most common. But human communities are perhaps unique in their use of speech in making persuasion a matter not always or exclusively of brute force, but also of mutual understanding, shared perceptions and interpretations, however temporary or tenuous. The power of persuasion, then, can be just as effective as – if not more so than – the force of arms. Indeed, organized violence is usually accompanied by some effort at justification to make it appear the right thing to do. It would be fair to say, then, that speech – the ability to address others and to define problems and their solutions – is the dominant medium of persuasion in human societies. Knowing how to speak – whether in voiced words, written text or a combination of both – in order to successfully persuade may be *the* fundamental political knowledge or skill, arguably the original 'political science'. The ancient name given to the body of knowledge whose object is the practice of speech and persuasion is *rhetoric*.

The purpose of this book is to introduce readers to the study of rhetoric in politics. That means grasping common ways in which techniques of persuasion operate in political life; how argumentative strategies are employed to shape judgements. But it also means understanding how the parameters of political debate are themselves conditioned, delimiting who can argue, about what and how. In this latter sense, rhetoric is more than just a collection of nifty techniques;

it is bound up with wider issues in political theory concerning the nature of power, authority and citizenship.

Rhetoric, I am suggesting, reveals to us the character of *the political*; that is, how, in speech encounters of various kinds, the limits of human association are acknowledged, fabricated and contested. Speech aimed at persuasion – whether in private or in public – is a powerful channel of energies, one directed as much at fashioning human subjects and the conditions under which they make choices as it is at moulding their judgements. To harness these energies is to lay claim to a power to generate a force of some kind – perhaps a force of agency, public opinion or community – to confront the uncertainties of the world.

In politics, then, speech mobilizes the power of persuasion. In the chapters that follow I offer a rhetorical approach to politics aimed at illuminating how persuasive speech garners this power and how rhetorical tools can help us understand it. But rhetoric – like politics itself – is riven with controversy and sometimes confusion. In the remainder of this chapter, I argue that its controversial nature alerts us to the intrinsically political dimension of persuasive speech and communication, the way in which these simultaneously disclose and mask relations of power. I then set out the approach to rhetoric adopted in this book and sketch the content of its chapters.

What is rhetoric?

The word 'rhetoric' derives from the ancient Greek *rhetorike*, meaning the 'art' (*tekhne*, or skill) of persuasive discourse undertaken by a *rhetor* (an orator or speaker) (see Burke, 1969: 49–55). It refers simultaneously to instruction in this practice and to the persuasive qualities of a discourse itself. That makes it – perhaps rather oddly – both a mode of enquiry and the object of that enquiry. Studying rhetoric can mean either learning about the skills of persuasion (that is, taking instruction in communicative techniques in order to achieve persuasion) or finding the persuasive element in a discourse (that is, examining 'its' rhetoric). Consequently, it is difficult wholly to separate subject and object, the human skill of persuasion from the intrinsic persuasiveness of a discourse. This raises a number of questions. When we are persuaded, is it because an idea or an argument just *is* persuasive? Or is persuasion a consequence of purposeful manipulation on the part of the speaker? Does the force of persuasion derive from a technique (that can be mastered by anyone) or from an independent quality (that only the gifted can know)? These questions, arising from the definition of rhetoric, underpin a deeper, fundamental uncertainty that haunts politics more generally. What is happening when people form their judgements? Why do they believe what they do? How can we know they are the right judgements? Can people be persuaded of *anything*?

These questions about the sources and validity of persuasion have come to warp our perception of the practice itself. Today the study of rhetoric remains present largely on the margins of democratic life, the preoccupation of classics scholars and, sometimes, nostalgic journalists. The word has an unfortunate, musty aura reminiscent of the book titles in the darker quarters of a university library. Indeed, more often than not these days the term is associated with speech oriented primarily towards deception, superficiality or manipulation. 'Rhetoric' is routinely contrasted with speech that adheres to 'reality' or with the 'truth' that can be found 'behind' words, the truth of real 'interests' or intentions that are deliberately obscured by language.

That rather negative use of the term is not how rhetoric is understood in this book. But let us not dismiss it without a thought. For it gives a clue to the ambivalent feelings we frequently have for persuasion in democracies, where speech is simultaneously an essential ingredient of politics but, quite often, the perceived source of its decline. Clearly, democracy means little without the opportunity to speak freely in public, to air our views, to persuade others of their value, to hold to account our politicians and governments and demand answers from them, perhaps even to become leaders ourselves and speak to, and on behalf of, our fellow citizens. Free speech, from this point of view, is not just a luxury in a democracy: it is its *sine qua non*, that without which popular judgements would be unable to influence public authority. But, at the same time, we are forever wary that free speech can result in the dissemination of the most ill-informed, repulsive and sometimes injurious views as contenders for public judgement. Democracy permits the spiteful, the prejudiced and the plain small-minded to have their say as much as it does the noble, the wise and the eloquent. It allows politicians to talk in simplistic 'soundbites' or grey, technocratic jargon so as to evade serious scrutiny. When they aren't pandering to public opinion, don't politicians regularly get accused of offering only 'hot air' precisely because we know it doesn't usually translate into practical change?

In modern democracies we despise and fear speech just as much as (if not more than) we honour it. We curse the 'liars' and the deceivers just as we desire inspiration and eloquence from our leaders. For every Rev. Martin Luther King Jr or Sir Winston Churchill there are many more, sadly less inspiring politicians to hand. Worse still, there are demagogues and firebrands only too willing to seduce us into endorsing the most despicable choices. Each uses the medium of speech, but how do we tell them apart? Persuasive speech, we might say, functions as both poison and cure to democracy. By consequence, the skill of rhetoric, where speech is deliberately manipulated to render it persuasive, is quietly cherished but – more often than not – dismissed and derided.

Politics, power and the political

The suspicion displayed by many towards rhetoric is a reminder that persuasion involves the exercise of power. But what kind of power is it? Not one whose effects and limits are always easy to define objectively. At one level, persuasion is a process whereby we are invited freely to give our assent, or not, to a point of view or claim. As the rhetoric scholar Kenneth Burke wrote: 'Persuasion involves choice, will; it is directed to a man only in so far as he is *free*' (Burke, 1969: 50; italics in original). Unlike propaganda or physical force, persuasion requires some independence of judgement, an ability to weigh up or assess an argument and choose or refuse to endorse it. In short, persuasion involves letting oneself be persuaded.

Yet, at another level, to be persuaded is a way of submitting to another. While we usually don't mind being persuaded by people we trust, or when little is at stake, in politics it is often relative strangers who seek our support, sometimes on matters of great significance. As Burke also points out, persuasion invites us not only to agree abstractly but, often, to *identify* with the point of view of someone separate from us: 'If men were not apart from one another, there would be no need for the rhetorician to proclaim their unity' (ibid.: 22). Yet because of this urge to identify or create a sense of unity between speaker and audience, we may also be conscious that to affirm another's arguments is also to approve of their authority over us – perhaps their superior intelligence or their right to make decisions in our name – or to link us to further judgements of which we may disapprove. Persuasion in politics is often a way of achieving or keeping office, of using resources in specific ways, of weakening opponents or sustaining alliances. To seek or to be the subject of persuasion is therefore to engage in subtle relations of power and to be complicit in some way with them. This complicity is all the more binding because we freely choose to accept it.

Uncertainty over the power of persuasion directs us towards a fundamental theoretical distinction that is of increasing significance to contemporary social and political theory and that will guide the discussion in this book: the distinction between 'politics' and the dimension of 'the political'. Hostility to rhetoric, I want to suggest, often represents an urge to minimize or remove altogether the political dimension from politics, to empty speech of the sense of power, contingency and controversy that the political arouses and to isolate judgement from the risks of possible manipulation. But first, what is the difference between these two terms? The distinction could be said to be between established social institutions and practices and the wider principles that 'ground' the polity and define its parameters and purposes (see Mouffe, 2005: 8–9). Politics refers, broadly, to the activities of administering and bargaining between organized interests, forming coalitions, developing policy and taking decisions on the basis of instituted relations and procedures (or the 'rules of the game'). The political, on the other hand, denotes the abstract frames or principles that define, for example, who gets represented, what kind of issues are legitimate topics of dispute and which social groups are recognized as 'acceptable' participants in politics, or not. The political names a dimension of controversy and, potentially, violence where some options are ruled in and others ruled out. It is sometimes argued to be 'ontological' in that it concerns the *being* – or basic identity – of social and political existence (Marchart, 2007). Thus we might say that the routine work of assemblies and parliaments, politicians and activists, government officials and civil servants largely comprises politics, while ideas about sovereignty, freedom or justice invoke the political.

Politics is always premised on the partial settling of political questions. Without some idea of what politics is for (to serve the common good, protect liberties or increase national glory, for example) or how different agents relate (as equal parts in an organic whole, a rigid hierarchy or a diverse plurality), politics would collapse into random exchanges lacking any coherence or durability. Politics therefore depends upon the political dimension to define limits to what can legitimately be said and done, not just in terms of law but also in terms of the ideals that inform the law. The political is not therefore a separate domain but a horizon inside which the myriad activities of politics are given coherence. Beyond the horizon, however, lies uncertainty and the threatening (or liberating) realization that politics might be done quite differently.

One reason why rhetoric is viewed with such suspicion, I want to suggest, is that it is frequently a marker of the contingency of our political horizon, its essentially groundless nature. That is to say, the basic structure of all political relations – the constitutive principles defining the space and time given over to the exchanges of politics – is founded not on eternal truths set in stone but on historical, fundamentally arbitrary and hence contentious decisions about who citizens are and how they relate to each other and the world. Judgements on these decisions are always, in principle, open to contest and reformulation, reflecting power relations that can be challenged and changed. But their contingency is something that is often resisted for fear that social order will be undermined.

The dismissal of rhetoric is one symptom of that concern. Sometimes it reflects an anxiety about what are regarded as 'basic truths' collapsing into 'mere politics' – that is, sacred principles being exposed to the amoral cut-and-thrust of party advantage and strategy. Thus the desire to eliminate rhetoric often comes in the form of a longing for certainty and security about these truths or via the image of a purified language that can eradicate scurrilous manipulation from judgement-making (see Garsten, 2006; Fish, 1989: 471–78). Or it might even take the form of a politics reduced to technocratic problem solving, removed from public life altogether and untroubled by controversial questions. At an extreme, such anti-political longing emerges as a violent refusal to accept that the organizing principles by which any group or society creates its shared world could or should ever be put into question. As we shall see later, eliminating rhetoric has been a feature of anti-political thinking for centuries.

Indeed, it is when the dimension of the political is brought into view – that is, when politics is understood as premised upon contingent decisions over basic principles – that the potential violence underlying human association is dramatically revealed. Such was the case, for example, during the so-called 'Arab Spring' of 2011, when a politics instituted around dictators was challenged by publics who no longer acquiesced to their rule. The political dimension that infuses all institutionalized politics is an uncomfortable, sometimes inconvenient reminder that such arrangements are premised not on nature, identity or universal agreement but, rather, on past decisions to coerce, exclude, suppress or ignore alternative arrangements. Often, public discourse can itself help repress such decisions, especially when such discourse is restricted to empty rituals, narrow routinized exchanges or formal procedures. But, as the rebels and protestors of Tunisia, Egypt and Libya (among others) demonstrated, new discourses can also reactivate the political dimension, exposing the habits and customs of institutionalized politics to the threat of their own dissolution.

Rhetoric is often dismissed because implicit to it is the nagging realization that there is always another argument to be made, an alternative point of view, that threatens consensus and order. It reveals public judgements to consist of certainties that have to be actively made, not assumed, and hence politics is ultimately a risky, uncertain and rather inconclusive business. But instead of eliminating the political from speech and persuasion, we could instead try to restore it and face up to its challenge. Rhetorical persuasion might properly be understood as a form of *mediation* between politics and the political. That is to say, argumentative practices link routine politics to essentially contentious judgements about the basic dimensions and limits of human association, reinforcing, contesting or even repressing them in varying degrees. In that respect, there is always a trace of violence (whether real or implied) that surrounds political rhetoric because 'matters of principle' invoke the limits of what is thinkable and do-able. As Slavoj Žižek has remarked, although language is often perceived as the medium for mutual recognition and peaceful exchange, 'there is something violent in the very symbolisation of a thing' (Žižek, 2008a: 52). Language, he argues, carves up the world into meaningful 'things', inserting them within one symbolic frame rather than another. In politics, the fundamentally arbitrary character of that frame is, to some extent, always partially exposed. We are never very far away, therefore, from the 'unconditional violence' – as Žižek puts it – which underscores all language and threatens to manifest itself materially in state repression, 'terrorism' or resistance, rebellion or dissent.

We can detect this underlying political dimension at work in rhetoric when the basic limits of association are perceived to be at stake, giving rise to controversy and a sense of unease or danger (see Marchart, 2007: 38–44). International politics is replete with such situations in which a precarious order is brought into question. Think, for instance, of Winston Churchill's wartime speeches as British Prime Minister in the 1940s. His powerful, sombre orations before parliament and on public radio are now widely admired for their steadfast determination to defeat the Nazi enemy 'at all costs' and to protect the independence of the United Kingdom. At stake here were the very foundations of civility, sovereignty and freedom. Churchill's rhetoric is routinely invoked as an exemplary patriotic and inspirational voice, rising above the fray of normal politics to express deeply felt common values and unifying its audience around the defence of fundamental principles – what Burke called identification. A profoundly political sensibility permeates these speeches, charging them with a sense of the underlying violence of the situation.

Yet it would be mistaken to think that Churchill's speeches expressed an entirely uncontentious set of values. In fact, his rapid rise to national leadership in 1940 came as a consequence of serious disagreement over the policy of appeasement followed by Prime Minister Chamberlain before him. A substantial part of the political class had been convinced that war could be avoided by negotiating with Hitler. The purported failure of that policy became a matter of public controversy in popular books such as *Guilty Men* (written by the anonymous 'Cato'; see Cato, 2010), which denounced erstwhile leaders and ridiculed their strategy. Churchill came to power on the heels of controversy and, certainly in the early period of his premiership, remained a figure of suspicion even in his own party (thus, in order to prevent instability in his government, he retained many of the pre-war leaders, including Chamberlain). Only after the experience of war, once Churchill's qualities as a statesman were confirmed, was 'appeasement' universally regarded as a derogatory term for poor international policy. We easily forget the controversy that prepares the way for the ascendancy of principle.

It is wrong, then, to think that the political dimension exists entirely in isolation from the strategic aspect of politics. In the daily flurries of institutional politics, the grand ideals and universal principles that are claimed to 'found' the community are always subject, to some extent, to the play of minor interests and struggles for advantage among competing parties. But it is also wrong to view the political dimension as simply reducible to a plaything of politics. Rather, the two are constantly interweaving and in rhetoric we find, simultaneously, efforts to foreground certain principles and close off others (the political) – and to do so without also undermining the 'relations of force', as the Marxist thinker Antonio Gramsci (1971) called them, upon which such choices are built (politics). In this meeting point between the political and politics we find the power of persuasion.

In this book I conceive of rhetoric through the mediated distinction between politics and the political. Persuasion is both a mundane business *and* a channel of wider power relations; a process of coalition building *and* an effort to define higher principles. Too often these aspects are separated off from each other, with 'empirical' politics and day-to-day debate divided from the considerations of political philosophy and theory. But to understand how persuasion functions we need to see the two at work together. When it is considered at all, rhetoric is sometimes associated simply with one or the other: for example, with a scurrying for advantage ('just rhetoric') or with the great statements of famous orators (the 'great speeches that changed the world'). The first invokes an image of politics without the political, while the second imagines the political without politics. If we are to have a better understanding of rhetorical persuasion, we need to see how each works with and affects the other.

Situating rhetoric in time and space

What exactly does the study of rhetoric comprise? Rhetoric is now an inclusive term for a wide range of themes related to communicating, arguing and persuading through symbols. A tremendous variety of scholarly books and journals are currently devoted to aspects of this expansive discipline. Its scope is simply too great for any one text to cover in sufficient depth. Rhetoric is studied in fields such as classics and history (see Habinek, 2005; Conley, 1990), literature (see Richards, 2008; Cockcroft and Cockcroft, 2005), law (see Brooks and Gewirtz, 1996; Goodrich, 1987), philosophy (Meyer, 1994; Grassi, 1980; 1983), cultural studies (see Brummett, 2011; Sellnow, 2010), organizational studies

(Hoffman and Ford, 2010), psychology (Billig, 1991, 1996) and even economics (see McCloskey, 1998). Traditionally concerned with written and spoken communication, the study of rhetoric now comprises visual forms, too (see Hill and Helmers, 2004; Kostelnick and Hassett, 2003). The approach adopted in this book is to introduce elements of rhetoric as they concern the study of politics and political theory. The main focus of the volume will therefore be on political discourses – that is, speech oriented towards relations of power and practices of citizenship.

In focusing on power and citizenship I do not mean to deny the political pertinence of the other areas of rhetorical investigation noted above. Rather, I seek to address a specific gap in political studies. Although rhetoric was originally an integral part of civic life in ancient Greece and Rome, the contemporary academic study of politics to a great extent neglects the role of speech and oratory (but see Skinner, 2002a: especially ch. 10; Garsten, 2006; Charteris-Black, 2005). There are many reasons for this, including the professionalization of politics, the proliferation of technologies such as television and the dominance in political studies of 'scientific' methods directed at measuring 'inputs' and 'outputs' rather than interpreting meanings (see Nelson, 1998). Despite these developments, politics continues predominantly to be an activity of communicating and arguing in order to persuade audiences. Certainly we live in a highly mediated age where texts and images are consumed in far greater quantities than ever before, but that does not diminish the relevance of speech and persuasion so much as it qualifies and transforms it (see Jamieson, 1988). Of course, we cannot simply transplant ancient ideas and apply them to the present, but we can let these provoke us into thinking more about what distinguishes the present. At the core of this volume, then, is a view that politics remains a stubbornly practical business of communicating and persuading.

It may, of course, be objected that to give attention to rhetoric is to take seriously politicians and the things they say and do. That is true, but it need not be an objection. A common prejudice is that politicians are utterly self-interested, amoral actors who neither merit close scrutiny nor require theoretical analysis. While that may be so in many instances, nonetheless it is a prejudice in need of correction. Not all political actors are professional politicians involved in the institutionalized processes of government and party politics. The term 'politician' can refer to any individual or group that seeks to promote a political position, whether inside or outside formal institutions. Moreover, politicians (in the broad sense) are usually self-appointed agents of social change and innovation. Their words are often themselves deeds, or ways of acting. As Kari Palonen argues, to understand what they do, we need to 'read politicians as theorists' in their own right (see Palonen, 2005: 359). Politicians use ideas, theories and arguments in a 'situated' way to define the present circumstances, to forge coalitions, judge policies, contest government actions or advocate alternative ways of thinking and doing politics. Unlike most professional theorists, politicians inventively navigate the constraints and opportunities of politics to re-fashion ideas as legitimation for action. A rhetorical perspective on politics invites us to discard our prejudices about politicians and to explore how political actors put theories and ideas to work (see also Wodak, 2011).

But why use rhetoric to examine what politicians do, rather than, for example, language, ideology or discourse? What is it that rhetoric offers that these more familiar categories do not? A preliminary answer is that *rhetoric permits an understanding of persuasive speech as a situated practice of argumentation.* To explore rhetoric is to consider how, at specific moments and locations, ideas are fashioned into arguments with a certain force and direction in order to win the assent of an audience. This definition underscores the dimensions of *time* and *space* as defining features of rhetorical persuasion, a point related to the idea of 'the political' as a horizon discussed earlier. Time refers to processes of simultaneity, change, speed and duration; space implies the co-presence of ideas and objects, relationships and distances between things. Speech aimed at persuasion is often a creative articulation of various times and spaces: the time and place of the speech occasion (the moment that gives rise to it and the event of its delivery), the time and space of the message (its sense of urgency, its ordering of priorities and so on) and the time and space of wider events into which it intervenes (the enduring effects it may have on politics in the future).

These temporal and spatial aspects interweave in rhetorical persuasion, helping to generate a sense of agency and purpose by mapping, via speech, a landscape of connections and hierarchies, certainties and risks, to shape judgements about how to proceed and to endow those judgements with affective force. In that respect, rhetorical persuasion is akin more to early cartography than to philosophy: it plots the terrain upon which we make our choices and alerts us to safety and danger ('Here be dragons!'), offering its audiences degrees of orientation in an otherwise unsteady world. Thus persuasion entails imaginatively recreating the context inside which a judgement is to be made about what to think or how to act.

A proper understanding of this jointly situated and resituating process undoubtedly overlaps with the study of language, ideology or discourse but, at the same time, it is not reducible to any one of these specialised discipline areas. Let me explain in more detail. In the past century, a broadly 'constructivist' idea of language came to inform a variety of philosophical and social scientific enterprises (see Taylor, 1985a: especially ch. 2; Rorty, 1989). Accordingly, language is the medium through which humans construct their cultural and material world and their sense of self. The grammars and vocabularies, concepts and categories of language shape what can be thought, perceived and said. To understand human beings, then, we must not only observe their behaviour but also interpret the meanings they employ to construct a world. Although it has ancient origins that long pre-date the so-called 'linguistic turn' in philosophy and the human sciences, continued interest in rhetoric today owes much to this conception of human action as linguistically mediated (Bernard-Donals and Glejzer, 1998).

But we should not equate rhetoric exclusively with language. Not all language is rhetorical – that is, used for persuasive ends – nor is rhetoric strictly linguistic (it involves gestures and sounds as well as words). Moreover, there is a danger of missing the way it is related to politics if we hold too strongly to the notion of language as fully constitutive of self and world. Rhetoric is important precisely because language regularly *fails* to constitute its object. It is because crises and dilemmas, conflicts and accidents occur that rhetoric is necessary. When established vocabularies cannot fully make sense of what has happened or how to proceed, then rhetoric helps to reassemble words and meanings in order for the world to make sense again. Of course, this work will of necessity involve language. But, as Sam Chambers argues, language is 'not merely a problem *for* politics but a problem *of* politics' (2003: 17): politics itself *is* the ongoing practice of reassembling self and world, given their repeated resistances to stable symbolization. Rhetoric weaves language and world together again and again because meaning is only partially stable, at best. Hence rhetoric is not identical to language but works through and around the gaps that prevent language from fully constituting a meaningful world.

We might say, then, that the spatial ordering of the world given in language is interrupted by time (or change). Some truths no longer hold; others don't hold for everybody or in all instances. That is why rhetoric is preoccupied with arguments. Arguments activate a preferred view of the relationship between symbols and the world, perhaps a hierarchy of values or an order of thinking, strengthening some connections and weakening others in order to reinforce or change a judgement where the durability of truth is in doubt. In rhetoric, ideas are given force and direction – that is, a sense of weight and purpose – within the work of an argument. It is, to follow J.L. Austin's famous title, a way of doing things *with* words (see Austin, 1962). But it is always a tentative and temporary kind of doing, with no guarantee that words can permanently hold down the meanings they are given (see Derrida, 1988).

If arguments are central to rhetoric, then why not look at political ideology? Ideology is a term used to describe an enduring constellation of associated concepts, values and arguments that orient political actors towards distinct programmes of government and social interests (see Freeden, 1996). This spatial arrangement of connecting concepts and making associations between them is typically recognized as partial in as much as it privileges some ideas at the expense of others, treating particular values as incontestable and universal while diminishing or contesting others. Ideologies such as socialism or ecologism are organized belief systems that may overlap in various aspects, but remain distinct in so far as they embody a selective preference for some principles or values, such as social and economic equality or environmental protection. Ideology therefore shares the argumentative orientation of rhetoric.

If there is undoubtedly a parallel between rhetoric and ideology, in its common usage the latter terms tend to direct us to established *systems* of ideas and arguments (liberalism, fascism and so on) and not to the practice of assembling them through forms of address to specific audiences. Rhetoric certainly is ideological in so far as it draws upon and adds to ideological systems but, again, it is not reducible to these (see Weiler, 1993). Sometimes speech and argument re-fashion ideologies in new ways, selecting elements that are thought to 'belong' to opposed systems and combining them in novel forms. On occasion there is no obvious ideological home at all for an argument; it may place itself simultaneously in a variety of ideological categories, or none at all (see Bastow and Martin, 2003). Nevertheless, ideology remains an important resource for the study of rhetoric in as much as arguments draw upon and rework enduring ideological configurations, which comprise already established scripts (see Finlayson, 2012).

What, then, of discourse? This term has become ubiquitous in recent social and political investigation, particularly in the fields of linguistics (especially critical discourse analysis; see Fairclough, 1993; Wodak, 2011) and social theory (see Howarth, 2000). Instead of referring us to stable systems of language or arguments, discourse usually places our focus on dynamic, often temporally changeable meanings that shape social practices and that are actively transformed across time and space. The emphasis on making meaning lends discourse a more fluid, inventive character than ideology. Like ideologies, discourses certainly have structure. But the term gives primacy to the malleability of that structure as it is reproduced in different contexts.

In that respect, discourse invokes the situated and 'at-work' character of rhetorical speech as a process of assembling ideas at specific moments. Discourse exceeds the closed system of ideas often associated with political ideology. In the work of thinkers such as Foucault, the term also has an ontological inflection. That is, it refers to ways in which social identity (the 'being' of human subjects, or subjectivity, rather than just their political values or interests) is itself determined through a combination of ideas and practices embedded in claims to knowledge and authority (see Foucault, 1980: ch. 6; 1972). As Foucault understood them, discourses are infused with power, conceived as a productive capacity, in that they create positions from which to speak. This is not power conceived as a force imposed on individuals from outside. Rather, it is a 'fluid' power by which selfhood is cultivated, perhaps even in resistance to dominant norms (see Phillips, 2006). Discourses 'recruit' (rather than trap) subjects, allocating them roles and shaping them in unconscious ways that often evade scrutiny. For example, discourses of race and gender shape the self-perception of subjects: the ways they are viewed by others, how they use their bodies and what they can properly say and feel about them. If ideology gives us scripts to argue from, then discourses position us on the stage, making us visible (or not) and authorizing us to speak (or not).

Yet the breadth of discourse (for instance of race, gender or nationhood) gives it a scope that extends beyond the situated encounters usually analysed by rhetoricians. Rhetoric is, undoubtedly, a form of discourse in that it disseminates meanings that shape experience and recruit subjects. But one key virtue of rhetorical study is its concentration on speech and argument in specific, situated encounters. Much discourse theory makes use of the terminology of rhetoric to talk about social groups and identities, but often at high levels of abstraction that refer back to complex systems of thought (see Howarth, Norval and Stavrakakis, 2000; Howarth and Torfing, 2004). It might be helpful, then, to regard rhetoric as a means to focus on discourses in their operation at the level of particular events, texts and encounters. If discourses organize social practices (that is, inscribe meanings on the activities that subjects undertake), rhetorical analysis explores the moments at which discursive 'regimes' are introduced and reproduced through argument. In that way, rhetorical study permits analysis of concrete interventions that aspire to become effective, perhaps dominant discourses. Like ideology, then, we can say that discourse is refracted through rhetoric, but it is not its primary concern. Rhetorical practices may introduce and, eventually, help to establish, extend or transform a discourse. But *as* rhetoric, its eventual outcome is still to be determined.

So if rhetorical study overlaps with the related concerns of language, ideology and discourse, it is nonetheless distinctive because it mobilizes aspects of all three in the generation of persuasive speech. Rhetoric describes the construction of meanings through language, often by drawing upon ideological associations to define that meaning in selective ways and discursively constructing the subjects who are to act through it. But these are achieved through *concrete* modes of address and argumentation, which are typically the concern of rhetorical enquiry. There is not a hard-and-fast distinction to be made between rhetoric and these other areas of analysis, so we should not see them as mutually exclusive. But, as we shall see later in the book, rhetorical study invites us to dwell on language, ideology or discourse as they are situated at intersections of time and space.

Chapter outline

The book is arranged in such a way as to introduce various aspects of rhetoric across a broad spectrum of issues. It does so in a series of steps: in Chapters 2 and 3 I discuss the relationship of rhetoric to political theory; in Chapters 4 and 5 I survey the classifications and techniques of rhetorical instruction; in Chapter 6 I reflect on how these techniques can be mobilized to analyse political strategies; and in Chapters 7, 8 and 9 I consider aspects of rhetoric in distinct domains where persuasive discourse is politically salient: namely democracy, the media and gender. Overall, I argue a number of things: rhetoric is central to a theoretical understanding of politics; the categories of rhetoric inherited from ancient writers remain illuminating and useful; and these categories can be supplemented with the help of contemporary theory to understand how judgements in politics are produced politically.

Let me now sketch the content of each chapter in turn. In Chapter 2 I explore the troubled relationship of rhetoric and political theory. Many classical thinkers believed rhetorical speech and its instruction to be central to the life of political association. This was the view promoted by Aristotle and later advocates of the republican form of government. Nonetheless, since then, political theory has tended to disparage rhetoric as a menace and even a threat to the maintenance of social order and authority. Thinkers such as Plato initiated this view by counterposing rhetoric to philosophical 'truth'. Modern political thinkers, such as Hobbes and Rousseau – although they reject Plato's notion of rational truth – retain the idea that rhetoric threatens political order and needs to be restrained.

Chapter 3 continues the examination of the status of rhetoric by focusing on its role as a tool of the citizen. I begin by noting the substantial difference between citizenship in the ancient and modern worlds. The classical advocates of republican politics regarded speaking and participating in public life as central elements of citizenship. But modern citizens are encouraged to look to private not public life as the source of fulfilment and rhetoric is no longer an explicit component of citizenship. Nonetheless, further reflection on the nature of modern societies – particularly the separation of a political authority from the rest of society – suggests how rhetorical persuasion remains important as a means of democratic representation.

Chapters 2 and 3 have set up a framework for thinking about rhetoric politically, underscoring the way in which persuasive speech is regarded as a threat to social order but also a means to contest and debate its parameters. The tension between these positions is evident in the way rhetorical strategies work today. Before we consider that further, however, we need to explore the content of rhetorical instruction itself. In Chapter 4 I explore the first two of the five classical 'canons' of rhetoric: the *discovery* of argument and the *arrangement* of the parts of speech. In Chapter 5 I discuss aspects of *style* and *delivery* (missing out the fifth canon, *memory*). These chapters provide a descriptive overview of the basic content of rhetorical advice inherited from classical times.

In Chapter 6 I consider how we can employ the techniques and classifications of the rhetorical tradition to analyse political action. Against the once dominant tradition of positivism in political science, I align rhetoric with 'interpretive' approaches that seek to understand behaviour by reference to the ideas and language of actors themselves. More than that, however, I follow others who claim rhetoric has a distinctive approach to ideas: namely, in the form of arguments. Political arguments never simply reflect stable cognitive frames by which actors see the world but, rather, are dynamic interventions that give force and direction to ideas. Rhetorical political analysis, then, is a way of examining how actors 'appropriate' situations by defining the issues at stake and orienting others in a given context.

In Chapter 7 I discuss the value of rhetoric for democratic theory today. Recent efforts to revive participation in democracy underscore active deliberation by citizens. But this has come with a strong critique of what are regarded as the disruptive effects of rhetoric, particularly the use of emotional appeals. Instead, so-called 'deliberative democrats' foreground the rational – and purportedly impartial – dimensions of communication. I discuss the difficulties and dangers of eliminating passions from persuasion and, with regard to developments in the disciplines of neuroscience and psychoanalysis, set out an alternative perspective that gives greater room to 'affective rhetorical strategies' to negotiate politics and the political.

The theme of Chapter 8 is the influence of mass media on political rhetoric. In many ways, media inherit the controversial status that rhetoric once held – simultaneously hailed as the channel of free speech yet frequently loathed as the obstacle to informed communication. To explore this ambivalence, the chapter identifies the contest over the meaning and limits of the 'public' as integral to communicative strategies undertaken in a mediated public domain.

Media platforms are never simply a neutral resource to communicate political messages; they themselves shape messages by appropriating situations according to selective values and nurturing their audiences' ongoing expectations. In this sense, media themselves undertake a rhetorical function. As we shall see, that enables certain rhetorical strategies over others and shapes public discourse in distinctive, often rather narrow, ways.

Finally, in Chapter 9 I discuss the gendered character of rhetoric. Classical ideas about speech and persuasion sometimes compared it to a form of struggle in which a heroic figure wrestled with an audience in order to win the 'war of words'. Such an outlook continues in modern politics where, as feminists have struggled tirelessly to lay bare, men and their speaking conventions dominate debating chambers. Political rhetoric, as we shall see, is gendered through and through, both in the way in which it is embodied in the person of a speaker and in how the wider 'body politic' is figuratively imagined. Yet a gender perspective also highlights the instability of the categories defining sexual identity, and thus also the ambivalent gendering of speech for the purposes of persuasion. Here I use the example of rhetoric about the nation to explore the peculiar ways that gender enters into political speech.

Summary

Persuasion, I have argued, is central to politics. But understanding persuasion lifts the veil on a practice that is more than just a set of techniques for communication. Rhetoric draws us towards the power relations, the contests over the parameters of space and time and the controversies that underlie and occasionally disrupt routine politics. Far from being concerned exclusively with a superficial level of speech, analysing rhetoric invites us to grasp the deeper political dimension that shapes how individuals relate to each other, what they can say, and how.

2 The truth of rhetoric

The controversial status of rhetoric is deeply rooted in the tradition of western political thought. Originally, rhetoric involved instruction in effective speaking for citizens of ancient Greece who participated actively in political affairs. Whether it was a genuine branch of knowledge, essential to the collective life of the Athenian *polis* or state, or merely a technique that could be employed by anyone, for good or ill, was a matter of heated debate. Rhetoricians classified different parts of speech, the forms of argument and the strategies that might help win over different kinds of audience. Rhetorical 'knowledge', therefore, was about controlling spoken communication, rendering it effective, memorable and even repeatable for other occasions. Speech was necessary to make the polity work, yet it often smacked of artifice and the absence of a genuine concern for the good of the community. Most famously, in the view of the philosopher Plato, rhetoric was an immoral practice that permitted unqualified people to rule by means of cheap argumentative tricks and the mimicry of genuine knowledge.

To this day, political theorists and philosophers have continued to feel uneasy about the value of rhetoric. At the heart of that unease, I propose, is a concern about the dimension of the political and its relation to politics. For many thinkers, politics must be founded on something firmer than the contingent, partial and unstable to-ing and fro-ing of speech and argument: preferably a universal order of values beyond the one-sidedness of speech. For others, speech itself – if properly aligned to the needs of the community – can channel the sentiments and values necessary to sustain political order. Either way, persuasion has long been suspected as a practice that has the potential to disrupt, even to destroy politics. In the modern age, we are heirs to this suspicion and its underlying 'retreat' from the political (Mouffe, 1993).

In this chapter I survey the troubled place of rhetoric in political thinking. This is not the place for a comprehensive history of rhetoric (but see Herrick, 2005; Kennedy, 1994; Vickers, 1988). Instead, I introduce some of the key arguments in western thought concerning its relation to politics. I start with a discussion of the classical origins of the controversy in ancient Greek democracy and Plato's criticism of the 'sophists', the ancient teachers of rhetoric. Next, I look at Aristotle's more generous view of rhetoric as an integral part of political life, a view that was central to the classical republican idea of politics handed down through

Roman writers and revived during the Renaissance in Europe. However, modern political thinkers – most notably Hobbes – announced the end of that idea of politics in favour of notions of 'sovereignty' and scientific truth. Even apparent republicans such as Rousseau conceived persuasion as a threat to the sovereignty of the General Will and sought to reduce the impact that unrestrained speech might have on politics. Thus we can see that the discomfort with rhetorical speech noted in Chapter 1 has a long history and isn't just a recent phenomenon.

The sophists and the origins of rhetoric

Like rhetoric, 'sophistry' has long been used as a term of abuse, and for similar reasons. To employ sophistry is to manipulate ideas deliberately in order to convince someone of something that is either not true or, at least, is only partially so. We inherit this use of the word from Plato, who dismissed the rhetorical skills taught by the sophists. We shall see shortly how Plato's opinion of the sophists informs much of our current suspicion that rhetoric is intrinsically deceptive. Plato's criticism had a manifestly political implication: human association, he believed, should be founded on knowledge of what is true, a knowledge accessible only by a certain number of gifted philosophers properly nurtured to discern it. Sophists, the argument went, merely taught people to feign knowledge and hence were not genuine philosophers.

But who were the sophists? The term refers to a category of teachers who were employed to educate citizens in ancient Greece from around 500 BCE. This was a period in which the system of self-government called democracy came into being (see Davies, 1993). Following the reforms of Kleisthenes, the *demos* – meaning the 'people', but also the 'rabble'; mostly tenant farmers, all of them male – were permitted to sit in the *ekklesia*, or assembly, as full citizens. Traditionally, aristocratic families had run Athens and, even after democracy was introduced, they tended to dominate political life still. With the arrival of new citizens, effective communication came to have a high premium. Many of these citizens – but, interestingly, often aristocrats – employed the services of the itinerant teachers known as the sophists.

The Greek word *sophos* means 'wisdom', and the sophists offered their wisdom about how to speak and argue in the public realm. That kind of knowledge was called rhetoric – from *rhetorike*, the art of speaking that they studied as a special 'science'. The sophists are thought to have originated with the arrival of Gorgias of Leontini, who came to Athens from Sicily in the fifth century BCE. Other important figures include Tisias, Corax, Demosthenes and Isocrates. The emergence of democratic politics in Athens presented an opportunity for teachers of this kind to offer their services. But they were not simply anonymous, travelling salesmen. Many were learned and original scholars in their own right, known for the important contributions they made both to rhetoric and to other areas of enquiry. Figures such as Protagoras, Gorgias and Isocrates developed important intellectual insights and contributed significantly to Athenian culture (see Dillon and Gergel, 2003). While little now remains of their teachings, they were famous for formulating notions such as Protagoras's claim that 'man is the measure of all things', implying that conventions rather than fixed, objective principles are the standards proper to human affairs. A claim such as this was relevant to a society in which public speaking had become a regular and widespread event. Individual sophists studied different aspects of argumentation and grammar, style and arrangement, compiled examples of speeches and passed on their knowledge in the form of what Vickers (1988: 14) calls '"how-to-do-it" manuals' to assist in the cultivation of effective public speakers.

Rhetorical instruction was not only a technical skill; it flowed from the Athenians' idea of moral and civil life. Let us note some key features of the democratic system in ancient Athens. The Greek *polis* is widely known for its highly participatory system of politics. To be a citizen in this system was regarded as an honour that bestowed important duties upon the individual. The freedoms of the citizen were understood to be closely associated with a commitment to a sense of the common good. The historian Thucydides reports the popular leader Pericles saying of Athens, in his famous 'funeral oration':

> Here each individual is interested not only in his own affairs but in the affairs of the state as well: even those who are mostly occupied with their own business are extremely well-informed on general politics – this is a peculiarity of ours: we do not say that a man who takes no interest in politics is a man who minds his own business; we say that he has no business here at all.
>
> (Thucydides, 1954: 118–19)

To be a citizen of Athens was to be part of a very special kind of association, one for which you would be expected to be highly active, often to fight and even to die. Membership was greatly prized and, despite our contemporary understanding of democracy as inclusion of *all* people, it was available only to males over the age of eighteen whose families originated from Attica (the region of which Athens was the capital city). Notoriously, women and slaves were not permitted citizenship status. Even citizens who broke the law or failed in some major public undertaking, such as winning a battle, were vulnerable to being stripped of their citizenship and exiled. So being a member of the Athenian polis was a significant marker of status, one defined by a powerful sense of obligation to the community and by an expectation to demonstrate one's worthiness. This was a competitive world dominated by the words and deeds of leaders who, crucially, were dependent upon winning the support of the *demos*.

Speaking in public was vital to Athenian life. It was a society where, traditionally, information had been carried by word of mouth via face-to-face encounters between individuals. Stories and histories had long been transmitted that way, as was news of battles and their outcomes. What people said mattered and Athenians had a high regard for the powers of oral persuasion, viewing the gifted orator as akin to a poet or magician. With the arrival of democracy, the teaching of rhetoric entailed a shift to a self-conscious use of speech in a culture already accustomed to valuing 'winged-words' – speech that was pleasing to hear and memorable (see Thomas and Webb, 1994: 7–9, 19).

Democracy did not just involve going along to the assembly to hear others speak. It was incumbent upon all citizens to engage in public debate both in and outside the assembly. The need for public speaking skills extended to committees to which citizens would be elected and, perhaps most importantly, to the law courts. All citizens would be expected to serve on juries and hear other citizens defend or accuse others. There were no lawyers available for hire: anyone accused of breaking the law had to defend himself in person, often from malicious accusations. It was vital, in this instance, that they had some experience of public speaking in order to protect their livelihoods. To be able to refute the charges effectively, to identify inaccuracies in the evidence of witnesses and to win the trust of the jury required some understanding of oratory and the best way to present a winning argument.

In his 'Hymn to Logos', the former sophist, Isocrates, expresses the peculiar veneration held by many in Athens for the activity of speech in civil life: 'the power to speak well is taken as the surest index of a sound understanding, and discourse which is true and lawful and just is the outward image of a good and faithful soul' (Isocrates, in Poulakos, 1997: 11). For Isocrates, speech was what distinguished the Athenian community from other societies and other animals. It was the distinctively civic orientation of speech and persuasion that gave Athens its moral superiority as a self-governing community (see Poulakos, 1997). Through speech, the community reflected upon, debated and judged its own activities. In so doing, it secured Athens its wealth and longevity.

Plato's critique of rhetoric

In light of the description above, we might think that the sophists were highly regarded as exponents of civic pride and public responsibility. But that was not so: the teaching of the arts of persuasion – and, indeed, democracy itself – was a matter of sharp controversy. The greatest critique of rhetoric came in the philosophy of Plato, an aristocrat deeply dismayed by the teachings of the sophists. As well as an opponent of democracy, Plato is also credited as a major source of western political philosophy: that is, the project of grounding politics on rational 'foundations' by means of which it is possible to separate out truth from mere opinion (or *doxa*). For Plato, a just state should be founded on knowledge of incontestable principles, not persuasion. That is, politics should have a metaphysical basis provided by the firm wisdom of philosophy, not by the arbitrary capacity of a speaker simply to woo his listeners.

It was precisely that ability to sway an audience – taught by the sophists – that Plato found objectionable, and to which he returned repeatedly in his dialogues. It had been their vulnerability to such manipulation, he believed, that resulted in the citizens of Athens unjustly condemning to death his mentor, Socrates (for supposedly corrupting the young). If public speech can persuade an audience of almost anything, then surely the greatest injustices can be served up in the name of justice? In all his work, Plato made clear his contempt for rhetoric as a form of knowledge. An 'expert in rhetoric', he warns in *Phaedrus*, is someone who can persuade 'the city to do something bad instead of good' (Plato, 2005: 43). Concerned only with technique and surface, rhetoric, he claims in *Gorgias*, is a form of 'sycophancy' or pandering to an audience, affirming opinion rather than delivering genuine knowledge (see Plato, 2010).

In the latter dialogue, Plato presents the rhetorician Gorgias boasting of his ability to persuade an audience on any matter, regardless of expertise: 'there is no subject on which the rhetorician would not speak more persuasively, before a large crowd, than any skilled practitioner you care to name. Such is the extent and nature of the science's power' (2010: 19–20). In response, Socrates disputes that Gorgias has a 'science' at all. Indeed, Plato has him compare rhetoric to cooking: a practice designed to bring pleasure to its recipients, but without any rational understanding of its own procedures and purposes! A genuine art or skill, he points out, is founded upon knowledge of its object. Rhetoric, as a mere practice of persuasion, has no object of its own – bar the substanceless goal of persuasion – and, by consequence, it is merely crowd-pleasing (2010: 27–28). Anyone with genuine moral intentions, argues Plato, would not use rhetoric: 'for the person who is not planning to act unjustly I don't think its use is very great – if indeed it is any use at all' (ibid.: 55).

For Plato – dismayed, as many traditional ruling families were, by imperialist Athens's low morals and belligerent lust for gain – rhetoric was a practice that exemplified relativism in public affairs and moral life generally. Without the guide of truth, persuasion was a rudderless boat leading people wherever seemed agreeable at the time. It lacked the firm compass of philosophy, which was always oriented towards the use of reason rather than pandering to prevailing opinions or appetites. In his many dialogues, philosophical leadership was provided in the figure of Socrates, whose critical interrogation of other people's views regularly exposed their limitations and drove their proponents through a rigorous, logically supported argument to a conclusion they had not expected. Socrates achieves persuasion by coming to clear definitions of concepts and then using these to infer conclusions that challenge the unexamined opinions of his interlocutors (see Plato, 2010: 43–44).

Socrates' type of speech was evidently Plato's model for a philosophical form of reasoning that connected everyday judgements about how to live with the higher realm of abstract reasoning. For him, that kind of reasoning was not a trick, but mirrored a stable order of essential ideas which he believed governed the cosmos and were embedded in the souls of all men. Rhetoric, however, 'relates to the soul as cookery does to the body' (ibid.: 31). The 'Forms', as he called them, were the unchanging and harmonious constellation of principles to which our finite ideas can only approximate. For our thoughts to reflect this higher order, he implied, took a talented and critical cast of mind.

Plato's preference, of course, was for a society in which rational thought, not persuasive speech, was at the helm. That wasn't a democracy but rather a community built upon the strict allocation of functional roles which he believed to be already distributed within the souls of men. In Plato's ideal republic – as set out in his dialogue, *The Republic* (see Plato, 1987) – citizens were allocated to their class in society and would dedicate themselves to their own natural gifts. Those with strong intellectual abilities would be given executive authority – the 'philosopher-kings'; those with 'spirit' would undertake a military role as guardians to protect the polis; and the rest would pursue their appetites by means of trade. A society premised on the veneration of truth could therefore dispense with public deliberation of the kind instructed by the sophists. Instead of the cacophony of voices mingling in the *Agora* and straining to be heard, there would be the quiet, orderly contemplation of reason among those with the expertise to do so, unswayed by opinion and mere appearances. For reason, or *logos*, was to Plato more like inward sight – a thoughtful reflection on images – than outward sounds. Truth was essentially indifferent to vocal communication. As Adriana Cavarero suggests, Plato's image of rule by reason is ultimately a silent order, for rational thought alone needs no outward expression through voice (Cavarero, 2005: 46). Indeed, in *The Republic* Plato made clear his contempt for those noise makers – the artists and poets – whose task it was to entertain and delight by 'mimicking' the truth. Such things, he argued, had no place in a rationally organized society and ought to be banished (see Plato, 1987: 335–53).

What are we to make of Plato's criticism of the sophists and rhetoric? What is its enduring message? Critics have long highlighted the illiberal, anti-democratic nature of his utopia. Plato wanted to replace politics altogether with a kind of priesthood of philosophers. For liberals such as Karl Popper (1966), this marks the early origins of 'totalitarian' thought, the urge to control society and limit the freedom of individuals on the justification that a special elite has access to a higher order of truth that ordinary people cannot attain. Writing in the twentieth century during the rise of Stalinist communism, Popper saw figures such as Plato as the philosophical precursors to a modern tendency to eradicate freedom in the name of a utopian vision of perfect order.

But if Plato was clearly no liberal, his writings represent a current of thinking that continues to inform political theory and philosophy today. As Jacques Rancière argues, Plato established an underlying tension between philosophy and politics whereby philosophy 'expels disagreement from itself' (Rancière, 1999: xii). That is, in its very purpose, philosophy eradicates the contingency of politics. Plato offered a theory of what Rancière calls 'archipolitics' – as the living embodiment of reason, all activities of the community manifest an ideal essence (ibid.: 65–70). The just state is one in which there is a proportionate distribution of functions among the citizenry, where everyone is allocated a role and accounted for according to a higher principle of order. Plato's rejection of democracy was not simply based on an illiberal tendency towards authoritarianism but, moreover, a refusal of the excess and disorder that democratic politics brings to the community. In a democracy, as he saw it, people exceeded their natural abilities and seek to undertake any function whatsoever (ibid.: 19). This is precisely the problem identified with rhetoric: the illusion of knowledge that upsets the 'proper' arrangement of roles, allowing anyone to claim anything. While we may dispute Plato's preferred vision of the just state, nonetheless his presentation of philosophy as a way of confronting and expelling the disruptive effects of the political remained exemplary for later forms of political thinking.

Of course, a more sympathetic reading of Plato might look beyond the urge to directly align politics with metaphysics. We might read Plato as offering us an *alternative* kind of rhetoric: one focused on rigorously examining our points of view and the conceptual definitions we use to reason, subjecting them to critique and exposing them to rigorous examination. It has certainly not failed to be noticed that for all his criticism of rhetoric, Plato was himself a master rhetorician. His dialogues demonstrated through elaborate, staged conversations and distinctive imagery the kind of argumentation he preferred over democratic rhetoric. This was a 'Socratic' form of reasoning that sought not to so much to eliminate speech as to guide it towards philosophically defensible claims. Today, we might not want to hand politics over to an intellectual priesthood, but we might find appealing an environment of rational, self-critical rigour, where public servants who have demonstrated expertise in their fields weigh up the consequences of certain choices. Indeed, that is very much the way in which modern democracies claim to work: that is, by separating complex public choices from the public (who participate primarily by voting) and handing them over to an elite of representatives and experts charged with the task of critically evaluating policy.

Plato's overt hostility to rhetoric, then, might be seen as an effort to persuade his audience to acknowledge, at a minimum, a certain kind of 'serious' argumentation as the basis to political order (see Lanham, 1976: 6–7). That view remains opposed to democratic politics, but it allows for some degree of speech and persuasion, albeit regulated by a sense of working towards 'higher principles' of knowledge. However we interpret his work, Plato established an opposition between philosophy and politics that contrasts the search for objective principles of truth with the dangerous rhetorical excess of democratic speech.

Aristotle and the republican tradition

Of the ancient Greek philosophers it is Aristotle, Plato's former pupil and founder of his own school – the Lyceum – who has had the most positive impact on the development of rhetoric. Unlike his teacher, Aristotle found a clear place for rhetoric in the business of the *polis*. He, too, was a firm supporter of the scientific quest for truth, and his many and varied writings are a testament to that objective. But in Aristotle's analysis, speech and persuasion had an undoubted, practical role in sustaining the political community and rhetoric could therefore be regarded as an acceptable ally of philosophy. Man, he famously claimed in his *Politics* (1988), was by nature a 'political animal'. It was speech that distinguished humans from the other animals and that enabled him to communicate moral ideas. It was proper, then, that speech and persuasion should be integral to the life of the political community.

For Aristotle, political association was founded not on fixed and eternal principles reflected in the soul, but on the natural orientation of humans to live together and share a common life. That foundation was conceived in a distinctive, 'teleological' way: all things develop in order to fulfil their essential purpose. Just as the purpose of the seed is to grow into a tree, so the purpose of the *polis* is to attend to the 'good life' of the families and communities that constitute it. Of course, in any specific instance political life could develop in pathological ways but, in essence, it was properly bound towards ends that could be rationally explored. In Aristotle's reasoning, the good life could mean a number of things to different communities, rather than any single thing universally. But it underscored his sense that debating the character of the common good was not an accidental or detrimental aspect of politics but an activity that belonged to the very essence of political association. To be citizens of such a community was, likewise, proper to mankind and in tune with its own distinctive abilities to speak and argue about issues of right and wrong, the expedient or inexpedient. Although Aristotle recognized various forms of political arrangement, such as monarchy, oligarchy and democracy (which he rejected as rule by the mob), he nevertheless endorsed a limited form of citizen participation in the ideal polity.

Starting from these premises, Aristotle made the case for rhetoric as a valuable skill for citizens and therefore a true 'art' and object of knowledge (see Olmsted, 2006: 12–14). In so doing, he aimed to systematize much of the previous knowledge of rhetoric developed by the sophists and to integrate it into a rational appreciation of political life. Rejecting the sophists' conception of politics as mere conventions open to manipulation, he presented rhetoric as a practical form of reasoning that complemented other, theoretical branches of knowledge. His work *The Art of Rhetoric* (1991) was assembled over several years and contains a rather uneven reflection upon various dimensions of speech. But it provides one of the most widely accepted sources for the later classification of the different aspects of rhetorical study that we will make use of in later chapters (see Black, 1978; Lawson-Tancred, 1991).

What does Aristotle say in *The Art of Rhetoric*? He opens with the assertion that rhetoric 'is the counterpart to dialectic'. 'Dialectic' is philosophical reasoning proper, whose purpose is to demonstrate the truth of things. The focus of rhetoric, he argues, is not persuasion per se but '*the detection of the persuasive aspects of each matter*' (1991: 70; italics in original). What does that mean? Aristotle rejects the sophistic view of rhetoric as simply about achieving persuasion, regardless of any other consideration. Instead, he limits persuasion to the worth of the resources at hand. Rhetoric entails an enquiry into how the best case can be put given the argument, the evidence, the audience and so on. This limitation was intended to prevent anyone overstating the possibilities of rhetoric and, in making it, Aristotle emphasized his intention to explore the ways in which rhetorical techniques could help in the pursuit of truth.

What then follows, however, is more an instructive exposition of rhetoric's fundamental elements than a purely philosophical account of the rationality of rhetoric. Aristotle takes issue with the sophists' attention to legal rhetoric. Instead, he insists on the primacy of political rhetoric, where what is at issue is the best course of action for the *polis* to pursue. Despite his insistence on rhetoric's alignment with dialectic, Aristotle insists on the significance of facing uncertainty – for deliberating in politics was usually a matter of hearing opposed arguments on an issue for which there was not a logical answer. Oratory therefore involved a demonstration of a reasoned course of action that would most likely be advantageous, and a rejection of the least advantageous. In that respect, his account of rhetoric complements his views of politics and of ethics: it concerns which policies serve the common good and the pursuit of happiness for the citizens as a whole. Those goals were the highest concern of the community, and therefore the supreme principle underlying a genuine 'science' of rhetoric.

The Art of Rhetoric provides an early but more or less systematic classification of the elements of rhetorical instruction that would influence later rhetoricians. That included the differentiation of the three 'genres' of rhetoric and the different types of argumentative appeal. The three genres referred to distinct kinds of persuasion for different occasions and comprised *deliberative* or political rhetoric, *forensic* or legal rhetoric and *display* or ceremonial (sometimes called 'epideictic') rhetoric. Deliberative rhetoric was the form of persuasion suited to arguments concerning the right course of action in the future, often argued in the Athenian *ekklesia*. Forensic rhetoric involved persuasion about the past, employed most often in the law courts. Display rhetoric, finally, involved persuasion in relation to the present, typically forms of praise or blame at moments of ceremony such as funerals or festivals. For Aristotle, deliberative rhetoric was the most significant of the three.

The different types of appeal distinguish between alternative sources of an argument. For Aristotle, those comprise the 'demonstrative' form, which appealed to an audience's use of reason, the appeal to the character or personal authority of the speaker and the appeal to emotion. Following their later Roman appropriation, these are now often referred to as the appeal to *logos* (reason), *ethos* (character) and *pathos* (emotion). Aristotle was mostly interested in reason and character, but he made an interesting case for appeal to the emotions in order to sway a crowd. We will consider these distinctions in more detail in Chapters 4 and 5.

Despite its pretensions to recruit rhetoric into the philosophical fold, Aristotle's *Rhetoric* has served primarily as a manual or guide to the practice of rhetorical instruction. Unlike Plato, he accepted the value for the community of persuasion through oratory. The real test was not the accordance of claims with some ideal principle accessible only by experts; rather, it was the ability of the orator to make a case in matters that did *not* admit of such ideal foundation. In situations such as these it was necessary for an audience to hear different sides of the argument and to make a judgement based not immediately on higher principles of truth, but on the weight of evidence. Aristotle drew attention to the importance of the 'enthymeme' in this process – that is, reasoning not from logical premises but from commonplace understandings that can usually be taken for granted. In politics, it was not necessary to defend every claim with rigorous philosophical logic. The good orator, instead, could assume certain ideas and values as already accepted.

24 *The truth of rhetoric*

But if in his account of the enthymeme Aristotle appeared to be a friend of rhetoric, there is an important lesson to be learned here. In order for commonplaces to work as hidden premises, the audience must be a community of likeminded people with whom such an understanding could be reliably utilized. In Athens, that meant exclusively male citizens who had wives and slaves attending to their private affairs. While there was no guaranteeing that this community would agree on every issue, it was reasonable nonetheless to assume that some matters (such as the need to sustain an order based on slavery) would not be criticized and hence did not need to be defended. This points to a common and serious problem for those who promote the idea of deliberation and the rhetorical arts today: the assumed existence of a community of likeminded people for whom argument and debate can be contained within a broad consensus on common principles (what I called a 'horizon' of political values in Chapter 1). For all Plato's railing against its dangers, political oratory has often been a rather elite practice built on a narrow community of speakers and listeners who can assume various ideas to be already agreed. Like Plato, Aristotle was suspicious of the mob entering politics and preferred that deliberation would be undertaken by a limited number of independent and wealthy men able to participate effectively in an informed discussion. Such a skill was hardly that of *all* people; a political community built on the teaching of rhetoric was never intended to introduce dangerous instability into politics.

Whereas Plato's approach to rhetoric was part of a deeply anti-political sentiment, Aristotle endorsed a limited form of politics that itself presupposed a limited community of citizens. This is what Rancière calls 'parapolitics', by contrast with Plato's archipolitics. Parapolitics also works from the idea of a stable, orderly community, but permits some degree of disagreement by partially incorporating the *demos* into the political order and making the management of their discord the task of government (Rancière, 1999: 70–77). A democratic contest of sorts is staged in Aristotle's vision, but it is also stripped of any destabilizing elements because, it is thought, a natural equality among citizens has already been established. This view remained very much the classical idea of politics transmitted from ancient Greece to the Roman republic and beyond; it was a 'republican ideology' of the state as a form of autonomous self-government. For later rhetoricians, Aristotle's *Rhetoric* was certainly not the last word, but it was a vital reference point for a view of rhetoric as a practice for deliberating matters of state.

In the work of Marcus Tullius Cicero – often hailed as the greatest orator and rhetorician of the Roman world – the skills of speech were central to the life of the *polis*. Cicero produced a number of treatises on rhetoric in his lifetime (as well as practising oratory as a lawyer and politician), where he extolled, in particular, the virtuous role of speech in sustaining the republican way of life (see Cicero 2001, 1949a and 1949b). The Roman republic was no democracy in the common sense of the word – it combined elements of representation with an aristocrat-dominated Senate – but it contained various opportunities for speakers to win over their audiences, and speech was a central part of its self-image as a self-governing community (see Connolly, 2007). As one commentator argues, the figure of the orator was a powerful motif in the republic and embodied the idea of a heroic protector from tyranny (Dugan, 2009). Yet Rome was a highly competitive and often rather dangerous and unstable order where success or failure in public speech, such as in the courts of law or the Senate, could have enormous implications. Riven with factions among the aristocratic elite and the plebeian classes, only a small number of individuals had the recognized right – that is, the personal prestige – to speak with authority. As a legal advocate and later a Senator and Consul, Cicero made his name with a famed ability for public speaking.

Cicero's contributions to rhetoric were less philosophical and more practically instructive, although he clearly endorsed a view of informed oratory as part of virtuous citizenship, where speech and the republican order were conceived as mutually supportive. Cicero also refused the sophistic idea that rhetoric could be used for *any* purpose. Rather, the 'ideal orator' was a virtuous man with a strong understanding of his topic, who could persuade his audience with reason, authority and emotion all combined: 'Surely it is one particular quality that marks good speakers: speech that is well ordered, distinguished, and characterized by a particular kind of artistry and polish. And unless the orator has fully grasped the underlying subject matter, such speech is utterly impossible' (Cicero, 2001: 70; see also 1949b: 357). For Cicero, it was the skill of the orator himself, rather than any techniques or ordering of the parts of speech, that mattered most. A good orator would judge the appropriate style of persuasion by the character of his audience and moderate his style accordingly. In that way, he believed, through oratory, reason and the higher needs of the community would prevail (see Kapust, 2011; Garsten, 2006: ch. 5).

Despite such noble intentions, in practice Cicero was a pragmatic orator, prepared to adapt his arguments to whatever seemed likely to protect the republic (Dugan, 2009: 187). His most famous speeches were delivered at moments of great crisis, such as during his campaign against Catiline and his co-conspirators. At such moments he was able to manipulate, in various ways, the idea of the republic and its needs in order to suit his vision of its best interests. Nonetheless, despite his inconsistencies, Cicero's figure of the ideal orator as a moderate and cultivated citizen who identifies with the good of the wider community persisted long after the decline of the Roman republic. For example, in the writings of Quintilian, himself a great admirer of Cicero, rhetoric was presented as part of the general moral and civic education of the citizen.

After the fall of Athenian democracy and, later, the collapse of the Roman republic, rhetoric largely disappeared from its prominent place in political life. But it reappeared again as part of the revival of classical scholarship during the period of the Renaissance, particularly in its most productive centres in Italy. There, as part of a reaction to external rule by autocratic princes and empires, Aristotelian and Ciceronian ideas were rediscovered and called upon in defence of the republican notion of politics. That included a re-elaboration of the idea of politics comprising self-governing cities where a limited number of citizens participated actively in the affairs of the community. Once more, rhetoric was regarded as an essential element for the purpose of debating the common good. The development of a 'humanist' form of enquiry into all sorts of areas of man's abilities shifted the focus from purely religious, 'revealed' teachings about the cosmos and man's predesigned role in it towards the knowledge and skills that mankind generated itself through its own endeavours (see Lanham, 1976). The works of Aristotle and Cicero were thus conceived as part of the heritage of human wisdom about human affairs that contributed to the establishment of political associations. Once more, then, rhetoric was considered integral to the self-founding and self-governing of political communities by citizens themselves, in opposition to the authority of theological dogma or rule primarily by force (see Grassi, 1980, 1983; Skinner, 1978: 28–48). Yet, again, the revival of the classical notion of politics – or parapolitics – and the place of rhetoric in it was not a defence of democracy, but rather a 'defence of liberty' by a limited number of citizens who alone deliberated public affairs (Skinner, 1978: 41–48). The contingency of politics – its potential to produce political disagreement, deception and instability – was therefore balanced by the narrowness of the body of citizens and the 'virtuous' qualities thought to be shared among them.

Hobbes, Rousseau and modern sovereignty

The change that brought the greatest threat to the survival of rhetoric in political life was the emergence of the modern, sovereign state. The arrival of centralized, immensely powerful authorities with distinct territorial boundaries and the capacity to enforce a uniform set of laws by the monopoly of the means of violence ran directly counter to the idea of politics promoted in the classical and humanist treatises on rhetoric – for sovereignty implies that public power is exercised through an autonomous and authoritative set of commands to be obeyed *without discussion*. Of course, public speaking and the rhetorical arts continued to have a part to play, but they became circumscribed by an idea of politics that severely limited their exercise in the public realm.

The principle of state sovereignty, which emerged across Europe from the sixteenth century onwards, involved subordinating existing assemblies and other opportunities for deliberation and persuasion to a final power whose will was indivisible. The outcome of that process was the nation-state model that now dominates the world, even if the principle of absolute sovereignty is no longer fully operative. What is important, from our point of view, is how the emergence of the idea of sovereignty was responsible for the eradication, or at the very least diminution, of rhetoric in politics. The two most significant political philosophers of modern sovereignty, Thomas Hobbes and Jean-Jacques Rousseau, offer contrasting interpretations of the nature of sovereignty as the basis of political order. Yet both firmly insist on the danger of rhetorical speech and the need to limit its effects. Let us look at the two thinkers in turn.

Hobbes's political theory, set out in his *Leviathan* of 1651 (see Hobbes, 1991), involved sustained criticism of the civic republican approach to politics that he himself had inherited as a youth. Famously, for Hobbes, political power was to be conceived as the formation of an independent authority fundamentally separate from the people who authorized it. Yet Hobbes's defence of absolute sovereign power was also theorized as a kind of 'social contract' – that is, as an agreement among those subject to power themselves. Once agreed as a legitimate power, however, the sovereign was free to decide the laws and determine the liberties – or not – of its citizens. A moment of deliberation, then, was brief but final. Thereafter, citizens were not to speak on public matters. Indeed, even the imagined moment of contracting was less a debate than a collective calculation of the optimal means of survival. At the heart of Hobbes's theory, then, we find once more a radical critique of rhetoric and the dangers it brings to civil peace.

Leviathan involved a sustained effort to reason from fundamental truths about the nature of human beings towards an idea of how they might live together. Hobbes's method was taken from geometry – the procedure of reasoning in logical steps from basic axioms – and his text sought to ground political theory in what he called a 'civil science'. That enabled him to develop a thoroughgoing scepticism about human ideas and values. For all the capacity to reason and imagine, humans could not be trusted to find peaceful ways of reconciling their common needs and desires. Driven by their passions and appetites, and by the basic need for survival, the 'natural condition' of mankind (that is, without an intervening authority) was one not of harmony but competition and uncertainty.

In Hobbes's sceptical view, although technically capable of rigorous thinking, people were as likely to take on trust the word of others as they were to reason from clear definitions or their own experience. Even if they reasoned independently, however, it was not possible to eradicate different interpretations of the world: 'For though the nature of that we conceive be the same; yet the diversity of our reception of it, in respect of different constitutions of body, and prejudices of opinion, gives everything a tincture of our different passions' (1991: 31). Such differences of interpretation were not minor. They extended along some of the basic dimensions of moral vocabulary:

> For one man calleth *Wisdome*, what another calleth *feare*; and one *cruelty*, what another *justice*; one *prodigality*, what another *magnanimity*; and one *gravity*, what another *stupidity*, &c. And therefore such names can never be the true grounds of any ratiocination.
>
> (Ibid.)

In the context of England's traumatic civil war, with its toxic combination of religious and political dispute, such differences could have dramatic, violent consequences. It was precisely the inability of men to agree naturally upon common definitions of the key moral concepts that determined the condition of uncertainty and competition that Hobbes described as the 'state of nature'. Indeed, Hobbes devoted considerable space to attacking precisely the 'absurdities' and misconceptions of religious advocates, the fallacious reasonings of ancient philosophers and, of course, 'the use of Metaphors, Tropes, and other Rhetoricall figures, in stead of words proper' (1991: 35). Such misunderstandings, misconceptions and misuse of words were the precursor to social and political strife. For Hobbes, the Enlightenment thinker, 'The Light of humane minds is Perspicuous Words' enabled by 'exact definitions [...] purged from ambiguity'. By contrast, 'Metaphors, and senseless and ambiguous words, are like *ignes fatui* [foolish fire or Will-o'-the-Wisp]; and reasoning upon them, is wandering amongst innumerable absurdities; and their end, contention, and sedition, or contempt' (1991: 36).

Hobbes is often thought a crudely materialist philosopher who reduces man to a self-interested automaton, unable to constrain his natural selfishness in the competition for survival. But as Terence Ball (1995: ch. 4) has argued, he was, on the contrary, profoundly aware of the linguistic dimension of human nature, the social character of language and its function as the basis of community. The uncertainty of the state of nature, as he depicted it, was a consequence not of humans with the speechless instincts of wild animals but, rather, of the surfeit of interpretations, ambiguities and misunderstandings among people who use language only too freely. The problem was that an ability to use language only extended passions into a confusion of concepts and values upon whose basic definitions they could not agree. Unable, unlike Hobbes himself, to use Perspicuous Words to agree a common way of living, it was subsequently necessary for them to generate a power who could intervene and make the final judgement of what was 'good', 'bad', 'just' and 'unjust' on their behalf.

Hobbes's account of the state of nature is, in part, a criticism of the Renaissance revival of classic notions of politics. The palpable evidence of religious and civil conflict demonstrated that there was no self-evident common good or all-embracing sense of community to which citizens would pledge their allegiance. Humans were capable of morality but they were not 'naturally' political, as Aristotle had claimed. They were naturally antagonistic, competitive and able, above all, to disagree over the kind of vocabulary that a stable community requires to exist at all. For that reason, Hobbes argued, it was rational to assume they would agree to authorize some person, or persons, to protect them from each other. The sovereign was therefore an 'artificial person' given the responsibility to decide and enforce the key definitions of civil vocabulary. The sovereign was the outcome of a contract between individuals to put survival above their preferred interpretations, abandoning their natural rights to decide such meanings for themselves. Of course, the contract was not a historical fact but, rather, a thought experiment designed to show how rational people would consent to such a power. Agreement was not a matter of deliberation and argument so much as a post-hoc calculation. Once it was recognized that a supreme power of some sort was rationally defensible, people would (at least, eventually) understand the legitimacy of such an authority.

Hobbes's political theory was a curious blend of absolutist goals (total power and authority in a centralized authority) with the language of civic republicanism (he made the case for a 'civil power', not some ancient or divine right) and the principles of liberal contractarianism (authority based on the acknowledged consent of rational individuals). Despite that peculiar combination, his defence of sovereignty has been extremely influential. Most states today are indeed regarded as independent powers irreducible either to the body of a king or the bodies of citizens, even if they are hardly absolute. We should not lose sight, however, of the fact that this conception of power is itself highly rhetorical. Not only was Hobbes a hugely gifted rhetorician – quite able to develop a rigorous argument and muster his own powerful metaphors, such as the 'state of war of all against all' or the sovereign as a 'mortall God', while simultaneously denying the value of rhetoric – but also, the sovereign power he defended was a way of organizing the space of speech and argument, granting primacy to *one voice* over all others. Unlike Plato, for whom political order should mirror the eternal – but speechless – ideal Forms, Hobbes conceived the state as the dominant voice in an otherwise crowded environment of interpretations. Likewise, today, we are accustomed to conceiving the state as the dominant voice, the source of authoritative commands and 'official' information that we are expected to acknowledge and obey, even if we disagree.

Writing around one hundred years later, Rousseau provides an alternative account of sovereignty to Hobbes's severe and distant figure of the Leviathan. For Rousseau, sovereignty entailed an agreement among individuals, but it could never be alienated from the collective citizen body. Returning to a classical republican theme (he was an admirer of the ancient Roman Republic and of Sparta), he recommended that the political order be founded on a community of citizens, each of whom participated in determining the General Will. But if Rousseau adopted a republican image of the political community, he nonetheless maintained a notion of sovereignty that had no truck with the rhetorical arts.

Rousseau's political theory and dislike of rhetoric were rooted in his view of the evolution of mankind. For him, the development of society had corrupted the settled and harmonious natural order of primitive man. Society had turned the 'noble savage' into a selfish and competitive individual. The only way to escape this decline and return humanity to any kind of harmony with its nature (a return to the primitive life of the past being impossible) was to reorder society in such a way that reduced the dissonance between the public and private worlds, between our consciences and our obligations to society. In his *Social Contract* of 1762, Rousseau set out a vision of a political community where citizens themselves collectively constituted the body of the sovereign (see Rousseau, 1968). Unlike in Hobbes's work, the principle of authority could never be externalized in a separate institution. Instead, for Rousseau, citizens of his ideal state would feel *internally* their common bonds and obligations to obey.

Rousseau pictured his state as a small republic or city-state, not unlike his native Geneva. As in Hobbes, the state would be constituted through a contract or pact between individuals to create an 'artificial person and collective body' (ibid.: 61) but, this time, made up of the citizens themselves. In that way, Rousseau believed, the state 'has not, nor could it have, any interest contrary to theirs' (ibid.: 63). As the source of law, the sovereign would determine what was just and unjust, and circumscribe individuals' duties but also enable their civil liberties in return for the individual giving up the right to determine such things privately (ibid.: 65). When submitting to the sovereign, however, citizens would obey not something wholly separate from themselves but, rather, what he famously called the 'General Will'. The General Will was the collective interest as determined by the citizens themselves, whom he envisaged meeting regularly in open assemblies to pass judgement on public matters. Submission to the General Will, then, did not mean handing power over to someone else to dictate all one's life choices (although it was reasonable, he thought, to delegate a government) but, rather, to align one's private interests with those of the community as a whole. That meant not being governed by one's own appetites alone (which was a form of slavery, he argued), but limiting them in order to fit with a wider sense of 'moral freedom' located in the self-governing community (ibid.; see also 76–77). The individual was entitled to private freedoms but it was the General Will that predominated, since only through that will are citizens free and equal: 'The citizen consents to all the laws, even to those that are passed against his will [...]' (ibid.: 153).

So far this might seem like a fairly democratic arrangement in tune with ancient ideas about democracy. But in the *Social Contract* and elsewhere, Rousseau qualified his account of what a virtuous modern community might involve. Among the preconditions he specified, Rousseau suggested it might help if the people were already in some kind of association (if yet without law); one where they all knew each other, where there was a moderate equality of wealth (he suggested Corsica as an example; ibid.: 95). Moreover, he made quite clear that this state should not be a democracy where *all* citizens could govern, since that was likely to lead to the importation of private interests and civil strife. Only a nation of gods, not men, could govern themselves democratically, he claimed (ibid.: 114).

Indeed, Rousseau indicated that it was better for the survival of the state if there was a high degree of unanimity to sustain the General Will: 'whereas long debates, dissensions and disturbances bespeak the ascendance of particular interests and the decline of the state' (ibid.: 151). He warned of the prospect of a 'sly orator' who could persuade the people against their better judgement (ibid.: 150). Under the rule of the General Will, 'there is no question either of intrigues or of eloquence' to manipulate others (ibid.: 149). Rousseau also suggests at one point that it would be better if, in their deliberations, citizens did not communicate at all (ibid.: 73)! Deliberation in his view was less a process of argumentative speech and more the outcome of internal reasoning from the standpoint of the General Will.

As Bryan Garsten argues, Rousseau preferred a language of persuasion that was essentially non-argumentative and appealed instead to the individual's conscience (see Garsten, 2006: 71–72). Particularistic interests could be avoided and a sense of 'generality of concern' unearthed only by bypassing reason. By consulting the 'secret voice of conscience' individuals would come, he believed, to make moderate and inclusive judgements that evaded the self-interest that modern reason had taught them. Thus Rousseau's figure of the 'lawgiver', whose task it was to guide the people towards their contract, was to 'employ neither force nor argument' but 'have recourse to an authority of another order, one which can compel without violence and persuade without convincing' (Rousseau, 1968: 87). To 'persuade without convincing' meant to appeal to common sentiments and not to bargain with individual interests. As Garsten points out, Rousseau believed community emerged from the underlying sentiments of pity and 'self-love' which brought a recognition of similarity with others and identification with them (Garsten, 2006: 74–75). To access these sentiments was to release a sense of virtue and fellow feeling independent of any argument, and it enabled Rousseau to regard sovereignty as the expression of a shared sentiment from within, not as an external order imposed from without. Yet, despite the disavowal of rhetoric, we might properly regard such arousal as an appeal to *pathos*, or commonly shared emotions. As such, Rousseau follows other republicans in assuming the presence of a pre-existing common bond as the basis to community. Garsten further suggests that Rousseau's anti-rhetorical image of political order invokes a 'prophetic nationalism' whose rhetoric is still heard today in the 'dogmatic' forms of speech that appeal to a natural community of sentiments. In forms of ethnic nationalism and religious speech, for example, judgements on issues are deemed to emanate not from the contingent play of arguments but from an incontestable harmony of values and feelings essential to citizens, whose desire for collective freedom may be expressed through a prophetic leader or guide (ibid.: 80–83).

In their different ways, Hobbes and Rousseau formulated ideas of sovereignty that sought to found political order on the presence of an incontestable will. For Hobbes that will was imposed from without, while for Rousseau it was cultivated from within. In both cases, however, the opportunity for argument and persuasion was halted so that political order could be firmly anchored in an incontestable principle. In these modern political theories, the moment of founding the order – when some degree of deliberation might be imagined – is limited to a rational calculation on the part of self-interested individuals or to the invocation of communal sentiment. As some have noted, modern western politics has oscillated between these two sources of sovereignty: the authority of the state being located either in an independent entity governing a society of atomistic individuals or in an underlying sense of community expressed through the state (see Taylor, 1985b: ch. 10). In each case, persuasion finds its absolute limit in an impermeable will that transcends politics.

Summary

Since its inception in ancient Greece, western political thought has largely constituted itself in opposition to the perceived dangers of rhetoric. This has been achieved either by treating rhetorical speech as wholly disruptive of political order or, more favourably, in need of alignment with intrinsic principles of social organization, such as the 'good' of the community (see Fish, 1989: ch. 20). In each instance, political thinkers have sought a point of reference, *outside political dispute*, that draws limits around what can be said, who can say it and how. Rhetoric is therefore contrasted with, or subsumed into, some eternal or basic 'truth' about humans and how they might live together. Persuasive practices must either vacate the space of the political community where that truth resides, or they must be so closely aligned with it as to not exceed its boundaries.

Rhetoric is controversial not because it is explicitly subversive but because it exposes the political order to a contingency that philosophers and theorists have tried to suppress. Philosophy's systematic organization of knowledge is supposed to reason from clear, rigorous principles and definitions that aim to have a universal scope. By contrast, rhetoric is thought to be concerned with partial points of view lacking in rigour. Left unchecked, many political philosophers and theorists predict that rhetoric will lead communities either to tyranny or chaos. But if some thinkers have tried to reason from fundamental truths, the underside of this claim is that the truth has been transmitted in ways that are themselves evidently rhetorical. From Plato's dialogues through to Hobbes's image of the Leviathan and beyond, political thinkers have, as Garsten notes, often *used rhetoric to argue against rhetoric*! That is, to get readers to understand the worrying truth about rhetoric and to submit to some higher order, it has been necessary nonetheless to utilize its techniques and devices. Philosophical and political reasoning therefore cannot be said entirely to lie outside the realm of rhetoric, as is claimed, but employs it at the very same time as it is disavowed.

3 The rhetorical citizen

Rhetoric is inextricably linked to a politics of the citizen. Citizens can be both speakers and audience in a community that governs itself. In the classical world, individuals granted membership of the *polis* had the freedom to attend assemblies, hear debates and speak as equals among their fellows. To be a citizen was – at least in principle – to be included within the speech community and to contribute to its sustenance. By contrast, modern political systems have done away with that dimension of citizenship. They have extended formal membership to a much wider range of persons, most notably women and people from all social classes and ethnic groups, but they have drastically reduced the degree of participation in politics demanded of citizens. In modern democracies, citizens are simply not expected to speak or to listen in public to the same degree as their classical counterparts. Not surprisingly, perhaps, rhetoric has diminished as a focal point of public life, substituted by a 'thinner' conception of citizenship and community based on codified legal rights and social entitlements. Paradoxically, opportunities for people to speak and persuade have multiplied vastly, but largely at a distance from the formal political arena, as private individuals and not as publicly engaged citizens.

We might see the contrast between ancient and modern citizenship as evidence of the ultimate triumph of efforts, noted in the previous chapter, to depoliticize public life and separate it from squabbling or easily flattered citizens. To an extent that is true. But we should not ignore the distinctive way that the political dimension presents itself in modern society. No longer are citizens perceived as the bearers of a common group identity for which they are regularly expected to demonstrate their support. Instead, in modern states commonality is achieved at a remove, through representation rather than physical presence: that is, common values are conjured and refashioned by actors (professional politicians and other political agents) who – formally or informally – represent citizens' needs and interests on their behalf and who make use of symbols, ideas and arguments to do the representing.

Rhetoric, consequently, is no longer framed primarily by a demand for an elevated or 'special' form of speech delivered by a virtuous citizen speaking to or for the *polis* (see Habinek, 2005). Instead, persuasion is sought through multiple strategies to shape the idea of the community itself and the place of the citizen within it. Rather than simply a means to the self-management of the community, rhetoric is now part of a *politics of representation* in societies that are much larger and more diverse and internally differentiated than in classical times. The separation of public authority (or the state) from society and the independent expansion of a bureaucratic apparatus mean that the formal public realm no longer coincides with the body of all citizens (conceived as a natural unity) but is, instead, permanently at a distance from that body and bridged by acts of representation that reduce but never eliminate the distance. That gives formal politics a relative independence and stability often lacking in pre-modern orders. But it also means that rhetoric relates to the political dimension in new ways: particularly in contests over the nature and limits of citizens' obligations to each other.

In this chapter I explore the above argument to think about how to conceive of the 'situated' nature of speech and rhetoric today. Even if it is no longer perceived as the primary skill of the modern citizen, rhetoric nonetheless remains important in mediating politics and the political – that is, in connecting the day-to-day choices and judgements in administering to society with the broader, 'universal' principles that shape its parameters and mark out its limits. But the separation of authority from society has opened up new opportunities to test, contest and remake such principles in ways unknown in classical times. As we shall see, different approaches in contemporary political theory offer alternative, often contrasting images of how citizens might participate in that process, with various degrees of attention to speech and persuasion.

Citizenship, ancient and modern

In its classical formulation, as we saw in the previous chapter, rhetoric denoted the civic skill of oratory or public speaking. The institutions of democratic Athens and republican Rome provided contexts for such skills to be at the centre of public life: political assemblies, public committees, open-air law courts, a large number of citizens freed from domestic concerns and hence able to attend meetings and a strong ethic of responsibility to sustain the community. Around such practices there developed a combative sense of citizenship as the prized membership of a community for which it was necessary on occasion to prove one's worth with a strong performance. In societies where the lives and deaths of individuals and communities were often closely related to a performance before an audience, being able to engage the crowd gave speakers a winning advantage.

Despite its vocal and articulate critics, rhetoric came to be regarded as a central part of the education of young citizens in the classical world. The ideal citizen was someone trained both in the skills of combat and those of grammar and rhetoric (see Habinek, 2005: chs 1 and 4). Such a view was expounded by figures such as Isocrates in Greece and, later in Rome, Quintilian, whose mammoth *Institutio Oratoria* (or the 'Orator's Education') set out a curriculum to nurture citizens on the basis of views derived from Cicero (see Quintilian, 2002; Connolly, 2009). Supporting that notion of rhetorical education was a view of public life as the object of a common obligation that bore down upon all citizens. To be a member of the *polis* in Greece or a citizen of Rome meant to take responsibility for public life over and above one's own person. Private life – which was more clearly set out in Roman law than it was in Greece – was not insignificant by any means but, by definition, it was not anyone else's concern. As Hannah Arendt once pointed out, the term 'private' stems from the notion of a 'privation'. To be in private, she argued, is 'to be deprived of the reality that comes from being seen and heard by others' (Arendt, 1959: 53). In the classical world, the purpose of living in large communities was to achieve a good higher than one's own personal success or, better, to make one's personal success translate into that of the wider community.

The assumption here was that the capacity of the community to govern itself freely meant overcoming external obstacles such as the power of other communities or tyrants. Thus Athens was perpetually at war with other communities, such as Sparta, and Rome was transformed over the centuries from a city republic into an enormous empire comprising half the world. The most cherished freedom, then, was that of the community as a whole, rather than of individuals alone. A citizen of communities such as these therefore took on duties to sustain and expand a collective identity that was the precondition of any liberties he and his family enjoyed.

In the classical conception of citizenship, then, to speak was to participate actively in an environment focused greatly on collectivity. Learning how to communicate by means of rhetorical instruction was an integral part of belonging to it. Performing well doubtless enhanced an individual's status in the eyes of others but, in the final instance, it was the wider group that was thought to benefit. Citizenship – although limited to a select number, all of them men – was functional to the community's survival. That is why, in the work of Aristotle (1988), the highest good of the *polis* was understood as the ultimate guiding thread for citizens. In his view, only a limited number of participating citizens were likely to defend the common good; a democracy in the fullest sense would end up as mob rule. Likewise, in republican Rome, full citizenship was not granted to everyone, nor were all citizens strictly equal in the powers they could wield; the political order was entrusted largely to a number of aristocrats who dominated the Senate from where ruling Consuls were drawn (see Connolly, 2007; see also Ober, 1991).

That sense of a powerful communal obligation had an impact on the teaching of rhetoric. Speech, too, was expected to conform to the higher need of the community for stability and survival in time and space. That expectation was expressed in concepts such as the Greek term *kairos* and the Roman idea of *status*. *Kairos* concerned the sense of 'appropriateness' of rhetoric to 'time, place and circumstance', that is, the accordance of an argument to what is given as true to the community at a given moment (see Lanham, 1991: 94). Contra Plato, rhetoricians taught speakers to address audiences in terms of what was reasonable for the community at the time, not what was rational outside of all time and place. Likewise, the later Roman concept of *status* (or *stasis* in Greek) denoted a deliberate effort to determine the space of conflict around an agreed issue (for example, whether a legal dispute hinged on a matter of fact, interpretation or motivation;

see Lanham, 1991: 93–94). By these concepts, speaking citizens in ancient times were encouraged to adopt strategies that worked within collectively recognized parameters (see Carter, 1988). Although there remained considerable room for disagreement about those parameters and how they were met, it was the responsibility of public speakers to demonstrate that they could align the content of their arguments to a common sense of time and space so that communal needs would remain paramount.

However, it is the close connection between citizenship and deference to the time and space of the community that contrasts with modern ideas of political membership. Although the classical idea of politics was still influential up to the early modern period in Europe, the notion of active, participatory citizenship was eventually supplanted by a more limited idea that only faintly echoes the earlier version. The rights-bearing citizen that emerged from religious wars and, importantly, the French revolution, although drawing upon the Roman idea of equality before the law, involved a wholly new conception of freedom, equality and responsibility (see Bellamy, 2008; Heater, 1990).

Let me sketch some of the important differences here. Fundamentally, the modern, broadly 'liberal' notion of citizenship dispenses with the embracing sense of community of the classical version. In the modern notion, membership of the political community entails a minimal obligation to observe the state's laws, not a responsibility to participate in the sustenance of a specific way of life or to pursue the common good. Here the state is not so much a higher moral community of which individuals are an integral part but, rather, an instrument for the preservation of order. Moreover, this independent public authority has the primary role of protecting the private freedoms and formal rights granted to citizens. As the institutional arm of public order, the state is typically constrained by constitutional law to prevent it from overly interfering with individual freedoms and encroaching upon rights. As we saw in the previous chapter, institutionally speaking, the sovereign is formally independent of the body of citizens over whom it governs. It remains the guarantor of individual rights and freedoms, but those are often regarded as embodying sovereignty too – that is, they are absolute and indivisible. So the politics of modern liberal orders usually entails a policing of the boundaries between citizen and state, with a strong emphasis on preserving the sphere of private right from illegitimate interference. That stands in direct contrast with the classical notion of politics, in which there was no fundamental boundary between public and private.

The modern state is therefore a political association promoting a distinct understanding of freedom: namely, individual freedom exercised outside the formal public domain. Individuals are thought to fulfil their personal sense of the good without regard to the concerns of public life. As many commentators and critics have pointed out – Karl Marx being the most famous (see, in particular, Marx, 1994) – this is a notion of private life congruent with market societies in which the pursuit of private gain is paramount. It is a notion that does not rule out *all* sense of collective belonging, but the demands of collectivity do not bear upon the individual citizen in anything like the same way as they did in the classical world. Above all, there is an assumption that society will endure more effectively if citizens attend to their own affairs, leaving the public sphere to a select group of experts. As the Swiss political writer Benjamin Constant put it in a speech of 1820: 'we can no longer enjoy the liberty of the ancients, which consisted in an active and constant participation in collective power. Our freedom must consist of peaceful enjoyment and private independence' (Constant, 1988: 316).

Formal citizenship in modern society therefore demands little of citizens as political participants. As a consequence, oratory and public speaking remain limited to the few who undertake a public function. The sense of a tight-knit community gives way to the more complex times and spaces of capitalism and the nation-state, with experts in particular fields working with degrees of independence from direct public scrutiny. In democratic parliaments, especially, debate and argument over political affairs is entrusted to representatives rather than the full citizen body. Of course, if the responsibility for political judgement is handed to an elite, nevertheless debate continues, which interested citizens share via public media such as newspapers and pamphlets and other public fora. While formal speaking is regulated and limited, mass literacy and the expansion of rights to assembly and free speech nonetheless grant modern citizens a considerable amount of informal opportunities to engage in debate.

In the modern notion of citizenship sketched above, speaking is not a central requirement. Indeed, direct participation in public life generally is not expected, at least not from everyone. The great merit of the idea is that it permits the individual to cultivate a private life and personal associations in myriad ways, much of which need not be justified in the name of a 'higher order' of values or made accountable to a prior conception of the good life. As citizens, individuals are free to determine their own interests without the burden of communal expectations, yet still under the protection of the law. Instead of emphasizing participation, modern (and usually western) societies have extended citizenship in other ways, by, for example, expanding the number of individuals with political rights and granting civil rights to protect them as they pursue their private freedoms. In addition, social rights have been added to enable more people to share in the benefits of private liberty by removing many of them from conditions of poverty and illness. Although supplemented by a growing variety of social, civil and increasingly 'human' rights, modern citizenship has remained relatively thin in relation to its political dimension (see Marshall and Bottomore, 1987).

The lack of depth to modern citizenship has led some to lament the loss of the virtues of the ancient idea. Indeed, a sense of solidarity with the community and a desire to speak to and for 'shared traditions' is common in the recurrent nostalgia for ancient virtues. The philosopher David Hume, for instance, remarked in an essay, 'Of Eloquence', that despite the great advantages of modern society and its application of reason, 'our progress in eloquence is very inconsiderable, in comparison of the advances, which we have made in all other parts of learning' (Hume, 1987: I.XIII.8). The 'sublime and passionate' oratory of the ancients, he argued, shines in comparison to the rational but dull public speakers and politicians of the eighteenth century. A similar but more substantial sensitivity to the loss of ancient virtues is found in the work of Arendt (1959). For her, the ancient idea of political association, where citizens meet to determine their common fate through speech, contrasts radically with modern political orders. The idea of sovereignty, she argued, makes politics a matter of the assertion of will – the indisputable and final judgement of a subject expressed through the state (see Arendt, 2000: 454) – whereas the ancients saw political judgement as an open-ended and creative process of collective deliberation among a plurality of citizens. Where today the freedom of the private individual is prized above community, in ancient times the freedom of the community had primacy. For Arendt, that was a genuinely political freedom, where speech and argument were central components of human action. Although neither Hume nor Arendt recommends a direct return to ancient citizenship (and, interestingly, Arendt says next to nothing about rhetoric), both regard the higher value of speech that characterized it as instructive of what is lacking in modern societies. Yet without a sense of communal time and space by which to regulate speech and maintain it within natural parameters, how can rhetoric continue to have a political role for modern citizens?

The politics of representation

The nostalgia that often accompanies reflections on rhetoric responds to an important, intellectual transformation in modern societies that distinguishes them from those of the past and profoundly alters the way in which the political dimension is now experienced. It is therefore worth thinking again about the difference between ancient and modern citizenship in light of this transformation. The difference derives from what is variably described as the loss of transcendent foundations, 'disenchantment' or the 'decentring of society'. It means that society is no longer conceived as an essentially harmonious unity centred on a fixed, transhistorical essence, such as God, and mediated by some privileged individual or collective body. Rather, it is exposed to the fluctuation of contingent forces without any secure anchor. Society – the social roles we are given, the nature of authority, justice and power – is no longer widely thought to mirror a higher or deeper order of values grounded in a shared sense of community. With no guarantee of the ultimate harmony of its different elements, society comes to be seen as fractured and unmotivated by any overarching purpose. Rather, as Niccolò Machiavelli was one of the first to point out, in *The Prince*, political action involves bringing order to a world that does not exhibit any intrinsic moral or objective cohesion (see Machiavelli, 1988). In those circumstances, political power comes to be understood as an intrinsically amoral and impersonal force, indeterminate in its specific content. Quentin Skinner argues that the idea of the modern state, conceived as a separate entity over and above its citizens, is informed by the perception that authority is no longer naturally embodied in the physical assembly of its citizens (as in classical republican thought) or in the body of the prince (as in monarchist absolutism; see Skinner, 1989). The state is an abstract agency – an artificial person, as Hobbes put it – whose authority rests on *not* being equated with any specific individual or group.

For Claude Lefort (1988: 17–19), that indeterminacy of authority – which found expression in the American and French democratic revolutions of the late eighteenth century – involves political power becoming what he calls an 'empty place' – that is, a location with no fixed content; rather, the place of power can be 'occupied' by numerous actors, but never fully and finally expressed by any one of them or in any agreed idea of the Good. With the advent of democracy, especially, no one can claim to mediate between society and the higher order, so guaranteeing divine or rational status to its pronouncements. Instead, authority is only partially and temporarily occupied by limited agents, who struggle to represent (rather than embody) the interests of all. As political philosopher Ernesto Laclau puts it: 'Incompletion and provisionality belong to the essence of democracy' (Laclau, 1996: 16).

The loss of a transcendent principle of society and justification for authority is at the heart of the modern idea of citizenship. It fundamentally alters the way citizens relate to the political realm and, consequently, alters the function of rhetorical speech. No longer are citizens members of a self-contained or 'organic' community; rather, they are part of an incomplete society whose unity is permanently in question and constantly needs to be represented anew. Rhetoric now functions not as the elevated speech of the community but, rather, as a means to represent society in its quest for an elusive social unity. There are two aspects to this representative politics that bear on citizenship and rhetoric, and which I would like to underline: first, the dynamic relation between the 'universal' and 'particular' aspects of community; second, the 'aesthetic' character of representation.

The universal and the particular

The distinction between universal and particular refers to the unifying and differentiating dimensions of a community. Modern societies are widely understood to have expanded the possibilities for legitimate differences in society (the element of particularity) while simultaneously loosening the hold of values and principles that, purportedly, transcend those differences and join them as equivalent parts of a whole (the element of universality). The weakening of religious claims on social and political life has steadily enabled a greater plurality of differences to emerge. That greater diversity, expressed in demands for liberty both in politics and in society more widely, does not eliminate the need for universal values. But the proliferation of particular liberties (economic, intellectual, sexual and so on) is increasingly in tension with what it is that makes them equal. The universal dimension of society comes to be a topic of dispute, its boundaries and shape constantly in question as new demands emerge (see Laclau, 1996: ch. 2).

How does this affect the idea of citizenship and rhetoric? Citizenship has always implied a confluence of particular differences (discrete individuals and their different needs and demands) and a universal identity, necessary to all, that makes people equal. As we have noted, in ancient Athens, priority was given to a universal dimension of existence, conceived as the substantive 'way of life' of the Athenian community. The particularities of citizens were certainly not erased, but they were subordinated to their shared identity as members of the *polis*. Citizens' private affairs, for example, were kept out of the purview of public debate to preserve the latter from corruption. Equally, the exclusion of women, slaves and foreigners from citizenship minimized the extent of potential differences. The democratic regime in ancient Greece therefore distributed speaking roles widely across its citizen body, but with clear restrictions that sustained a strong sense of the universal dimension.

The ancient primacy of the universal is clearly mirrored in explicit attitudes towards rhetoric. As we saw in the previous chapter, rhetorical practices were conceived by many as integral to the life of the community – that is, as necessary to its identity. On the other hand, critics such as Plato saw universality as eternal Forms accessible only to the most gifted intellectuals. For him, ancient democracy undermined the universal by allowing particularity to corrupt it. There could, in his view, only be one kind of society that adhered to universal principles – a hierarchical one where philosopher-kings ruled and everyone else fulfilled their allotted roles. Yet, for all their stark differences, both perspectives saw the stability and purity of the universal dimension as having priority over the particular.

In modern societies, by contrast, universality remains but has softened its connection to one, exclusive way of life, so transforming citizenship and, as I shall argue, the standing and function of rhetoric. Without a fixed order of social ranks and hierarchies premised on a societal essence, modern democracy postpones the idea of a complete or self-contained society and that, in turn, allows a variety of particular groups to demand inclusion. The indeterminacy of power permits a greater variety of images of the common good and hence invites a diversity of agents to enter the fray. The result has been an increased plurality of citizens and their voices, but also a constant struggle of competing conceptions of social order and the universal principles that purportedly give it coherence. It is no surprise that the democratic age is also an 'age of ideologies', since democracy not only offers the possibility of membership to different groups but also provides space for competing representations of the society citizens are members of. Contrasting ideological programmes present alternative conceptions of the proper boundaries of societal relations: the 'balance' of state and society, the public and the private, liberty and discipline, and so forth. In each, we find variations in the ways in which universal values – which promise the achievement of social harmony – are combined with particular differences.

In the history of modern democratic states, then, we find a variety of different groups struggling for citizenship – workers, women, ethnic and religious groups – mobilizing or redefining universal ideals that promote varying degrees and terms of inclusion and exclusion. As Marx and other critics of liberalism remind us, these universals are often particular elements of society writ large: the self-interested bourgeois, the white male European, the 'ethnic' national, the working man and so on. What is universal is never without some grounding in the particular. Universal principles are often presented as being founded upon the underlying 'truth' of society, whose full realization guarantees the future reconciliation of all (legitimate) differences between citizens.

As Michael Freeden (1996) argues, ideologies both contest and 'decontest' universal values. That is, they promote certain universal ideals (individual liberty, social equality, national identity and so on) as intrinsically superior to others that they diminish or oppose and, in so doing, treat those ideals as incontestable principles whose validity is self-evident. Thus ideological rhetoric is heavily principled – mobilizing values supported by vast constituencies – but also deeply antagonistic. The political is experienced less and less as a privileged time and space of deliberation based on common premises and fellow feeling, and more as a sharp contest of competing arguments representing ideas of how a good society can properly be accomplished (see Balibar, 2002: ch. 8).

Aesthetic representation

Aesthetic representation refers to the way in which the political dimension in modern conditions relates to society, now conceived as an inherently incomplete order in search of unification. As Frank Ankersmit (1996) has argued, modernity entails the steady loss of the view that political authority directly 'reflects' a transcendent order of truth, and its replacement by the notion of *re*-presentation of society by contingent actors (that is, elected or appointed political representatives in parliament or elsewhere, such as the media or culture). In his view, such representation must be distinguished from 'mimesis': even in liberal democracies where 'the people' are supposedly sovereign, politics does not directly reflect society; it is not a mirror or measure of it. Rather, like a painting and its object, politics is an 'aesthetic' representation of society, a partial and fabricated version of the people and its demands, one that never fully corresponds to it in its totality: 'representation is essentially a process of depiction' (Ankersmit, 1996: 45; see also Laclau, 1996: ch. 6).

Ankersmit underscores the point that the distance between society and its representation can never be overcome. Rather, representation relies on that distance and the opportunities it creates to vary, perhaps reimagine altogether, what society is. Like the visual arts, politics substitutes for society rather than mirrors it. For that reason, Ankersmit criticizes schools of thought that seek to install an identity between politics and social interests, whether through rigorous electoral systems or ethical rules that try to make politics transparently reflective of something 'more real'. The 'aesthetic gap', as he calls it, creates a space between represented and representatives, people and the state, that cannot be judged according to objective criteria (just as paintings should not be judged as to whether they accurately mirror their object): 'That is why the elimination of the aesthetic gap between the voter and the representative is not the realization of democracy, but an invitation to tyranny' (Ankersmit, 1996: 104). The drive to create an identity between state and society – to fill the gap or substantially embody the place of power – is the source, he claims, of totalitarian thought.

Politics, continues Ankersmit, is a creative activity – an 'art' – in so far as seeking to represent others (through elections or communication) is a matter not of following preconceived rules but, rather, of style and taste (ibid.: 54).

Representatives are not 'delegates' of their constituents but substitutes for them. Their success relies on their ability to creatively style themselves according to the tastes and feelings of their voters, shaping themselves in ways that invoke a seemingly 'authentic' relationship between them (see Saward, 2010). Of course, representatives often *claim* to be accurately reflecting the interests or needs of their constituents, as though representation was indeed mimesis, a simple identity shared between the one and the other. But that claim is illusory, not least because representatives do not regularly consult with their constituents to make decisions or secure seamless continuity with their views.

Ankersmit's idea of aesthetic representation helps to clarify the relationship between modern citizenship and rhetoric. Citizens who are represented, rather than themselves embodiments of the public good, are able to view themselves from the point of view of others, to locate themselves in a wider set of relations outside of themselves. To Ankersmit, that condition is potentially a 'civilizing' one in so far as it decentres the citizen from public life and therefore permits a greater tolerance for others whose demands must also form part of the act of representation (1996: 56). But, we might add, the aesthetic gap can also result in conflict and efforts to narrow the distance between public and private realms by prioritizing a narrow set of values, feelings and styles over others.

As regards rhetoric, or the character of public debate, we can understand the antagonism of modern ideologies as part of the 'friction' between state and society that the aesthetic gap entails. The state becomes a permanent terrain of contest over different ideals, the repository of numerous political strategies and the arguments that inform them. Far from reflecting the outcome of rational syntheses of opinion or the formation of shared premises, public policy is a selective process which, as Ankersmit points out, as much involves ignoring or dismissing an opponent's views as it does confronting and answering them (ibid.: 106–11).

Rhetorical speech (and, indeed, other forms of representation) can be understood as part of the aesthetic bridging of the gap between state and society. In principle, democratic rhetoric enables alternative styles of representing (and hence shaping) opinion and contrasting conceptions of the shared parameters of time and space. Undoubtedly, some styles predominate over others – white, male, middle-class representatives have been the norm in most western democracies and consequently give parliamentary rhetoric a certain hue. Nonetheless, as the enormous attention paid to the public image of politicians and parties testifies, style and the shaping of public taste for partisan political purposes have both become fundamental elements of communication in modern democracies. This is especially so following the expansion of communicative technologies in the twentieth century (which we consider in Chapter 8).

In summary, then, we can say that modernity involves a transformation of the experience of political life that wholly recasts the ancient idea of citizenship and the practices of rhetoric. What appears as a depoliticization of the citizen and a diminution of rhetoric is better conceived as a reconfiguration of the dimensions of political encounter. In this new environment – built around the essential incompleteness of society – membership does indeed become more formal than solidaristic and participatory. But citizenship is also removed from attachment to any one specific community or way of life and becomes an open-ended project where different types of solidarity may be imagined, though often in a fraught relation to established parameters of the state. Likewise, rhetoric loses its status as the elevated speech of a civic community of citizens. It, too, is pluralized and becomes more open to the vernacular and popular traditions, again always in potential conflict with the social order and established values and customs. Oratory and rhetorical persuasion are diminished as the primary medium of public power, replaced by bureaucracy, written text and force (see Ong, 1982). But social relations in general (that is, traditions, customs, social roles and conceptions of the world associated with them) are increasingly revealed as conventional and open to rhetorical contest, or what Richard Rorty calls 'redescription' (Rorty, 1989; see also Vattimo, 2004).

In the modern environment, oratory has lost its centrality to political life and yet, because of this, rhetoric permeates society in more diverse ways than ever before, as part of multiple efforts to represent citizens and their common demands. Rhetoric is no longer key to the self-government of a polity by its citizens but is part of a wider politics of representation in which citizenship and the limits of the modern community become open to redefinition.

Contemporary political philosophy and rhetoric

In this final section I want to survey ways in which citizenship and rhetoric are figured in key contemporary approaches in political theory. At the risk of simplification, these can be categorized as approaches from liberalism, critical theory and postmodernism. Although they occasionally overlap, unlike other theoretical positions such as communitarianism or Marxism, each takes up the challenge of modernity to find a way of conceptualizing citizenship without invoking a substantial concept of community or common good (see Kymlicka, 2002 for a general discussion).

Liberalism

Modern political orders have been substantially influenced by liberal political thought, especially the work of thinkers such as John Locke and John Stuart Mill. Liberals such as these embraced the separation of state and society as the essential condition for individual freedom. Without a single conception of the good life, a plurality of projects can freely co-exist. Liberated from the bonds of public duty but protected by their rights, individuals thrive in the private sphere and choose to participate in public life at their own will. For liberals, the absence of a transcendent authority requires us purposefully to draw a balance between the particularity of individuals and the universal preconditions of their association. The co-existence of separate public and private domains is achieved by constitutional controls on government and mediation between government and society by an informed elite. In that way, government is prevented from overreaching itself by imposing unwarranted universal values and principles on society. However, undergirding much, though not all, of liberal political philosophy has been a rationalism that understands universal values – primarily the value of individual liberty – as founded upon the implicit direction and development of society itself, which is understood to entail the progressive expansion of freedom and the ultimately harmonious reconciliation of differences (see Bellamy, 1992; Gray, 2000).

For much of the first half of the twentieth century, however, liberalism seemed at odds with the prevailing direction of society. War, economic crisis and class conflict all indicated that liberal principles were not written into history but were the outcome of contingent circumstances not universally shared. Liberal philosophers later sought to overcome this deficiency by making explicit the reasoning behind liberal ideals and by demonstrating their capacity to mediate different demands on government. Perhaps the most significant liberal thinker in the second half of the twentieth century, in this regard, was John Rawls, whose *Theory of Justice* aimed to reconcile the liberal defence of individual liberty with social democratic ideas of wealth redistribution (see Rawls, 1999).

Famously, Rawls claimed that redistributive measures were philosophically defensible for liberals only in so far as they improved the circumstances of the worst off. That is, it was just to treat people differently (that is, tax some more than others), rather than as strict, formal equals, if doing so permitted those with less wealth to improve their lot and so exercise their rights and opportunities with greater success. That conclusion was rationally demonstrable by means of a purportedly 'impartial' form of reasoning: Rawls invited his readers to imagine themselves being behind a 'veil of ignorance', unaware of the circumstances into which they might be born and the opportunities that would be available to them. From the perspective of that imaginary 'original position', claimed Rawls, it was reasonable to argue that wealth should be redistributed to allow those who are born into poverty or inherit other circumstances that limit their ability to live free and autonomous lives.

How did Rawls view the relationship between rhetoric and citizenship? At its heart, his argument defends the idea that particular private needs can be reconciled because a universal rationality demonstrates the justness of redistributive measures. In that argument, rational judgement is a subjective exercise and not a practice of actual individuals communicating and persuading each other to shape their judgements. The 'impartial' reasoning that Rawls expounds is deemed to be transparently available to all rational individuals and does not require active debating among citizens (see May, 2008: 11–13). Rawls's philosophy therefore leaves little room for the aesthetic gap in which style may intervene in forming judgements: in the original position we are bereft of any such distinguishing features, and thus reason alike on the basis of logic alone. Like other liberals of the late twentieth century, Rawls's approach is that of a legal philosopher, concerned with abstract principles and their application. In Ankersmit's terms, Rawls presents a view of public life in terms of mimesis – that is, the mirroring by political orders of rational principles deemed universally valid.

In Rawls's liberalism, there is little room for a dynamic rhetorical interaction of universal and particular – where different, perhaps opposed versions of public reason are contested and one view comes to achieve dominance. In his later work, however, Rawls agreed that his account of justice could not be claimed, in strictly Kantian terms, as universally valid for all. His was a 'political liberalism' – that is, contingent upon particular societies and not necessarily shared by all (see Rawls, 2005). Yet, despite this, Rawls saw no real problem with the idea that rational citizens might come to what he called an 'overlapping consensus' about the rules by which they agreed to live. Again, that consensus was presented as the product of a purely subjective reflection in which people set aside knowledge of who they actually are, not an actual process of discussion by citizens, with all their distinguishing features and abilities (see Mouffe, 1993: 41–59).

Of course, not all liberals adopt Rawls's philosophy to justify their outlook. Many are happy to accept that politics is a rhetorical activity where representatives vigorously compete to persuade citizens to endorse the principles they promote and so vote for them accordingly. The virtue of a liberal order is not that it is philosophically grounded but that it sustains a common allegiance to individual liberty (however defined) and refuses the alternatives of moral coercion (as in Plato) or endless, disruptive conflict and insecurity (as in Hobbes). Such is the view, for example, of Richard J. Burke, who confidently claimed that 'modern American politics is best understood […] as a sort of ongoing debating society in which everyone is trying to score points according to the agreed-upon rules' (1982: 54). Yet that perspective requires there to be a settled consensus over the value of individual liberty and what it practically means. The political dimension – the aspect of controversy over principles – is here radically diminished so that rhetoric appears as a kind of harmless exchange of opinion. In light of the historical struggles to bring civil and political equality to all US citizens, more recent conflicts (physical as well as verbal) over race and gender and the authoritarian response to the 'war on terror', such a consensus seems not to be settled at all.

Critical theory

Against the apparently complacent view that citizens would be happy to put aside their differences and agree common principles without actually communicating or conflicting, the tradition of thought known as critical theory has sought to inject greater practical involvement of citizens in the formulation of shared principles. In this, its proponents have been open to the interaction of universality and particularity and to the place of aesthetics in shaping public life (see Bronner, 2011). The dominant figure in this enterprise has been the philosopher Jürgen Habermas, although that is not to say that all who work under the label of critical theory agree wholeheartedly with him. Nonetheless, Habermas provides the primary points of reference for a critical theoretical approach to citizenship and the positive value of public argument, and it is therefore worth dwelling on his ideas.

Habermas, like his earlier critical theorist predecessors, emerged from a Marxian theoretical framework that aspired to the liberation of individuals from structures and systems of oppression (particularly economic oppression under capitalism). In that vein, Habermas developed a theory of 'communicative action' that would advance on Marxism's traditional focus on labour by setting out a conception of intersubjective dialogue as a precondition for human emancipation. In communicative action, argued Habermas, citizens debated and held to account the authorities and powers that shaped their lives. His model for that conception came originally from his studies on the 'bourgeois public sphere' that emerged in the late eighteenth century in the form of cafes and salons where merchants and businessmen freely discussed and criticized public policy (see Habermas, 1989). In this they formed a mass of self-generated critical opinion that could bear on government and influence its direction. While that opinion slanted in favour of particular interests, nonetheless, argued Habermas, the key to legitimizing public power is to rebuild the public sphere, where free 'opinion formation' might occur, and keep a check on the otherwise autonomous and potentially pernicious systems of the state and capitalism.

We can see, then, that Habermas's response to the separation of state from society, unlike that of liberals such as Rawls, is to advocate an intermediary space of dialogue where public life is exposed to the critical interrogation and opinion of its citizens. Habermas's project has been to define the preconditions that permit critical dialogue among citizens and between them and the formal public sphere or state. He, too, accepts that there is no preconceived common good. Like many contemporary liberals, he proposes a 'deontological' ethics – a conception of morality divorced from an explicit account of the good life. Citizens themselves ought to formulate moral principles via democratic procedures that structure their communication and enable them to test the 'validity' of the normative claims they make (see Habermas, 1996a). Collective moral discourse, then, rather than Rawls's 'monological' justification, is the basis for forming binding judgements of a universal nature:

> If moral argumentation is to produce this kind of agreement, however, it is not enough for the individual to reflect on whether he can assent to a norm. It is not even enough for each individual to reflect in this way and then to register his vote. What is needed is a "real" process of argumentation in which the individuals concerned cooperate. Only an intersubjective process of reaching understanding can produce an agreement that is reflexive in nature; only it can give the participants the knowledge that they have collectively become convinced of something.
>
> (Habermas, 1996b: 186)

Habermas calls the procedures for testing validity 'discourse ethics' – impartial rules designed to be inclusive but also to constrain dialogue in such a way as to eliminate 'distortions' that impede reaching a 'rational consensus'. For him, validity claims are intrinsic to any 'speech act' in so far as they are always presupposed but can be actually tested by participants raising objections and demanding further justification (see Habermas, 1996b: 147). The content of any dialogue will vary, but implicit validity norms are deemed universal to communicative acts aimed at reaching mutual understanding. By instituting forms of deliberation based on discourse ethics, he argues, citizens can – together – reach common judgements about their shared arrangements, eliminating claims that are untrue, inappropriate or insincere. The achievement of a rational consensus is, of course, only an ideal; any actual dialogue may fall short of fulfilling all the criteria to everyone's satisfaction, but that does not, in his view, undermine its value as a democratic answer to the conditions of modern societies.

Habermas's ideas have been extraordinarily influential in the development of the theory of 'deliberative democracy' (to which we shall return in Chapter 7). In that view, citizens are active participants in debating, contesting and ultimately agreeing the principles that govern them collectively. Discourse ethics are designed to uphold the separation of state and society, yet also to mediate between the two in such a way that particular differences can be reconciled by means of (discursively revealed) universal principles. But, as many critics have pointed out, the claim to have grounded discourse ethics in reason radically narrows the possible kinds of communicative encounters and, at worst, threatens to exclude ways of arguing and persuading that do not fit with it – that is, claims that cannot be 'rationally' justified. Such claims might be dismissed as distortions of the truth, inappropriate or insincere because they do not fit with preconceptions of what is rational. In short, far from being impartial rules, discourse ethics may well pass off forms of power and control under the guise of universal reason (see Calhoun, 1992). Moreover, the demand for rational justification does not admit much in the way of aesthetic play or stylistic variation which, though not entirely ruled out, are deemed irrelevant to the fundamental goals of agreement. Indeed, Ankersmit himself sees Habermas's ethics as a way of overcoming the aesthetic gap by securing a mimetic relation between state and society.

Postmodernism

Although, again, a very broad term, so-called 'postmodern' philosophies have involved a quite distinctive approach both to citizenship and to the place of speech and rhetoric. Central to postmodern thought is what Jean-Francois Lyotard called 'an incredulity toward metanarratives' (Lyotard, 1984: xxiv); that is, a scepticism concerning totalizing conceptions of society and history that imply a coherent structure that unifies their parts and which a properly elaborated rational outlook alone can grasp. For postmodernists, broadly speaking, neither society nor history can be anchored around a stable principle independent of language and symbolic representation. The historical separation of state from society, then, was the precursor not to a more rational correspondence between the two, but to a destabilization of all authority. Postmodern thinkers therefore tend to enhance the significance of 'rhetoricality' in general and often emphasize the ultimately linguistic and arbitrary character of universal principles (see Richards, 2008: ch. 3; Bernard-Donals and Glejzer, 1998; Rorty, 1989; Fish, 1989). For many, that is an opportunity for a citizenship of much greater particularity, but also controversy and conflict. While there is no single dominant thinker in a postmodern approach, 'poststructuralist' figures such as Michel Foucault and Jacques Derrida stand as influential representatives. Central to their work is a rejection of the idea of the human subject, or self, conceived as a naturally autonomous, self-sufficient agent directed by its own conscious purposes and free will. This so-called 'anti-humanism' undermines the view that universal principles can ever be finally found by gaining access to an uncontested truth free from contamination with particularity.

Foucault, for instance, argued that the subject was itself an effect of various forms of knowledge and institutions that shape human desire and selfhood in particular ways. The individual, in his view, is not born self-sufficient and only later confronts pressures to conform in one way or another with society; rather, the individual is the product of various 'disciplinary' practices and discourses that shape it from birth and impress upon it certain truths and abilities (Foucault, 1980: 117). Famously, Foucault saw these pressures as forms of power – not a repressive type of power that blocked a pre-existing freedom, but a productive or 'positive' form of power that enabled the subject to accomplish certain things. In that respect, power is different from 'domination' (see Foucault, 1997: 283). Institutional discourses around sexuality, education, crime and punishment, and health and illness, for example, nurture subjects amenable to techniques of self-control and allow individuals to operate 'freely' in society. Power, in this conception, is not opposed to individual freedom but is, rather, a condition of it. Indeed, for Foucault, we need to dispense with the idea of power as a repressive instrument concentrated in the state – for him, power (in the form of discourses about knowledge) circulates throughout society and is never located exclusively in the hands of political authorities or the wealthy (see Foucault, 1980: 115–22; 1977). In his view, society is not a total structure operating around a power centre that amasses control, but a diverse and uneven assemblage riven with forms of resistance and subversion (Phillips, 2006).

Similarly, Derrida rejected the view of an implicit structure to society or history (see Derrida, 1978: 278–93). In his philosophy of 'deconstruction', he refused the view of language as a transparent medium of communication by means of which an autonomous actor could represent an independent reality to another without in some way interfering in it. That is not to say that we cannot communicate but, rather, that all meaning is bound up with – and therefore inflected by – its mode of representation (see Derrida, 1976; 1988). Thus Derrida disputed the view that human speech was somehow superior to writing because it emanates in an unmediated way from the consciousness of the speaker (whereas writing makes use of graphic signs that, by definition, function at a distance from the original intentions). Indeed, speech is itself a form of writing because it also tries to represent by means of signs, such as sounds, pauses, emphases and so on. Thus there is no communication that is not open to the inflections and figurations of language, but also to their possible misunderstanding or reinterpretation in different contexts. It is therefore wrong to think in terms of a pure and transparent language that does not delay or interrupt meaning in some way.

With their criticism of humanist accounts of subjectivity and the idea of representation-free and power-free communication, poststructuralist philosophers appear to undermine the classical rhetorical focus on the persuasive speaker. Moreover, they imply that modern politics can never fully resolve clashes between citizens, since no universal reason or stable moral principle can genuinely be established. How, then, might a democratic political theory build upon these ideas?

Postmodern political theorists tend to see the impossibility of universal reason as an opportunity not for chaos but for a radical democratic politics that legitimizes a plurality of social differences (see Laclau and Mouffe, 2001; Little and Lloyd, 2009). In that conception, the presumed stability and coherence of universal values are brought into question, as is the coherence and stability of the very groups whose identities are marginalized or oppressed by those values. The decline of philosophical and cultural supports to dominant principles, however, does not mean they disappear overnight; rather, their grip on society is increasingly open to contest (see Vattimo, 2004; Martin, 2010). Thus, for example, feminist criticisms of patriarchy do not do away with patriarchy, but render it ever less tenable as a naturalized belief and source of commonplace judgements.

So a postmodern politics does not dispute the effect of all rhetoric and rhetorical strategies. Rather, it disputes the claim that there is a single language of communication that can stand outside of power relations and arbitrate between all voices without remainder. There is no one style of speaking, no one set of universal principles, no one actor that represents all. Postmodern theorists therefore emphasize the dynamic interaction of universal and particular, exposing universal principles to greater variation and transformation rather than renouncing them entirely (see Rorty, 1989, 1999; Corbin, 1998; Fish, 1994). That is not to say that all interpretations are equal (the common charge of 'relativism'). Rather, it suggests that all universal claims are – at least in principle – open to dispute and controversy. The emphasis in postmodern political theories is often therefore on legitimizing difference and conflict in rhetorical encounters among citizens rather than harmonizing them (see Mouffe, 2005, 1992; Isin, 2009, 2008, 2002; Balibar, 2004; Phillips, 1996). Like critical theorists, postmodern thinkers see contemporary society as open to greater democratic involvement in the formation of common ways of being. But unlike critical theory, postmodernism refuses the idea that democracy can be anything more than a temporary and contingent stabilization of conflict.

The three general approaches sketched above do not exhaust all forms of contemporary political theory, but they provide a clue as to its broad orientations. Each approach accepts the institutional and symbolic separation of state and society as the starting point for reflecting on the character of contemporary citizenship, but each adopts a different perspective on the place of rhetoric and its part in the life of citizens. Contemporary liberalism endorses a plurality of citizens and conceptions of the good life, but more than the other approaches it minimizes the place of public speech in formulating judgements on universal principles. In its typically analytical and legalistic language, universal principles are often defended as a matter of reason. Critical theorists, by contrast, emphasize the importance of citizens' collective deliberation in formulating universal principles. Yet, as

Habermas's work indicates, such deliberation remains guided by the idea of rules of communication thought to be universally grounded. As with liberalism, then, there remains a suspicion of rhetoric entering the fray and distorting communication. Postmodern thinkers, on the other hand, reject the idea of universal reason and point to the multiplicity of representations such that no *final* foundation is achievable. All human relations are imbued with a potentially political character in so far as they can be disputed and recast according to new principles. Of course, for some that invites a relativism that undercuts any genuine solidarity based on shared truths and makes postmodernism a deceptively conservative outlook (see Habermas, 1987). Postmodernists, however, retort that refusing speech, argument or representation any automatic or intrinsic priority actually permits a radically pluralistic democracy to thrive.

Summary

Rhetoric started out as an integral part of the repertoire of skills for citizens actively participating in the public life of ancient communities, whose unity and survival was felt to be paramount. While today something remains of the idea of elevated speech in the formal political arenas and especially in law courts, I have argued that the state's separation from society has fundamentally altered the relationship between citizens and the dimension of the political. No longer are we so automatically deferent to a singular, hierarchical sense of community whose boundaries must be respected. Public authority is now open to contest over the source and character of its representation. In the gap opened up between public power and citizens, different voices contend to define the unifying principles of the community and offer up competing styles to represent them.

In the modern era, then, the political dimension is no longer concentrated exclusively in the *polis* but, rather, concerns the wider articulations of state with society, public power and popular opinion, universal and particular. If citizenship no longer demands direct participation and rhetorical engagement as a condition of membership, citizens are nonetheless exposed to the rhetoricality of society more generally – that is, to the contestability and variation of identities, principles and values. Paradoxically, then, the decline of rhetoric as the privileged realm of political discourse coincides with the dispersal of its effects across society more generally. Many people now live in societies that, curiously, permit citizens to talk about almost anything in private; yet those societies remain suspicious of the public value of speech and unwilling to instruct people in it as a condition of citizenship. Contemporary political theories have responded to this situation in different ways: most welcome the division of state and society because of the opportunity it affords for a plurality of ways of life. But there are important distinctions among those theories concerning the role citizens might play in formulating common judgements and how they communicate with each other in so doing. In the next two chapters, we shall turn our attention to the advice on this matter offered by ancient rhetoricians.

4 Techniques I
Discovery and arrangement

What does the ancient study of rhetoric teach us and how might it be relevant today? Classical rhetoric offered its students a series of practical observations and classifications to help the would-be speaker navigate the successive steps and dimensions of public speech. Rhetorical advice was designed to enable a speaker to master a situation by anticipating the occasion and preparing in advance a strategy to achieve successful persuasion. That advice consisted of technical instruction rather than philosophical investigation, typically delivered by word of mouth or via a handbook (sometimes referred to as 'a rhetoric'). Designed to be applicable on numerous different occasions, rhetorical instruction was a mobile body of knowledge – a kind of communications toolbox of many instruments – and varied from teacher to teacher. Today it comprises a vast collection of practical techniques and terms gathered under a range of headings and applied, beyond oratory, to all forms of communication in fields such as politics, law, poetry and literature (see Lanham, 1991; Olmsted, 2006).

In the next two chapters I survey key rhetorical classifications and techniques handed down from antiquity in order to underscore their continued relevance to politics. Unlike the previous chapters, then, the two that follow will serve as a direct resource for undertaking rhetorical analysis and criticism. But we should also bear in mind the earlier discussion concerning rhetoric's mediation of politics and the political. Contemporary handbooks for public speaking and speech writing tend to limit themselves to the immediate concerns of the moment – effective techniques of communication within familiar contexts (see, for example, Atkinson, 2004; Lancaster, 2010). But we need to remember that rhetoric also contributes to shaping such contexts – that is, it helps to set the parameters of debate by representing the community and orienting the audience towards it. Later, in Chapter 6, I combine the elements discussed in these two chapters to discuss the analysis of rhetorical political strategies. In Chapters 4 and 5, however, I consider separately the techniques that make up such strategies, taking as my point of reference four of the five 'canons' of rhetoric (see Table 4.1): *discovery*, *arrangement*, *style* and *delivery* (the fifth, *memory*, concerns how to memorize a speech. It is not significant for us and will not form part of the discussion).

52 *Techniques I: discovery and arrangement*

Table 4.1 The five canons of rhetoric

Latin name	English name	Concerns
1. *Inventio*	Discovery	The argumentative claim and how it is defended
2. *Dispositio*	Arrangement	The structure of the parts of speech
3. *Elocutio*	Style	Techniques of language and linguistic expression
4. *Pronuntiato*	Delivery	Techniques of performance
5. *Memoria*	Memory	Techniques to memorize speech

Source: Corbett and Connors (1999: 17–23).

In this chapter I look at the 'discovery' and arrangement of persuasive arguments. Any speech or contribution to a dialogue is likely to have an argument – that is, a distinct conclusion or point of view of which the audience is to be persuaded. It might advocate a universal claim ('all poverty is wrong'), or define that claim in a distinctive way (by expanding or contracting it: 'poverty leads to crime'), or argue the case for how some particular example fits with it ('high crime rates are a symptom of poverty'). The 'invention' or discovery of arguments, as it was called (in Latin, *inventio*), refers to the choices a speaker makes about the issue at hand in order to convey effectively the desired point of view. Arrangement (or *dispositio*), on the other hand, refers to the procedure of the speech, the combination of various structural elements in a certain order. Like all the canons of rhetoric, however, the two are closely related to the context and to what precisely is at issue. I mentioned in Chapter 1 and in the previous chapter that this sensitivity to time and space – expressed in concepts such as *kairos* and *stasis* – was central to the 'situated' character of rhetoric. So, before we look at these dimensions of persuasive speech, let us first consider the question of occasion and issue.

The occasions of speech

Rhetoric is concerned with persuasive speech as it relates to specific contexts. Aristotle famously distinguished three 'genres' or occasions, according to which different types of persuasion will apply (see Aristotle, 1991: 80–82). These are the ceremonial ('display' or *epideictic*), the judicial (or *forensic*) and, finally, the political (or deliberative; see Table 4.2). All forms of persuasion, he assumed, fall into at least one of these categories. What distinguishes them is their audience, their general orientation towards action, and hence the kind of argument (or message) that suits them.

Ceremonial discourse concerns action oriented towards events in the *present*. The kind of arguments appropriate to such circumstances typically concern praise or blame; or, as Aristotle put it, 'to laud and censure' (Aristotle, 1991: 104). Funeral orations or rousing speeches prior to military battles are ceremonial moments, when the orator is given the task of taking stock of the prevailing situation and of persuading the audience to acknowledge a certain sentiment.

Table 4.2 The genres of speech

Type of persuasion	Occasion	Orientation	Type of discourse	Example
Epideictic	Ceremonial	The present	Praise or blame	Wedding, funeral, presidential inaugural, opening of parliament, national celebration
Forensic	Judicial	The past	What happened? Who did what and what was the motivation?	Court proceedings, committee hearings
Deliberative	Political	The future	How to act? Advantageous or disadvantageous?	Election campaign, public debate, legislative discussion, media debate

Source: Aristotle (1991: 80–82).

Judicial discourse is concerned with action in the *past* and is recognizable in the arguments for prosecution and defence given in courts of law (see Aristotle, 1991: 80–111). Here the audience is often a jury who must be persuaded to form a judgement about what is deemed to have happened in a specific circumstance now past. This will involve re-description of the event and a discussion as to whether the conduct that took place coincides with the law or not. The 'forensic' examination of evidence is a very common feature of this style of argument. It involves picking over the details of an event reconstructed before the audience.

Deliberative discourse, finally, is concerned with action in the *future* and, for Aristotle, involved the properly political style of argument over issues such as legislation, revenues or war (see Aristotle, 1991: 84). Debate over policy or its goals concerns matters that have yet to happen, and hence cannot be treated with the same degree of objectivity as judicial speech. Here persuasion is typically about probabilities (the possible outcomes of a policy or judgement and its potential benefits) and argument is usually directed towards affirming one possible choice of action over alternatives.

Aristotle distinguished these three speech genres but, of course, any single effort at persuasion may utilize elements from all three. A political argument may contain not only advocacy of a specific policy (future) but also a critical dissection of a government's record (past) and, very often, an affirmative celebration of the group gathered to hear the speaker (present). So we ought not to regard the classifications as mutually exclusive. Clearly, the three reflect the type of events that people living in ancient Greece would have regarded as familiar. We may no longer understand these as exemplary forms of public gathering (we might add the realm of public debates occasioned by the media, for example) but, given that much of modern politics was built on images of public life inherited from the ancients, they still provide a useful point of reference.

In contemporary societies we still find events that match or combine Aristotle's threefold distinction. Political debate is obviously driven by the desire to promote preferred policies and visions of collective action. This is what we find in debating chambers in most democracies, but also in the wider media and in the less formal spaces of dialogue and deliberation, especially when the debating chambers either don't exist or are not receptive to an issue. But we also find forensic analysis of the past mixed with political debate – for instance when political leaders and office holders are held to account for decisions they have made – as well as in the law courts. Indeed, debating the past is a constant activity in democratic life, especially now that we can retain so much information in text and digital records. As a consequence, interpreting the past can become an issue with direct influence on the present and the future – as evidenced by the International Court of Justice, which deals with 'crimes against humanity', or the heated debates about the decision to go to war in Iraq in 2003.

Finally, in politics we also find regular forms of ceremonial discourse where a collective sentiment is endorsed. In many democracies today, the head of state or the prime minister will undertake a role as the focus of national attention following a disaster or tragedy, at a moment of national celebration or commemoration. Here the function of speech is not to argue about the future or past so much as to praise or blame certain agents, affirm feelings and rally people behind an ongoing cause. Similarly, political leaders will engage with their own supporters at conventions and public rallies designed primarily to fulfil a ceremonial function. Party conferences and conventions are precisely the place for leaders to show their sympathy with the grassroots organizations that support them. Such ceremonies may look like harmless, non-political celebrations, but they are vital in generating an attentive audience for the future-oriented discourses that follow. Without a sense of common feeling it is difficult to encourage the audience to accept controversial political positions.

If the occasions of speech are never made quite as simple as to fall exclusively into one or another of the three of Aristotle's genres, it is nevertheless worth retaining the analytical separation. For the distinction between ceremonial, forensic and deliberative pinpoints distinctive modes of representing certain principles: ceremonies tend to assume certain shared values; forensic examination may assume certain (legal or factual) principles but question how particular details fit with them; and political debate holds open the possibility that shared principles can be contested or redefined. Even if all three are present on any one occasion, one will often dominate over others. A ritual occasion such as the US President's State of the Union Address, held every year of the term of office at the start of the calendar year, will be partly ceremonial and assume certain values as universal (such as the need to hear the President, the authority of the legislature and so on). That is because it is a ritual with a distinct and widely understood purpose from which the speaker rarely diverges. But it also serves as an occasion to set out the President's own political arguments, if only in general terms, about how government will proceed in the future. Common feelings, particularly with Congressional representatives, will be strongly affirmed, but often as part of the process of elaborating a distinct policy agenda or defining the kind of attitude or style that will orient the presidency. Here the usually uncontroversial affirmation of sentiments in the present will function as a platform to set out preferences for the future.

As we shall see in Chapter 6, if we are to understand any particular use of rhetoric it is important to grasp the kind of occasion that predefines the speech event and the mode of persuasion taken up by the speaker. Speeches and other prepared forms of discourse are usually formulated with a distinct occasion in mind. This is largely so that they conform, at least to some extent, to the expectations of the audience who, it is assumed, will be prepared for a certain kind of event and will respond warmly when its expectations are met. Of course, it may be that the speech is deliberately written *against* the grain of expectations in order to surprise the audience. But that is a risky decision to make and demands not only audacity but also skill. For example, we rarely find wedding speeches dwelling in intimate detail, and at great length, on the past conduct of the bride and groom, because the occasion largely demands the affirmation of goodwill and a deliberate forgetfulness about the past. To diverge radically from the expectations of the audience and the assumed goal of the occasion (what is called *decorum*) is to risk being thought inappropriate and to show poor judgement (being 'indecorous'). On some occasions, such as the proceedings of law courts, close adhesion to expected standards is strictly policed and any serious divergence may be punished. A more effective way of subverting the occasion might be, instead, to insert into a public address comments that diverge only mildly or suggestively from the expected form. In that way, a veneer of formality is maintained but another kind of persuasion can be alluded to. As we shall see later, this 'layered' use of speech occasions is very much the norm in modern democracies.

What this insistence on the speech occasion tells us is that arguments are *social* and not strictly logical activities. Any utterance may be incontrovertibly true – as a statement of fact or logic – but if it is delivered at an occasion that does not suit it, its truth may be lost on the audience. Formulating an argument means acknowledging the constraints of the occasion, the way in which convention makes some things socially acceptable and others not. For example, many people are disappointed if they attend a law court as a witness or even as a defendant only to discover that it is not arranged simply so that they can 'have their say in court'. To think about the formal expectations of an occasion is to begin to shape an argument according to power relations that pre-date the event – sometimes to affirm those relations, sometimes to exploit them, perhaps even to subvert them. Either way, the occasion will give us some clue as to what kind of audience will be faced and to what type(s) of message it will in all likelihood be receptive.

The issue

The 'issue' refers to what is at stake on any speech occasion. Of course, the type of occasion will give us some idea about the roles taken up by participants (for example, in a judicial setting: audience as jury, the presence of a judge, lawyers as the main speakers, plaintiff and defendant) but it will not tell us exactly what it is that needs to be argued or how speakers approach their designated roles. This all concerns 'the matter at hand' – that is, what is in question or doubt – and that is particular to the specific event. Nevertheless, understanding the issue is vital for working out what kind of 'stance', or attitude, to take as a speaker. If I am supporting an argument against critics, rather than proposing one, my stance may be defensive, cautious even, and responsive to certain claims made against me. If I am recounting the factual details of a past event, I will need to be precise and able to discriminate what might seem to be the case from what is so. If I am celebrating some common sentiment I will be positive, assured, maybe expressing a degree of joy.

All these are examples of a stance taken in relation to what is deemed to be at issue. They imply that speakers need to judge the appropriate tone and their comportment towards the task of persuasion by adopting an attitude that fits with the problem in hand (on 'stance' see Cockcroft and Cockcroft, 2005: ch. 1). To fail to do so, again, runs the risk of accusations of improper conduct. To appear uncertain or defensive when calm reassurance was required can be unsettling to an audience. Aggressive, forceful argumentation will be out of place in circumstances where people are not yet convinced of the premises of an argument. All speakers at some time run the risk of accusations of smugness, over-confidence, excessive flattery, patronising attitudes or lack of sincerity, to name only a few failures of stance associated with politicians. Getting the tone right is a matter of judging, on the specific occasion, how to approach the issue, given what is at stake.

But what can be 'at stake'? Our division of occasions gives us a clue here. In ceremonies it is usually praise or blame. In judicial settings it is usually a question of ascertaining facts and evidencing transgressions of the law, either in prosecution or defence. In politics it is most commonly a question of how, or how not, to proceed in policy. But even within this classification there are many variations and shades. As we noted in the previous chapter, the theory of status (or stasis) is a commonly utilized framework for thinking about what is at issue in legal contexts (see Table 4.3). Cicero distinguished between the statuses of 'conjecture', 'definition' and 'quality'. A conjectural issue concerns matters of fact – whether something did or did not occur. A definitional issue concerns the interpretation of the fact. An issue of quality concerns the nature itself of the fact. In a court of law, a defence counsel needs to determine precisely what will be defended: whether something happened (a murder, for example), whether what happened has an interpretation that mitigates the defendant's behaviour (not 'murder' but manslaughter), or an account of the crime in relation to its particular quality (murder in order to prevent greater loss of life). A final option is the status of 'circumstance', where the issue is regarded as inappropriate for the type of trial (for example, a civil rather than criminal case) and hence not to be defended in that court at all. In each instance, the stance adopted will vary with the issue.

Status theory can be extended to other kinds of occasion, not only those of legal defence. In political affairs, speakers need to adopt a stance in relation to commonly accepted principles and values. That is, they need to work out whether such a principle is at stake (from which certain deeds may depart: conjecture), whether a nuance of interpretation needs to be taken into account (definition), or whether there are good grounds for overlooking the transgression of the principle

Table 4.3 Status theory

Status	Question	Example
Conjecture	What is the truth?	I did not do it (e.g. take the money)
Definition	What does it mean?	I did it, but it's not what you think (I borrowed the money)
Quality	What is the nature of the act?	I did it, but for a good reason (I used it to help the poor)
Circumstance	Is it relevant?	You can't ask me that here (you have no authority)

Source: Cicero (1949a: 21–25).

(quality). For example, Tony Blair's defence of his conduct to an enquiry in relation to the 2003 Iraq invasion could be said to have shifted the issue from one of conjecture (over whether he propagated 'lies' about the threat from Iraq's weapons of mass destruction) to one of definition (how we interpret his role as a leader uniquely burdened with the task of making judgements with imperfect evidence), but also of quality (it was useful to invade Iraq despite its alleged threat or otherwise because it got rid of a dangerous tyrant).

Establishing the issue, then, permits the speaker to adopt the stance that appears most conducive to persuasion. This is not a failsafe approach in politics (Tony Blair's critics still maintain he 'lied'), but it accounts for much of the manoeuvring of speakers prior to an event when they seek to determine what questions might be asked in an interview, or who in a debate can ask questions and how (in advance rather than spontaneously, for example). In political arguments speakers often talk past each other precisely because each defines what is at issue in a different way, usually the one most conducive to the stance they wish to adopt. Being able to 'frame' the argument by determining what principle is at issue can allow one speaker to dictate the way in which others will respond and close off awkward questions that are difficult to explain away.

The discovery of the argument

Having understood the type of occasion and the issue upon which a speaker might take a stance, it is possible to select a fitting argument(s) to achieve persuasion. The discovery of argument involves selecting, from a range of options, a form of reasoning that addresses the audience in such a way as to encourage them to reach (or, as Kenneth Burke argued in 1969, identify with) the conclusion offered by the speaker. Aristotle claimed that this range consisted of three types of appeal or 'proof': the appeal to *logos*, *ethos* and *pathos*; that is, to reason, authority and emotion (see Table 4.4).

The appeal to reason involves an argument based on a logical procedure through which the speaker leads the audience, often by employing evidence of some kind to demonstrate the veracity of the conclusion. This, of course, is the process with which many trained philosophers are familiar. The appeal to authority involves

58 *Techniques I: discovery and arrangement*

Table 4.4 The three types of appeal

Type of appeal	Meaning	Methods
Logos	Appeal to reason	Demonstrating logic (inductive or deductive) of an assertion, using empirical evidence, statistics or examples
Ethos	Appeal to the authority or character of the speaker	Explicit or implicit reference to qualities of speaker
Pathos	Appeal to emotions of the audience	Expressing feeling, identifying shared emotions

Source: Aristotle (1991: 74–75).

pointing to the appropriateness of the speaker to speak at all. That is signalled in various ways: perhaps by announcing one's distinctive experience, qualifications or job title. Finally, the appeal to emotion involves invoking the sentiments of the audience: a sense of moral outrage, of hope or of humour, for example.

Each appeal constitutes a way of arguing that is recognized as legitimate in certain contexts. We often associate argument with a logical procedure that demonstrates, or at least indicates, rational truth. While this is certainly a dominant, perhaps even preferred, form of appeal, we should not dismiss arguments based on authority and emotion. A sense of authority, perhaps in the form of expertise or experience, is effective – perhaps even necessary – at times of crisis. Likewise, emotion is a powerful, if frequently underestimated, dimension of persuasion, as we shall see later. The capacity to 'lighten the mood' or, by contrast, to invoke seriousness or even danger is an impressive tool when used effectively. While the latter two may not always appear strictly like arguments (with a specific thesis that is promoted with explicit reasoning), they have what Ruth Amossy (2005) calls an 'argumentative dimension' in that they help orient their audiences towards an issue.

The three different types of appeal might be more or less appropriate to certain contexts, but they rarely function entirely independently of each other. In any oration or process of argumentation, each appeal will be used to a degree, if only subtly. It is difficult to imagine any political communication where reason is not used in so far as valid conclusions are shown to follow logically from certain premises. Likewise, the authority of the speaker needs to be maintained, at the very least by speaking well. And all forms of persuasive argument will seek to satisfy the feelings of the audience, perhaps only by avoiding provoking discomfort. What is important to note, however, is that any speech moment will involve at least *one* kind of appeal. Let us look more closely at each.

Logos

The appeal to reason entails leading the audience through certain logical steps so as to reach a specified conclusion. In politics, this is a key dimension when policy options have to be deliberated, when principles and ideologies are asserted, defended or attacked, when past or potential consequences are examined and, finally, when explicit decisions have to be made. For Aristotle (1991: 75), the appeal to logos was a vital form of argumentative strategy in politics, since it involves reasoning about the future (whether in the long or short term) and thus requires the use of particular intellectual processes such as abstraction and calculation. To encourage an audience to reason their way to a conclusion therefore requires an understanding of what reasoning involves.

In very general terms, a rational argument can be said to involve a procedure by which we defend a specific thesis, or conclusion, by making logical connections between the conclusion and certain premises or supporting grounds (see Weston, 2000: 1–9). The claim that 'hand weapons sales should be banned', for example, might be defended on the premise that 'hand weapon usage accounts for an enormous number of deaths every year'. Or the same claim might be defended on the grounds that 'weapons designed to kill are morally repugnant'. The first is a form of 'inductive' reasoning whereby the conclusion is based on a particular case (the number of deaths in *this* country in the past ten years, perhaps). The second is a form of 'deductive' reasoning whereby a specific conclusion is reached by way of a general principle (*all* weapons designed to kill are morally wrong, wherever we are). In the first, reasoning comes from an external form of evidence – that is, a claim about the empirical world. If the empirical evidence changed (that is, if the number of deaths radically reduced), the conclusion would not reasonably follow. In the second, the conclusion is deduced from a general principle that is assumed to hold at all times in all places. In that instance, the premises are abstract – that is, they are assumed to be acceptable by any reasoning person.

In both examples, the argument is drawn from premises that we are required to accept if we are to reach the same conclusion. The speaker's task is often to *demonstrate* the connection between the premises and the conclusion such that the reasoning is shown to be one that an auditor can legitimately follow and, as a consequence, agree to be fair. The effectiveness of rational argumentation lies in the speaker's ability to make this connection appear as smooth and unforced as possible. In that way, even if the listeners do not like the conclusion, they are compelled by their own reasoning to accept it as valid. The assumption, then, is that having been taken through certain logical steps, listeners are unlikely to disagree with themselves. That is, if they are rational they will seek logical coherence in their views and feel compelled to accept coherence as a sign of validity even when it contrasts with their own preferences or preconceptions.

This is what Richard Dawkins implies in *The God Delusion* (2006) when, in his argument against religious explanations of life on earth, he contrasts a Darwinian form of reasoning based on the principle of evolution with arguments drawn from religious texts. If we are reasonable, he claims, we will see that religion offers only dogmatic (that is, unsupported) assertions about the design of all life by means of a divine source. Meanwhile, Darwin's theories demonstrate, through the use of empirical evidence and theoretical hypotheses, that life evolved over the course of millions of years through a process of trial and error through which only those organisms that could adapt to their external conditions could survive, so passing on their genetic code. For Dawkins, Darwin's theory is a superior contender for universal agreement because it draws its conclusions from empirically verifiable premises. However much we might recoil emotionally at the conclusion, we are compelled by reason to accept it as true.

Dawkins' polemical encounter with religion exemplifies a (frequently rather shrill) form of scientific argumentation that seeks persuasion through reason. Yet, like all forms of reasoned argument, it demands we accept the logical connection between premises and conclusions. However, this is where *logos* reveals its vulnerability as a strategy of persuasion. Few premises are self-evidently true and, if examined or brought into question, they can show themselves to be open to criticism. Much of scientific enquiry demands we isolate empirical evidence and reduce it to a series of 'objective' features that can be enumerated, quantified and labelled. That is what Darwin spent much of his life doing before he came up with his theory of evolution, and it is common practice for members of scientific communities. Most other people, however, do not engage in this exercise and simply have to accept such claims to scientific objectivity and evidence. We are not usually in a position to contest the accumulated findings of scientists and therefore we accept the premises because they *appear* valid and in tune with prior ways of thinking that we endorse. Having done so, however, our ability to contest their conclusions is also limited. Once we accept Darwin's premises, it is difficult not to accept as valid his conclusions about the development of life on earth.

In politics, however, argumentative premises are much more likely to be disputed, not least because they rarely have the same weight of evidence as do scientific theories. That demands that we think about reasoned argument in political life being characterized by less rigour than is the case for scientific theory. To make this point, Aristotle distinguished between the 'syllogism' and the 'enthymeme' as two forms of logical reasoning (Aristotle, 1991: 75–77). The syllogism is an abstract form of deductive reasoning that makes a logical connection between conclusions and premises. As the famous example goes:

Major premise:	All men are mortal
Minor premise:	Socrates is a man
Conclusion:	Socrates is mortal

Here the conclusion, 'Socrates is mortal', follows inexorably from the major and minor premises. Of course, it may not actually be true that Socrates is mortal. The conclusion here is 'logically valid', that is, it is the product of a correct form of reasoning. We might dispute the truth of either of the premises, in which case the reasoning would be wrong, or 'fallacious' (see Pirie, 2006). But if we accept them, then the conclusion must follow. In philosophical logic, this is thought to be a rigorous demonstration of abstract deduction. Thus we might replace the contents of the premises and conclusions with other claims such as, for example, 'Murder is wrong. Killing animals to eat them is murder. So killing animals is wrong'. As long as we accept the premises here, the conclusion is valid. But if we dispute either of the premises, then the conclusion will seem fallacious. We might disagree that murder is always wrong or we might dispute that killing animals for food necessarily amounts to murder. In such cases, the conclusion cannot claim to be based on a logically rigorous form of reasoning.

Few political or moral disputes are conducted in this way. It is rarely possible in the heat of an argument to set out premises in neat, orderly steps. Indeed, it is not always desirable to do so. Hence Aristotle (1991: 77) named a lesser form of argument: the enthymeme. In the enthymeme, the premises might be missing, merely implied or hidden so that only part of the argumentative structure is visible. Sometimes premises are just assumed, taken as accepted fact, and the conclusions are reached without having to demonstrate every logical step. For example, the saying that 'money follows power' is a conclusion that involves premises which are suppressed. These premises could be 'those with wealth always seek the conditions to make more wealth' or 'those in political office always provide the conditions to make wealth'. Yet, as an enthymeme, the saying takes the premises as assumed, implicitly understood and accepted such that it is not necessary to state them explicitly. This is the power of an enthymeme: it is a form of reasoning that invites listeners silently to acknowledge the truth of a claim, to make the logical connections themselves, and so become subtly complicit with the speaker's reasoning.

It is the informal logic of the enthymeme, rather than the strict logic of the syllogism, that characterizes moral and political debate, as contemporary rhetoricians usually accept (Perelman and Olbrechts-Tyteca, 1969; Burke, 1984). Sometimes that is because certain premises or conclusions are so widely held as to not need recounting in detail. We find this in the aphorisms and popular idioms that stand as collective wisdom in certain communities: 'in this country we all believe in free speech', 'all men are born equal', 'there's no smoke without fire' and so on (see Morrell, 2006). Classical rhetoricians often provided lists of formal argumentative structures called 'topics' (*topoi*) that enumerate recognized rational formulae for speakers to fill out with their own content (such as topics of cause and effect, association, contraries or similarities; see Aristotle, 1991: 183–214; Corbett and Connors, 1999: 87–130). Topics provide ready-made structures that, like aphorisms and idioms, give rational *plausibility*, rather than strict logical validity, to rhetorical reasoning (see Burke, 1984). At other times, it is useful simply to assume agreement on issues, or an association between ideas, that might actually be contentious but which the speaker wants to pass over without controversy. Sometimes that might be achieved by suppressing the conclusion rather than the premises: 'we all know where high interest rates lead …'. Either way, enthymemes remind us that political and moral debate often involves appealing not to explicitly demonstrated logical truths but, rather, to implicitly assumed matters of fact or agreed principle that, if tested, might prove contentious and may even need to be further defended.

A similar approach to argumentation is set out by the philosopher Stephen Toulmin (2003). Most arguments, he claims, refer us not to absolute, final truths so much as to 'local' truths: accepted reasonings about how things are to be conceived. It would be wrong, he claims, to test most forms of reasoning by the highest standard of logical validity. Instead, he argues, we must see truth claims as being restricted to certain 'fields' or collections of understandings that rarely need to be set out. Of course, taking certain matters to be true – by using off-the-cuff remarks and figures of speech, for example – often reflects power relations in society, where commonplace understandings, or what Gramsci referred to as 'common-sense' thinking (see Gramsci, 1971: 432), have come to crystallize around certain practices and domains. 'Common sense' is a type of shorthand for an accepted way of reasoning that does not lay itself open to question but relies on our implicit acceptance or deference – and hence our complicity.

In order to evade such complicity, it is necessary for an opponent to make explicit the hidden premises of an argument and so dispute them, thereby bringing into question the conclusions that 'naturally' follow. Much of politics in debating chambers, as well as in society at large, involves precisely this identification and disputation of hidden and/or faulty premises and the offering of alternative premises or new conclusions in their place. The dialogical nature of many public arguments also permits speakers to anticipate potential counter-arguments when making their own case so as to deflect them in advance (hence humanist rhetoricians taught their students to argue *in utramque partem* – on both sides of the case – to strengthen their ability to defend themselves). This image of argument as a rather clever academic seminar may reflect the character of some political debate today. But we should note that it is a lot easier to contest conclusions or their premises when aspects of the central issue are already agreed. Such a debate might occur if we are arguing about the correct approach to welfare policy, which may involve evaluating the foreseeable costs of withdrawing benefits or programmes and directing funds elsewhere. Heated disputes might well arise here about potential effects on certain sectors of society, the use of statistical evidence to justify the policy or the moral reasoning informing it.

But if the issue is shifted from the question of *how* to undertake a specific policy to the issue of *whether* such a choice should be taken at all, or whether the problem to be resolved is not one of how to reduce costs but instead how to raise revenues, then the framing of the argument may substantially transform. In such circumstances, debaters may fail even to find common ground upon which to contest premises and conclusions. Such is often the case when entirely opposed ideological viewpoints come into conflict: neither party comes 'close enough' to the other to test their reasoning. That may sometimes be an opportunity: allowing one to advocate anew the terms within which premises and conclusions are posed. But it can also be severely disabling of any kind of reasoned deliberation and, if it persists, can create the conditions for hostility and violence. Alternatively, rival parties can find some common ground – in the form of constitutions or agreed principles (peace, equality or national self-determination for example) – by which to institutionalize and regulate their disagreement within relatively settled parameters.

Ethos

The appeal to ethos is, as with pathos, not an alternative to the appeal to reason but something that typically accompanies it. Nevertheless, it is worth dwelling upon since all argument demands a sense of confidence in the speaker by the audience. Ethos refers to the speaker's character or authority, which gives his or her words some degree of persuasive force. We typically understand this when we hear 'experts' speak (see Aristotle, 1991: 172–79; Cockcroft and Cockcroft, 2005: ch. 1). Sometimes, ethos works on the basis of the recognition of prior authority (for instance, being someone who already holds public office and hence having the right to speak), but often it is because an authoritative character is demonstrated in speech itself (see Amossy, 2001).

Demonstrating or even seeking to enhance one's ethos need not mean explicitly claiming to be an expert on the topic on which one is speaking. But it does involve giving the listener a sense of the speaker's *entitlement* to speak. Witnesses at a traffic accident are not experts in accidents, but their views have force because they saw what happened. Alternatively, people who can demonstrate an unblemished record of efficiency and hard work will be more appealing to employers than those who cannot. Ethos is a reminder that a sense of entitlement to speak is a vital addition to a reasoned argument, for the perception of the speaker as a worthy and truthful character, at least in regard to the topic in question, is a way of making an argument seem plausible. In short, as listeners (or readers), we need to trust our speakers as genuine and reliable sources of the judgements they defend. To experience this trust means not to have to examine the validity of every sentence but, instead, to feel confidence that whatever is said is worth hearing. Thus ethos contributes to making arguments seem plausible.

In politics we see the appeal to ethos regularly, though sometimes it can be very subtle. Politicians and political activists wish to enlist the support of members of the public with whom they are usually not familiar. To do this, merely setting out a reasoned argument is not always enough. It is necessary to ingratiate oneself with an audience, to supply them with reasons for thinking this person or group is worth hearing or that it is worth hanging around long enough to hear their argument. For many professions this is not a problem: people go to medical doctors, surveyors, police and lawyers precisely because they accept such people are entitled to speak on certain matters. But in politics, things often work the other way around. Politicians, at least in electoral campaigns, come to us (either in person or via the media) for our votes and our continued support (financial or moral). For this they need to win our trust, not just by telling us what they think but also by demonstrating in some way that they have the right to be heard.

Appeals to ethos can be either explicit or implicit. An *explicit* appeal will involve saying why the speaker should be trusted, perhaps by listing existing accomplishments or by recounting his or her past experiences, family upbringing and moral values. The point here is to bridge the gap between listener and speaker, to generate a sense of identity with the audience that assures it of that entitlement. Sometimes politicians do this by claiming to have much in common with the audience, maybe that they belong to the same community. At other times ethos might be achieved by differentiating themselves from the community, perhaps by indicating a distinctive experience or ability that grants them knowledge or expertise in judgement. Such explicit claims include the recounting of war experience, being a parent in 'difficult times' or a past history of holding public office.

Implicit appeals to ethos, on the other hand, involve employing subtle indicators of character that an audience will understand without them having to be explained. These might include a general eloquence and control over one's words, indicating a capacity for moderation and thoughtfulness. Or, by contrast, it may involve using one's local accent or a vernacular vocabulary to imply a connection with 'ordinary people'. Notable politicians are often those who communicate with distinctive traits that make them seem less 'polished' than typical politicians, but perhaps also more 'authentic'. Likewise, a capacity to quote sources suggests erudition and intelligence, while plain speaking may suggest honesty.

It is also true that ethos extends far beyond the words used. Throughout much of the past century the use of the media, and particularly visual imagery, has grown in significance and is regularly exploited to enhance the ethos of speakers. Backdrop and context, the style of dress and the mannerisms of a speaker are all assumed to be important in defining character and many professional politicians hire image consultants at some point in their careers to assist them in this department. Failure to consider such things, particularly in an age when embarrassing photos can be distributed across the media within minutes of being taken, can puncture the public image of a speaker, undermine their credibility and dent the degree of seriousness with which he or she might be received by the public.

Pathos

The appeal to sentiment is a pervasive element of rhetorical communication, though often those who prioritize *logos* diminish its significance. Pathos involves seeking to shape the feelings rather than merely the thoughts of the audience (see Aristotle, 1991: 139–71). That may involve seeking to generate laughter, concern, fear or even anger. Doing so helps to create a context for arguments to have greater persuasive effect. Encouraging a public sense of anger or hurt might make a forceful or extreme policy option seem reasonable. Using humour can lighten an atmosphere and dispel discomfort or nervousness. These effects are often regarded as cynically manipulative by critics – especially in relation to efforts to express passionate feeling – and more in keeping with theatrics than serious argument, perhaps even distracting an audience from the intended misdeeds of the speaker. It is certainly the case that tyrannical dictators have employed strong appeals to the emotions as way of generating popular support for terrible crimes. But it is also true that many do not. Passion can sometimes be distracting but so, too, can dull, bureaucratic reason. Pathos need not always be thought an effort purely to manipulate the audience; it is also a way of demonstrating a connection with shared sentiments and an ability to channel them towards a constructive judgement.

Cicero claimed that good speakers need to argue not only rationally but also eloquently in order to delight the audience: 'all who desire to win approval have regard to the good will of their auditors, and shape and adapt themselves completely according to this' (Cicero, 1962: 323). Increasingly, today, neuroscientists and others are coming around to the view that emotion is not a brake on reason so much as a necessary and ever-present stimulant (see Damasio, 1994). To reason effectively, it is argued, we need to be in the right emotional disposition rather than not being emotional at all. Certain emotions may place the audience in dispositions that enable receptivity to particular arguments. Thus well-deployed humour can allow an audience to deal with serious issues that might otherwise be experienced negatively. A certain register of anxiety in a speaker alerts us to danger, while anger or rage encourages us to be decisive or resolutely principled (see Marcus, 2002).

A speaker's use of the appeal to pathos is revealed in a number of ways: in the vocabulary, or *lexicon*, and in what we might call 'tone'. The vocabulary of emotive speech is largely self-evident. Specific words invite certain responses: some words have violent connotations and invite intense reactions (for example, 'rape', 'fight', 'slaughter'), others invite concern ('crisis', 'corruption', 'disaster'), and still others imply routine business ('discussion', 'agreement', 'procedure'). This aspect of pathos is closely related to rhetorical *style* (the use of words), which will be examined in the next chapter. Tone, on the other hand, refers to the general resonance of communication rather than to specific words and relates to other qualities related to *delivery* (which we shall also examine in the next chapter). Hurried speech, for example, may imply anxiety and invite listeners to feel concern, while gently paced speech indicates control and invites feelings of assurance. Other differences can be found when arguments are shouted or gently spoken, delivered at a distance from the audience or close up, savagely critical or accommodating and friendly and so on. There is no guarantee, of course, that changes to words or tone will induce the expected response from the listener. Sometimes things can go badly wrong with the feelings of the audience: being booed off stage, being politely ignored, or just not 'hitting the right note' with an audience is always possible. In such circumstances, a negative, or at least neutral, emotional reaction can make it difficult to get across an argument.

Appeals to reason, authority and emotion are essential to the craft of rhetorical persuasion and, it might be said, form the substantial matter of any political intervention. To mobilize an argument by means of these appeals is not only to make and defend a reasoned case; it is also to shape the way in which that case is received and digested by the audience (see Tindale, 2004). In short, it is to *create a relationship* and, in so doing, recruit others into the process of acknowledging certain qualities in the community. The discovery of arguments involves judging the best means by which to connect – or, indeed, disconnect – particular issues, ideas and claims with a wider horizon of principles.

Arrangement

Discovering the right argument or combination of argumentative appeals may be the essence of a speaker's task. But the argument still needs to be assembled into an order of presentation that delivers its full force. This aspect of rhetoric was known as the task of 'arrangement' or, in Latin, *dispositio*, which deals with the positioning of the various parts of speech and the way speech flows from start to finish. There is much advice in the classical canon on the proper forms of arrangement for different types of oration, so let us stick with a fairly typical schema. The varied parts of the speech can be broken down as in Table 4.5.

What are these parts expected to do? The *exordium* opens the speech with some preparatory comments designed to achieve two things: first, to prepare the audience generally, perhaps by greeting them, thanking them or announcing the significance of the event; second, to inform them of what is about to be said. The latter might involve any number of things, such as directly stating the conclusion of the argument and setting out how it will be reached. Less directly, the speaker might quote a famous saying, pose a question or state a paradox or some observation that will capture the audience's attention and prepare it for the argument. Look at the introduction to any speech, pamphlet or book and you will usually find some effort to hook the audience's attention by inviting them to consider a problem or a question.

But the task here is not simply one of capturing attention. The introduction also offers an opportunity to present the speaker's view of the issue at stake and the stance to be taken on it. Sometimes this will be very simple and uncontroversial – at a wedding, the presiding official will welcome and announce the purpose of the event – but on other occasions it might involve broaching a controversial or difficult subject, such as giving bad news, resigning or announcing a failure of some kind. At these moments, introductory remarks function to allow a topic to be approached by adopting a tone that signifies what will come without saying it directly. Of course, getting straight to the point is frequently desirable, especially when the speaker or the general purpose of the speech is widely understood. In such instances, preparatory remarks might be unnecessary. Often, however, the speaker will need to establish an initial relationship with the audience, if only by greeting them. Such is regularly the case at political campaign rallies, where different constituencies can be addressed individually and thanked directly, allowing everyone else to recognize their own presence as a distinct part of the whole. On other occasions, such as governmental committee hearings or in legal contexts, the speakers may not dwell for long on their introductory remarks, given that the purpose and function of the event is already clear.

Table 4.5 The parts of speech

Latin name	English name	Function
Exordium	Introduction	Prepare the audience and inform them of what follows
Narratio	Narration	Set out the 'facts', interpret facts selectively
Confirmatio	Proof	Present the argument(s)
Refutio	Refutation	Reject alternative argument(s)
Peroratio	Conclusion	Close the discourse by summarizing argument(s) and/or gesturing a sentiment

Source: Cicero (1949a: 40–161).

The *narratio* involves the setting out – or narration – of the facts. In law courts this occurs in order to let the jury know what the known facts of the case are so that lawyers can then proceed to develop their interpretation. But the narration of facts takes place in all sorts of other speech contexts, too. News reports are dominated by this part of speech, and broadcast interviews with politicians will also involve reference to events that involve recounting factual information upon which they might then be asked to comment. In so far as politics involves responses to events in the world such as wars, military conflicts, natural disasters, financial crises and the success or failure of policies, there will be, by necessity, a place for narration.

But narration is never simply a matter of neutrally setting out agreed facts. In political life (and doubtless elsewhere), facts are always bound up with interpretations. To set aside a part of speech devoted to what is officially known is also to take the opportunity to decide what ought to be known. That is, facts can be *selectively* narrated. If facts supply a good part of the empirical premises of inductive forms of reasoning (for instance, facts about what other politicians said or did, about the economy, or facts in the form of statistics), being able to define them is a vital part of securing persuasion. This is what Quentin Skinner (2002b: 270–74) refers to as 'rhetorical redescription': redescribing reality according to one's own preferred view. Others may just call it 'spin'.

Narration may involve attributing certain causes to events, identifying blame, emphasizing some aspects of an event over others, appealing to statistical data or just restating known but controversial facts that place an event in a wider picture. Whichever choice is made, narration provides an opportunity to define the situation and, hence, details that are purportedly beyond dispute. Perhaps the important point here is that one's own preferred interpretation should not seem to be uppermost in the speech. To describe the world simply as one prefers it will appear absurdly prejudiced and crudely manipulative. The *narratio* works as an account of the facts if it is represented as an *objective* description that others can agree is true.

Confirmatio is the part of a speech devoted to setting out the 'proof' or argument of which the speaker is seeking to persuade the audience. In different types of speech event, this will have a greater or lesser role to play. In politics and political debate, the proof is usually the centrepiece of the event, but in ceremonial speeches, it need not be at all elaborate, and sometimes not even explicit. In celebrating births, deaths or marriages, the essential argument (often of praise or blame) will likely be already understood and so simply needs saying only once, if at all, and then succinctly. In matters of greater controversy, however, the moment of proof will require more effort and maybe demand attention to the aspect of discovery. In these instances there will often be several proofs, and so it is necessary to decide which is the most important and in which order to present them. In classical rhetoric it is often claimed that, in order to stay in the memory of the audience, the most important, or 'clinching', arguments will come last, while the lesser proofs will be presented first.

But here much depends on the context and the nature of the speech event. A debate with another speaker (or more than one) will likely often require responding to their arguments, too, contesting their premises or conclusions. Inevitably that will detract from a speaker presenting his/her own arguments, or it may require repeating the preferred argument after aspects of it have been disputed. In contexts where a speaker is given free rein to present his/her own proof, it will be necessary to calculate how rapidly the central argument needs to be set out. If there is time, a number of minor proofs might be made, premises developed and conclusions elaborately defended. But if there are tight time constraints, minor proofs may be set aside in order to deliver the clinching argument. Furthermore, not all proofs will appeal to logos, or not exclusively so. If ethos and pathos are also part of the proof, then the moment to employ these, too, needs to be calculated in order to have the optimum effect.

Closely related to the presentation of proofs is the *refutio* or refutation of opposing arguments. It is not always possible to separate the refutation of alternative arguments from the confirmation of one's own, and it may even precede the proof. Nevertheless, we can treat this as a separate part in so far as it is a distinct element of many speeches and arguments. Sometimes the refutation will be of distinct claims by specified individuals, but it can also involve the rejection of anonymous claims (such as 'it is said that …'). Either way, refutation is an important way to enhance the persuasiveness of one's own argument by permitting it to be set alongside the limitations of another. Thus a speaker's proof can be made to substitute for another, less effective argument by exposing its fallacies or answering its deficiencies.

There are many ways to develop a refutation of another's argument. These are clearly related to the aspect of *discovery* and the kind of proof upon which the (real or anonymous) other relies. A speaker might criticize the other's premises and conclusions by highlighting the faulty reasoning of the argument. Or the speaker may attack his or her ethos, demolishing the opponent's character and thereby his or her right to speak with authority. Finally, the speaker may dispute the sentiments aroused by the opponent, perhaps dismissing their seriousness by ridiculing them or, in a reverse movement, by suggesting they do not take seriously enough the issue at hand. Either way, the audience will be presented with a stark contrast between one supposedly proper emotion and another that is deemed inappropriate.

The *peroratio* concludes the speech by signing off in a way that closes the argument effectively. Closing abruptly may leave the audience in expectation of more and unaware of why things have stopped. So a deliberate conclusion provides an ending that releases the listener's attention by bringing the speech to a final point. That point may involve a neat summation of the argument, a return to some issue (or quotation) raised at the start or a gesture of some kind that embodies a sentiment for the audience to take away with it. The conclusion is the 'last word' of an oration and, depending on the context, speakers can find it difficult to let go. We often notice this in broadcast interviews or public debates where speakers want their own views to be the last words heard by the audience. There is nothing more frustrating than to find oneself cut off in mid-flow and hence unable to give some final, emphatic flourish to one's argument. The *peroratio* is the moment at which a 'final frame' is placed on the speech and the place where its essential qualities may be invested. Once finished, the audience will start to reflect on what has happened, so this final frame is important if the speaker wishes to ensure the audience remains in tune with the spirit of the argument.

Not every persuasive speech follows the pattern of exposition above. Depending on the occasion, various parts may be missed out altogether, while at other times some parts will be elaborated at great length and in a different order. We can see that ceremonial speeches will involve little or no *confirmatio* or *refutio*, while judicial speeches (concerned with elaborating facts) will devote much attention to *narratio* and political speeches may dwell on *refutio* and *confirmatio*. Among these occasions there may be a wide variety of differences, too. It is possible to identify certain 'genres' of arrangement in politics in the same way that we can define genres of literature (see Cockcroft and Cockcroft, 2005: 139–60). Thus we can point to party conference speeches, resignation speeches, campaign speeches or presidential inaugural speeches as examples of distinctive genres that arrange their parts in similar ways (see Freedman and Medway, 1994).

The arrangement of a speech is significant not because there are fixed models to follow in each and every circumstance, but because there are choices to be made in any occasion, and often examples that can be followed. Rhetorical reflection upon arrangement is a way of mapping out the structure of possibilities for making this judgement. When we listen to, or read, a speech we tend not to see this aspect and it passes by without our noticing, partly because we are caught up in the flow of the argument, registering its effects moment by moment and responding to specific phrases, concepts and sentiments as they arise. Yet it is precisely this 'flow' that helps shape our reception of speech – that is, our reaction to the speed and fluency with which it covers its various parts and the sense of tension and release, movement and intensity it conjures by the arrangement of the parts in a distinctive way. Although we might not reflect much upon it, all speech moments involve an economy of feeling and desire: the management of our expectations as an audience; of our desire, perhaps, to hear the facts or get a sense of the overall point, or maybe just to hear acknowledged certain sentiments and values. An effective speech is one that selects an arrangement to both stimulate and meet those expectations. Sometimes that involves holding off the clinching argument, but at other times perhaps it means saying it straight away. In delivering bad news, for example, one is rarely thanked for saving the crucial information right until the very end! In the defence of a policy, dwelling on the deficiencies of other policies might appear a rather negative way to promote one's preferred approach. Getting these details right is a matter of judgement and doing it effectively – that is, in a way that does not jar with the audience or encounter disabling criticism – will reflect well on the speaker (and the speech writer).

Summary

The importance of discovering the argument and arranging the parts of speech can be understood by returning to the toolbox metaphor I used at the beginning of the chapter. *Discovery* and *arrangement* provide tools to craft the substantial dimensions of speech. Defining the argument gives us the precise focus to the stance we wish to take on an issue in any particular occasion, supplying a coherent purpose to our discourse. Arranging the parts of the speech permits us to structure our words so as to effectively deliver their focus.

This toolbox metaphor should not be taken too far, but it does convey an idea of what the first two rhetorical canons are about. Without a clear view of the argument or a structure, persuasive discourse is likely to fail. Of course, political life is full of occasions when people argue unclearly or without a strongly defended argument and when they talk without brevity, concision or proportion. Classical rhetorical advice, however, provides a means to think and prepare one's strategy in advance. This is not simply a matter of producing an eloquent and pleasing discourse. Nor, indeed, is it just a technically effective way of transmitting information. Discovery and arrangement are instrumental in shaping the basic terms of the relationship between audience and speaker; they disclose the message that the speaker wishes to convey but also help position the audience to receive that message. As we shall see next, the effort to shape the relationship between audience and speaker is further enhanced in the canons of *style* and *delivery*.

5 Techniques II
Style and delivery

This chapter explores the technical elements of rhetoric related to *style* and *delivery*. Whereas discovery and arrangement concern the substantial content and shape of rhetorical speech, the next two explore what often makes it distinctive and memorable. Style (in Latin, *elocutio*) concerns the use of language and delivery (in Latin, *pronuntiato* or *actio*) deals with the techniques and qualities of performance. In some respects these are the most outward, perhaps even 'theatrical' aspects of persuasion. They are dimensions that give it distinctive qualities as an event. By consequence, they might seem rather superficial aspects, especially if the central part of speech is thought to be its argument. But given that speech is typically a public performance of some kind and not just a thought experiment, outward qualities take on a greater significance than might otherwise be expected.

Style and delivery could therefore be said to concern primarily 'aesthetic' qualities of speech – that is, the evocation of sensation – whereas discovery and arrangement concern the rationality of argument (that is, its logic and order). This holds to some extent, but we should not think that style and delivery do not impact at all upon the qualities of the argument (or its 'argumentative dimension', as Amossy put it; see Amossy, 2005). On the contrary, they are particularly important in influencing ethos and pathos, each common forms of argumentative proof. In domestic and international politics, the dimension of theatre – or the aesthetic dimension – is widely recognized, if not always positively endorsed (see Bleiker, 2009). Speeches are not infrequently delivered as exhortations from balconies to admiring crowds or in apparently impromptu public settings to provide the speaker an immediate and uncritical reception. Of course, it is always possible to be understood if we simply communicate in plain prose delivered in a formal, undemonstrative manner, but what is said might not be experienced as an argument with sufficient intensity or appeal to be fully grasped. Persuasion – as opposed to mere understanding – often involves making emphases, expressing urgency or conveying degrees of moral significance to help make auditors identify, if only momentarily, with the speaker and the claims being made (see Burke, 1969). These are possible only if speech takes an outward form that presses its argument in such a way as to make it moving (see Spence, 2007). That need not always demand excessive exuberance or heightened theatricality, which may diminish the reception of the argument, but a flourish here and there can sometimes help the argument find its target. As is commonly said about effective rhetoric: it not only makes you agree with what is said, it makes you *want* to agree. That task is the responsibility of style and delivery.

Style

Style is the most overtly 'literary' part of rhetoric. It is the part that concerns language: the choice of words (diction), the figures and forms of speech and the overall tone of a discourse. It is through the choices made about style that speech not only delivers its argument but also, indirectly, conveys the ethos of the speaker. Clarity and precision without extensive ornamentation or wild flourishes can convey a simplicity of purpose that suggests resolve, while the use of dense language with technical jargon may isolate the hearer behind a veil of apparent expertise that implies distance. When we hear political actors communicate, the style of language makes an immediate difference to the way we hear and appreciate what is said. It will shape our trust in the speaker and our sense of attachment to the argument(s) being put. As well as contributing (or not) to the ethos of the speaker, therefore, language may also have an effect on pathos: the emotional disposition of the audience.

That link between language, ethos and pathos is of particular importance in political life, especially in democracies where the connection between citizens and their representatives is desired but never assured. When a leader speaks with little attention to style – when, for instance, unprepared verbal responses are given to questions – the audience can easily generate negative feelings and the speaker can lose authority. If a consistently poor performance is put in, then the speaker may even become the object of ridicule. Former US President Ronald Reagan's occasional failure to respond coherently to direct questions from journalists (sometimes without the prompting of his wife, Nancy) for which he was not prepared was often regarded as a sign of weakness. President George W. Bush's occasionally mangled phrases and lack of grammar regularly brought him much criticism. Interestingly, however, it could also be argued that this lack of perfect diction and eloquent style endeared him to some of the public, making him appear unpolished but genuine, a 'regular guy'. President Obama's control of language and his thoughtful, well-prepared orations reflect a more 'intellectual' style that has mostly met with public approval. In each of these instances it is never wholly certain in advance how language will play with the audience on any given day. But once politicians have found a style that works for them, they are likely to continue with it as much as possible.

But what is it about language that makes it so important to find the right kind of style? This is a difficult and complex question to answer, and it has been an issue for philosophers, linguists and literary scholars (among others) for a very long time. One way to start to think about answering it is to recognize that language is never simply about words or signs designed to 'pass on' information. The instrumental view of language treats words as though they were vehicles carrying discrete meanings from one person to another (see Chambers, 2003: ch. 1). While that is true of words to some extent, language is so much more than simply intended meanings travelling from A to B. Like colours, words have different effects depending on how they sit alongside each other in combination, in what order they come, how different words might substitute for each other and what happens when some are missed out. Language involves complex and varying systems of combination and substitution that can alter meanings in diverse ways just as a painter's palette can select and blend different colours and tones. Just as blues look subtly different when tinged with green or with purple, so concepts and ideas come across differently when combined in different ways.

Rather than thinking of language exclusively in terms of vehicles containing information, then, we might conceive it also as a way of blending meanings in different ways to produce different types of sensation. That effect can be discussed in terms of the distinction between 'denotation' and 'connotation'. Words are denotative when they seek to represent directly the objects they name. Thus the word 'oil' is used to represent the dark material extracted from under the ground. However, words are connotative when they make associations between objects and ideas. For example, to call someone 'oily' is to imply moral untrustworthiness by connoting the way in which oil is slippery and prevents a firm grip, or to say that someone is 'fishing around' for new ideas is to convey a sense of speculative searching rather than actually employing a hook and rod.

In speech we regularly employ denotative and connotative aspects of language at the same time, indicating actual things but also conveying a more abstract representation through indirect associations. For instance, to say 'he signed the contract' is a denotative statement about someone actually signing a piece of paper setting out the legal terms of a partnership. But to say 'we want a new contract with the people' is to signify the spirit of a legal arrangement, an agreed relationship to which each party willingly submits and takes on a duty to fulfil, rather than an actual document. If lawyers deal with the first kind of contract, politicians often deal with the second by using the connotation to make abstract associations that invite confidence and trust. The connotative dimension of language associates indirectly rather than indicates directly. That can make it easy to miss, especially if we are not familiar with the kinds of association being made. But it reminds us that language is a rich fabric of meanings that never merely sends us information; it also 'dresses' its content or colours it in ways that provide layer upon layer of sense that we cannot always penetrate in the moment that we hear it. Like the informal reasoning associated with the *discovery* of arguments, it requires the audience to infer what is being suggested by drawing upon its stock of common sense or cultural knowledge. It is no surprise to find that *elocutio* is an aspect of rhetoric that has been influential in the study of poetry. Speechwriters, it has been said, are the poets of public discourse (see Clark, 2011; 2009).

Of course, politicians are not always known for their precise arguments but, rather, for the simpler ways in which they put things in speech. The 'soundbite' – the formulaic phrase or saying that concisely sums up an outlook or idea – has been a trusty component of politics in the age of the mass media, where it is possible to distribute widely a neat, condensed package of meaning in a short collection of words. But even before soundbites came to prominence, the stylistic flourish that connotes a complex blend of meanings was a common feature of public orations. Clichés and platitudes, for example, are, like aphorisms, part of that stock of pre-digested common sense that needs only be repeated to elicit widespread recognition. Speeches are themselves often the originating source for such well-known phrases. For example, students of politics have long repeated Abraham Lincoln's celebrated definition of democracy in his Gettysburg Address of 1863, as 'government of the people, by the people and for the people'. Aside from the likelihood that many who repeat the phrase do not recall its original location in a specific speech (perhaps they do not even recall the author), it is often missed that the repetition of 'the people', divided only by prepositions and conjunctions, gives the phrase an uncomplicated but insistent affirmation of the principle of popular sovereignty (despite the fact that it was uttered after a devastating and violent civil war, when the people were hardly united). The appeal here lies less in Lincoln's formal definition of democracy (which is fairly vague) and more in the rhythmic alliteration, which exquisitely performs in words democracy's claim about the primacy of the people (try replacing the three prepositions with any others to see that the effect is largely the same: 'at', 'in', 'on', for example).

However critical we might be of the simplicity of soundbites today, they are a reminder that much of what we know of speeches in the past is often reliant upon a single, repeatable phrase that can be extracted and used as a *motif* for the whole message (Clark, 2009: 115). This is what dictionaries of quotations typically comprise: famous lines taken from bulkier orations or writings that articulate an outlook in a concise but memorable way. Many of the speeches with which we are familiar are referred to in terms of single lines that are used as titles: Sir Winston Churchill's many war speeches, for example, such as 'We shall fight them on the beaches' (speech to the House of Commons on 4 June 1940) or 'Blood, toil, tears and sweat' (speech to the House of Commons on 13 May 1940; the phrase was originally used by Garibaldi). Or think of key policy approaches: for example, Gordon Brown's 'No more boom and bust'. Such titles sum up certain emotional or aesthetic qualities connoted by a speech or a proposal rather than offering a precise argument. We find a similar thing in the use of the *epithet* in political discourse: the short adjective that names something or someone and simultaneously attributes particular qualities to it. Trading insults, for example, is a regular feature of democratic conflict: a good name can carry associations that are hard to shake off. Australian Prime Minister, Paul Keating's labelling of his opponent as a 'feral abacus' because of the economic rationalism of his party's policies helped him win the 1993 general election (see Clark, 2011: 5). Alternatively, Margaret Thatcher's appellation as the 'Iron Lady' probably enhanced rather than diminished her appeal.

So the peculiar effect of style can often be the way in which it makes speeches and their ideas memorable and repeatable in other contexts. This might have the consequence of obscuring the logical force of any argument, but it transmits a sentiment or an idea that endures beyond the speech occasion. Prime Minister Margaret Thatcher's claim that 'there is no such thing as society', for example, has come to sum up the type of neo-conservative liberalism she promoted. President George H.W. Bush's fateful campaign phrase of 1992, 'Read my lips: no new taxes' (a claim he did not fulfil), reminds us that quotable phrases transmit unfortunate as well as inspirational ideas.

Figures of speech

What makes for a memorable style of language? Here rhetoricians often point to the use of 'figures of speech' – that is, distinct ways of shaping language to enhance its connotative and denotative effects. This is accomplished by using words and sentences that deviate from normal discourse in some way, making them stand out and catch our interest, as well as blend together different kinds of sense. Listing figures of speech has been central to the rhetorical tradition, with new figures continuously being added (and, like other terms we have seen, often labelled in Latin or Greek – a helpful list can be found in Lanham, 1991). Nevertheless, figures are typically divided into two categories: 'schemes' and 'tropes' (see Corbett and Connors, 1999). Schemes are ways of arranging words within the sentence; tropes are ways of using particular words. Let us look at each category in turn, using examples to illustrate their effects.

Schemes

Rhetorical schemes arrange words in ways that heighten their effect – that is, they draw our attention to the way we read or hear them. Nowadays these effects are mostly associated with the study of literature but, because rhetoric is in certain respects a literary approach to speech, they are important in public life too. Although formal speech has become remarkably less ornate in the past few hundred years, and hence less inclined to sound what we might call 'poetic', rhetorical schemes are still regularly employed. In such schemes, the words themselves do the performing by virtue of their peculiar presence in a sentence.

There are very many named schemes and so I will list a few recognized examples. Schemes concern the *phrasing* of sentences and produce their effects primarily by way of techniques of repetition, word order and even the omission of words. In this they attend to the flow of meaning that an audience hears, creating movement between ideas through word sequences that slide, stop, interrupt and sometimes deliberately reverse the sense of what has already been said. Such techniques permit the selection of emphasis in order to shape the auditor's process of reasoning, but they also offer a certain ornamentation that can make the mundane seem otherworldly or more meaningful than we might otherwise think. In repetition, the most common techniques include: *anaphora* – the repetition of the first words in successive clauses of a sentence (for example, Churchill's 'Blood, Toil' speech: 'no survival for the British Empire; no survival for all that the British Empire has stood for; no survival for the urge and impulse of the ages, that mankind will move forward towards its goal'; see Churchill, 1940: 188); *epistrophe* – repetition of the final words of a clause in successive clauses (for example, 'live young, die young'); and *antimetabole* – repetition of words in reverse order in successive clauses (for example, JFK's famous line from his inaugural speech: 'Ask not what your country can do for you, ask what you can do for your country'). Other forms of repetition include *epanalepsis* – the repetition at the end of a sentence of the words from the start, or *anadiplosis* – repeating the last words of the previous clause to start the next.

Word order techniques can involve deliberate deviations from a familiar arrangement. For example, Jesus' reported line at his crucifixion 'Father forgive them, for they know not what they do' (Luke 23:34) is an example of *anastrophe*, the inversion of normal word order. The sense here remains intelligible but the poetic 'know not' (rather than the regular 'do not know') adds an alliterative emphasis with a simple rhythm that helps make it memorable (similar to the 'Ask not' in the JFK example). On the other hand, the use of *antithesis* places emphasis on contrasting terms (for example, 'we seek freedom, not tyranny'). The dramatic contrast between one thing (idea, principle or objective, for example) and another is clearly central to political debate, where arguments typically aim to differentiate themselves from and declare their superiority over each other. Such antitheses can be found in unbridgeable dichotomies such as them/us, friends/enemies, not(this)/but(that), either/or and so on. Alternatively, speakers who wish to avoid a confrontation will try to eliminate the antagonism with terms that do not directly contrast – for example, by using 'and' instead of either/or. This was a notable aspect of former UK Prime Minister Tony Blair's style when trying to evade the ideological antithesis of the state versus the market (see Bastow and Martin, 2003).

The omission of words is effective in altering the sound but also the sense of speech. *Parallelism*, for instance, involves creating a balance or sense of structural equivalence between terms (words, phrases or clauses) by omitting intervening words (for example, 'our cause is just, our goal is clear'). *Asyndeton* is the omission of conjunctions between clauses to create a continuous flow (for example, Julius Caesar's reported 'I came, I saw, I conquered' instead of 'I came, then I saw, and then I conquered'. The absence of 'and' between the terms enables an effortless movement through each action, rather than adding new, unrelated elements one by one).

Among the most well-known types of rhetorical scheme in political speech is the *tricolon*, or three-part list. Three sometimes seems like a magic number in rhetoric, since it involves orderly steps that become increasingly emphatic (two is often an antithesis, which creates an immediate hierarchy). The tricolon can involve three parallel words ('Friends, Romans, Countrymen') or phrases ('I came, I saw, I conquered'), which build to a powerful conclusion. Again, like most schemes, the effect is partly in the ordering of words, which simultaneously colours their connotative meaning. The third step is usually triumphant in relation to the others; it both adds to the order of their succession and completes them. Thus the final '*for* the people' in Lincoln's famous phrase accomplishes in the form of *tricolon* what it cannot as *epistrophe* (the mere repetition of the word 'people'): namely, to emphasize the primacy of government serving the people above all else.

Finally, schemes enable a degree of interaction with the audience that invites them to anticipate the reasoning of the speaker. This is achieved in phrases that either explicitly or implicitly elicit a response. The most well-known of these is the 'rhetorical question', in which the speaker explicitly asks a question that she then goes on to answer herself. Churchill's famous 'Blood, Toil' speech, for example, involves him twice asking and responding (with tricolon) for his audience:

> You ask, what is our policy? I can say: It is to wage war, by sea, land and air, with all our might and with all the strength that God can give us; to wage war against a monstrous tyranny, never surpassed in the dark, lamentable catalogue of human crime. That is our policy. You ask, what is our aim? I can answer in one word: It is victory, victory at all costs, victory in spite of all terror, victory, however long and hard the road may be; for without victory, there is no survival.
>
> (Churchill, 1940: 188)

Contemporary speechwriter Max Atkinson lists a variety of similar techniques that he classifies as 'puzzle–solution formats', which pose problems rather than ask direct questions, inviting the audience to anticipate a solution that the speaker then gives (Atkinson, 2004: 190–92). The puzzle may consist in a curious anecdote or statement of paradox that implicitly poses a problem whose next step is a resolution. For instance, then UK Labour leader Neil Kinnock's Bridgend speech of June 1983 set out a puzzle in the form of a warning: 'If Margaret Thatcher is re-elected as Prime Minister, *I warn you*'. He then solves the puzzle with a long series of anaphoric repetitions that answer the implied question concerning the nature of his warning: 'I warn you that you will have pain […] I warn you that you will have ignorance […] I warn you that you will have poverty' (Kinnock, 1983: 439). In Atkinson's analysis, to be effective, contemporary speeches often combine various schematic techniques (such as lists, contrasts and puzzle solutions) that work to constantly engage the audience and create regular bursts of applause by prompting them to anticipate resolutions that, to their satisfaction, the speaker then provides (see Atkinson, 2004: 198–210).

Tropes

Tropes involve the use of particular words to connote certain meanings. Here effort is directly focused on creating or specifying meaning rather than arranging words and phrases for effect. By consequence, tropes are often closely connected to the premises and conclusions of an argument. Again, there are many possible examples of these figures and I will draw upon only a few notable examples.

One of the most significant tropic figures in rhetorical analysis is *metaphor*. Metaphors abound in political discourse, although they are not always recognized as such (see Carver and Pikalo, 2008; Charteris-Black, 2005). They involve the substitution of one or more terms for another in order to invoke a kind of comparison. I say 'kind of' because metaphors are stronger than *similes*. In a simile we explicitly claim something is 'like' something else (for example, 'the defeated candidate was cowering *like* a dying animal'). But the word 'like' indicates only a partial similarity between things that are basically different. By contrast, a metaphor implies an identity between otherwise different things (see Black, 1962). Thus to call a political experience a 'journey' or to talk of a 'new dawn' in international affairs involves comparison by asserting an identity between particular events and certain, evocative ideas. This is a stronger claim than mere similarity and permits a much more powerful use of imagery. It invites the audience to have the same direct reaction and response to the metaphor as it would to the thing described.

Metaphors have such a strong effect on communication generally that they are rarely used just to embellish an already established argument (see Lakoff and Johnson, 2003). The substantive content of a speech may well use a metaphor either as a premise or even as a conclusion. For instance, after 11 September 2001 the claim to be undertaking a 'war on terror' was used as a premise to enable some fairly extraordinary uses of military and legal powers by western states against 'terrorism' (see Redfield, 2009; Brecher *et al.*, 2010). Here the strength of the metaphor lay in its ability to make a series of discrete actions all relate to the goal of 'preserving security' by treating them as elements of an ongoing war. Of course, this was no war in the strictly literal sense of one state undertaking a military assault to subdue another (although that formed part of it, in Afghanistan and Iraq). Rather, it was an ongoing utilization of state power in various ways *as though* there was actually a war with a defined enemy. That metaphorical definition became a premise for arguments to alter the established legal entitlements of citizens and to undertake military action of various kinds (against purported terrorists). The use of the words 'war' and 'terror' – dramatically charged terms, but with no precise target – heightened the effect of the phrase in order, it might be argued, to invoke a sense of principled purpose behind a collective mobilization (as war implies, even when it is a 'war on poverty', for example) and to raise fears of a generalized nature about an imminent attack on civilians. Interestingly, the phrase was eventually withdrawn, as it came to be widely dismissed as excessive and inaccurate.

The use of metaphor to sustain an argument can also be found in what is called 'analogical reasoning'. This is an inductive style of argumentation that works by presenting a particular case as 'being like', or sharing features, with another case such that we should react in the same way: for example, referring to an international negotiation as 'appeasement' (invoking comparison with the appeasement of Hitler in the 1930s). Such arguments are common in the pragmatic world of politics, where practical examples rather than universal principles are employed to make sense of specific issues (see Musolff, 2004; Aronovitch, 1997). Analogy functions metaphorically to connect a specific instance with others that it is assumed to resemble, encouraging an audience to infer the resemblance and respond to this instance in the same way they would to the other. Analogies of war, 'rape', 'theft' or being on a 'battlefield' are common in international politics and conflict, but so too are more cooperative analogies, such as appeals to 'family', 'humanity', 'special relationships' and so on. Analogies permit an argument about an issue to unfold as an enthymeme: by allowing the metaphor to serve as an implied or unexplained premise or conclusion and relying on the audience to make the connection. In adopting the analogy, distinctive features of the object are suppressed and a selective connection with other qualities is stressed. In day-to-day politics, such analogies are often unquestioned and may form part of an underlying consensus. But when the metaphor is exposed as partial or inadequate, the analogy might then be contested and its accuracy or hidden prejudices laid bare.

We have already noted the journey metaphors, which can be seen to help define change in terms of positive movement. But other analogies for change are used in political contexts, such as the activity of 'building' (to achieve peace between divided communities, for example), developing 'road maps' (in the Palestine–Israel conflict, in order to have a journey at all) and so on. Metaphors such as these are not necessarily controversial, but they assist the elaboration of arguments by framing the context and, as a consequence, orienting the audience towards a distinctive, associated quality of an issue. Thus it is easier to invite people to make a decision when there is a sense of urgency, which might be assisted by talking of the train being ready to 'leave the station', as happened in debates about the European Union in the 1990s (see Musolff, 2004). To disagree, as Mrs Thatcher found, meant tackling the metaphor that defined the situation, rather than just the arguments built around it. Thatcher discovered to her cost, however, that if everyone else sticks with the analogy of departing trains, there lies a risk of being isolated in a discourse that no one else is hearing.

Metaphors are often connected to two other tropes that connote meanings: 'metonymy' and 'synecdoche'. A metonym involves the substitution of a word or concept with another that has particular connection with the object in question. In that way, related aspects of the thing described come to stand for it as such. Here there is room to generate connotative associations and to define the thing(s) in question. Thus, for example, governments are often referred to in the media by the location of their executive seats (for example, 'Washington' for the US, 'Beijing' for China). These substitute names give political authority and its decisions a distinct sense of place. Where metaphor invokes an identity between different things, metonymy uses close associations, and these are often a matter of convention. For instance, the saying 'the pen is mightier than the sword' uses pen and sword metonymically to symbolize the things these objects actually do (writing and fighting, respectively). Aphorisms and other commonplace sayings in political speech often rely on metonymic conventions such as these to convey their meanings.

A synecdoche, on the other hand, is a type of metonym for which an actual element of an object comes to stand in for the whole, or the whole for a part. A typical example is the use of a sail to represent ships, or, keeping with the nautical theme, the command 'all hands on deck', where the hands of people stand in for the people themselves. Synecdoches therefore keep a direct association with the object represented either by taking one part as its defining feature or using the whole class to reference one element of it. This can be a rather controversial way of reducing things to one aspect of their many features, such as reference to individuals by the colour of their skin ('blacks' or 'whites') or by their clothes (for example, 'suits' to refer to businessmen). But it can also have a powerful effect, because it defines the qualities of a thing by eliminating all complexity and magnifying one trait over others. Referring to whole groups or communities by distinguishing one feature, for example, is a common use of synecdoche: 'gays are demanding equal rights', 'Muslims are under threat', 'the French capitulated to the Germans' and so on. Here an element of group identity – be it sexual orientation, religion or nationality – is taken as the unifying trait of the group. Synecdoches therefore provide a recognizable shorthand that can be either narrowly reductive or helpfully clear, depending on how they are employed.

Metaphors, analogies, metonyms and synecdoches are therefore powerful devices for stylistically shaping not just the tone but also the content of an argument, because they permit speakers to redescribe situations, objects, agents or experiences in selective ways that subtly shape how judgements about them are to be made. One way for political actors to escape a downturn in their fortunes – such as hostile public opinion or a series of events that go against stated aims or principles – is to redescribe the situation by changing the dominant metaphors. Thus the designation by President G.W. Bush of certain states as part of an 'axis of evil' helped to turn a sense of potential weakness or isolation in the international environment into a moral struggle against not just specific regimes or a military alliance, but the embodiment of moral wrongdoing itself. 'Evil' is a common term in political discourse in so far as it magnifies what otherwise might be regarded as discrete difficulties into conflicts where what is at stake is the very principle of moral order. Such rhetoric is often criticized for being overly simplistic and certainly unhelpful if technical solutions to problems are thought to be available. But its effect is to lever its audience into making a choice – possibly quite unconsciously – or taking a principled stand on some issue, often to adopt the judgement of the speaker by having little option but to take the side of the Good. Again, to resist such arguments means taking issue with the metaphor and having the resources to sustain an alternative description of the situation.

As we shall see further in the book, politics involves a constant negotiation of competing metaphors to define contexts and actions. These metaphors often function as premises to assist the deployment of certain arguments. Metaphors prepare audiences for arguments to which they might not otherwise be receptive, to acknowledge conclusions that, without the metaphors, may seem alien or inappropriate. Even the most anti-rhetorical speakers will use metaphors of some kind to make their arguments – think of Hobbes's definition of the state of nature as, in essence, a 'warre of all against all' to be resolved by the 'mortall God' that is Leviathan. Often, however, the use of metaphors fails. The appeal to the symbol of the British pound, for example, by the Conservatives in the 2001 UK general election failed to ignite sufficient interest among the public. That synecdoche was intended to mobilize support in defence of British economic sovereignty in light of the purported threat that the Labour government would adopt the euro as its currency. Doubtless there were many external reasons for this failure (the Conservatives were still in general popular decline), but it is clear nevertheless that the choice of metaphor takes place in a context of uncertainty where the readiness of the public to invest their aspirations or fears can vary significantly. Not all situations are characterized by such chronic anxiety or accumulated discontent that new metaphors can capture the audience in sufficient numbers.

I have devoted considerable space to discussing metaphors because these figure greatly in political life. But other tropic figures are worth mentioning, too. For example, *hyperbole* involves the deliberate exaggeration of a point to magnify its significance. For instance, to argue that 'permitting greater immigration will gradually murder our way of life' adds a metaphor (murder) that overstates but undoubtedly enhances its thesis. Hyperbole dramatically raises the stakes in political debate, putting something fundamental at issue. The danger, of course, is that such a technique will be regarded as an overstatement deployed to paper over the weaknesses of an argument. Alternatively, the use of *irony* – stating something that is not true in order to draw attention to its implied lack of truth – is a common device that relies on an audience's understanding to work (for example, 'We all know how politicians abhor media attention ...'). Irony is a regular technique used in the mockery and ridicule of others.

Another trope that is important to political argument is *paradiastole* – the reevaluation of an action by 'replacing a given evaluative description with a rival term' (Skinner, 2002a: 183; see also Lanham, 1991: 107). For example, a coward might be called 'cautious', vacillation might be called being 'fair-minded' and so on. The effect here is to reverse the moral significance of an act or object, making negative what was once viewed positively, or vice versa. This is an argumentative manoeuvre to which Skinner makes reference in his discussions of post-Renaissance politics and Hobbes in particular (see Skinner, 2002a: 175–87; 2002b: 273–85; 2002c). Paradiastole was a common technique in 'rhetorical redescription', whereby a creative redesignation of persons or actions altered their public evaluation. But it was precisely the capacity to stretch or narrow a moral vocabulary that, for Hobbes, allowed rhetoricians to manipulate their listeners. Only the Leviathan state could ensure that words had fixed meanings, he claimed (see the discussion in Chapter 2).

In politics, we regularly come across contests over the way a term is used evaluatively. Paradiastole is an inventive practice whereby a speaker may extend a moral vocabulary to include something with which it usually isn't associated, thus making that something seem morally acceptable or, by contrast, repugnant. Common examples of this device include designating violent suppression as 'law enforcement', calling the state's receipt of taxes 'theft' or defining terrorists as 'freedom-fighters' (or vice versa). In that way, the audience's appraisal of certain ideas, activities or agents is encouraged to alter by applying terms whose application elsewhere is already understood. What on the surface often looks like an agreed vocabulary among opponents can turn out to involve quite opposed understandings of the meaning and application of evaluative words. Thus during the peace process in Northern Ireland in the 1990s, the very term 'peace process', although widely shared among different parties as a positive goal, had a variety of interpretations. For some it meant the total eradication of any organized violence without exception (and hence the immediate and unequivocal relinquishing of all weapons), while for others it meant a process of gradual movement towards that situation (and hence permitted the retention of weapons by certain groups until an appropriate time). Use of this imprecise but shared vocabulary eventually succeeded in overriding differences of interpretation over what it actually meant (see Shirlow and McGovern, 1998). In other contexts, however, such differences can be exclusionary and generate serious disagreement. For example, should the vocabulary of the 'family' and 'marriage' only apply to heterosexuals or can it reasonably include homosexual couples, too? Debates in the US (and elsewhere) about how to apply these terms involve rhetorical strategies over whether and how certain actions are valued or which kinds of persons can legitimately be associated with them (see Chambers, 2003: ch. 6).

Finally, a noted alternative to paradiastole, where moral approval and disapproval is contested around a common vocabulary, is *catachresis* – the introduction of a new term altogether. This new term has the effect of providing an alternative point of reference to an established vocabulary and is often associated with the introduction of an inappropriate term whose novelty arises from the way it jars with existing usage (see Lanham, 1991: 31). Examples include the term 'democracy', which in ancient Greece was a term of abuse indicating, as Rancière (1999) argues, a scandalous assertion of equality by subjects not thought fit to govern. Similar catachrestical terms in social and political life include words that sometimes have a jarring effect but that also offer new, unifying categories – 'justice' or 'freedom' in authoritarian regimes or 'the people' or 'proletariat' elsewhere. In post-revolutionary France, for example, the term 'citizen' became a new and radically egalitarian term of address for new political subjects in a society hitherto accustomed to hierarchy and markers of distinction. To call others 'citizen' was to publicly remind them that they were now equals. These examples are all what Ernesto Laclau calls 'empty signifiers' that function to unite various political demands by not referring to any specific groups or set of arrangements as such (see Laclau, 1996) – that is, they are presented as universal principles or qualities that apply to everybody. Their very emptiness permits numerous demands and aspirations to coalesce around a common name that then stands in opposition to the existing order.

As I noted earlier, style is often associated with ornamentation. That makes sense in so far as it is a dimension linked to poetry or the deployment of words (in any form) so as to have some kind of aesthetic effect, shaping sensations and the meanings built upon them. But in political rhetoric, we should not dismiss it for this reason. As I have tried to argue, stylistic devices such as schemes and tropes shape the way in which an argument is perceived and understood by its audience. This is not, then, simply a harmless matter of surface appearance or agreeable-sounding words and phrases. Style involves reflection on how to fine-tune speech for the purposes of persuasion, to get around the strict logic of an argument to access the softer range of sensations that always accompany reason. Some devices are doubtless used as a matter of personal preference or needless ornamentation and have little substantial effect on how an argument is received. But others can have a vital part to play in determining the issue and conveying the stance of the speaker. Stylistic devices are therefore important 'moves' in strategies to achieve persuasion.

Delivery

The performance of speech might, at first glance, seem like a matter that pertains only to the speaker on the day rather than to the speech itself. In a predominantly oral culture we can understand that much of the reception of a spoken performance would have hung on the qualities of its 'live' delivery. In today's rhetorical performances, by contrast, where so much is written and communicated textually and electronically, such things are now heavily managed (often with specialist expertise). But the delivery of speech remains crucial to its reception and plays an important part in shaping ethos and pathos – that is, the authority of the speaker and the emotional reception of the audience. Indeed, if anything, delivery has become equally as important as the content of speech, since recordings remain in circulation long after the actual performance and can be distributed much further than the immediate audience. As we shall discuss in a later chapter, the formation of mass media may have fundamentally shifted the balance away from argument in favour of image and performance.

On the question of delivery, we are likely to find the advice of the ancients rather anachronistic. Cicero, for instance, had much to say on the topic. In *De Oratore* he noted that 'Delivery is, so to speak, the language of the body' (Cicero, 2001: 294). 'Every emotion', he claimed, 'has its own facial expression, tone of voice and gesture' (ibid.: 292). Physical presence was therefore crucially important and speakers should adopt a 'vigorous and manly attitude of the body derived not from stage actors but from those who fight with weapons' (ibid.: 294). Continuing with the military analogy:

> The hands should not be too expressive, accompanying rather than depicting the words with the fingers. The arm should be extended forward a bit, as if our speech were employing it as a weapon. And you should stamp your foot at the beginning or at the end of energetic passages.
>
> (Ibid.)

Techniques of delivery, then, are likely to vary from age to age and from culture to culture. That makes it difficult to generate common expectations or advice. Nevertheless, it was clear to rhetoricians such as Cicero that delivery was of great significance, and it is still worth taking seriously: 'Delivery [...] is the one dominant factor in oratory. Without it, even the best orator cannot be of any account at all, while an average speaker equipped with this skill can often outdo the best orators' (Cicero, 2001: 290).

Delivery involves the manipulation of the 'paralinguistic' (or non-spoken) tools directly available to the speaker to help sustain the point being argued. These tools are, in most cases, the body and the voice (conceived as a device for making sounds). Orators can move their limbs to direct the audience's attention through gestures and can modulate their voices to convey various degrees of emotion and force. The recordings we have of political orators such as Adolf Hitler or Benito Mussolini underscore their distinctiveness in oratorical delivery. Hitler's lengthy speeches often built up into shrill demonstrations of intense anger, his voice almost squealing with rage as he denounced his enemies. Mussolini, on the other hand, chose to swagger, jutting out his chin and often crossing his arms and staring at his audience with contempt. Of course, these were the performances of megalomaniacal showmen and firebrands, deliberate crowd-pleasers looking to stir up popular feelings with pronounced oratorical displays that now seem rather overstated, comical even. Leaders in liberal democracies tend, by contrast, to downplay their physical and vocal abilities in order to display calm and control.

Nevertheless, today's politicians and leaders are often given quite sophisticated advice about how to deliver their speeches in ways that enhance rather than detract from their argument. Mrs Thatcher notoriously lowered the tone of her voice in order to affect a more reassuring and less hectoring vocal tone than before. Similarly, political leaders are taught what to do with their hands when speaking (a problem for all public speakers at some point), perhaps relaxing and placing them to the side or behind the body rather than, say, jabbing the air aggressively. The most difficult techniques, however, are often to do with the voice. Scientists are increasingly aware of the intense sensitivity of humans to the pitch, speed and volume of the human voice and the differences in reaction that variations can stimulate (see Karpf, 2006). Being able to modulate vocal tone (that is, to go up and down the high and low notes at will) is desirable but not always easy. Nor is knowing when to do it. A modulated voice enables emphases to be made at the right time, permits irony and generally shapes the tone of the oration in harmony with the kinds of arguments being made. Celebrated British orators such as Aneurin Bevin or his protégé, Michael Foot, were impressive modulators of tone to create a probing, questioning and sometimes mocking tone. Churchill, on the other hand, exuded statesman-like authority via a deep, gruff voice. Similarly, speakers need to learn how to pace their orations, avoiding excessive speed, undue length, unclear words or stumbling over multiple syllables. These are all simple, basic issues but they can make a great difference to the tenor of an oration and how the audience receives the speech.

While advice and expectations may vary, it might be possible to distinguish types of performance by the classification of the speech occasion. Different events, we might say, demand certain modes of delivery. Ceremonies, for example, rely on the affirmation of common feelings and therefore a certain degree of pathos is to be encouraged. But the precise form of delivery will vary if the ceremony is one of sympathy and goodwill (a marriage, for example) or one of loss (such as a funeral). Likewise, a judicial speech demands clarity in the delivery of a narrative about past actions and evidence to sway the jury, but the delivery may adopt more or less aggressive styles depending on the lawyer's perception as to what kinds of evidence the jury will be receptive to. Finally, political deliberations may often involve aggressive, heated and emphatic argument. But, equally, 'the voice of reason' can be found in the speaker who rises above the fray with gentle serenity and only the most modest of vocal and gestural inflections. Selecting the right style of delivery, then, is not exclusively associated with the type of event so much as the kind of tone a speaker wishes to adopt. What is 'right' in any instance will vary in light of all sorts of conditions – not least the natural abilities of the speaker.

There are also choices about delivery that might be made on the occasion itself rather than prepared in advance. Bold gestures, the use of props, sudden halting and silence, coping with hecklers or an angry crowd, perhaps even crying might be deemed acceptable given the nature of the event. In the 2008 US presidential election, for example, Hillary Clinton interrupted an interview to shed some tears. Whether that was feigned or entirely genuine is not easy to tell. But it certainly draws attention to a candidate if he or she is deemed to be burdened with emotions that cannot be contained inside the oratory. On other occasions, delivery might be unduly interrupted or rendered less convincing by bodily events that might not have been expected. Richard Nixon's notorious unshaven appearance is thought to have made him look less presidential than his opponent (and eventual winner), John F. Kennedy, in 1960. Tony Blair's visible sweating during a party conference in 2001 doubtless drew attention away from the content of his speech.

It is for these reasons that contemporary politicians often have image consultants. When things are going well, we tend not to see the manufactured, carefully coiffured aspects of a speaker's appearance and delivery. The 'image' and the 'substance', as they are often distinguished, merge into each other effortlessly. When they don't, however, appearance and argument compete for attention and the argument can so easily get lost. Achieving a sensation of 'authenticity' and honesty so as to deliver the argument effectively is a constant struggle for politicians who are permanently in danger of being regarded as insincere or superficial. That struggle is visible in recent efforts by some professional politicians to speak without the use of notes, to roll up their shirt-sleeves and appear informal or, by contrast, to communicate with the faltering speech of 'ordinary' conversation.

Outside of the well-known techniques of routine politics, the issue of performance has an increasingly significant place in contemporary political theory. In particular, the work of Judith Butler has drawn attention to the importance of performance in generating and sustaining social, particularly gender, identity. Butler has argued, following Foucault and other poststructuralist and feminist thinkers, that human sexual identity is not a fixed or universal set of qualities and orientations but, rather, a contingent phenomenon dependent upon regular (or 'reiterated') bodily performances (see Butler, 1999). Butler develops J.L. Austin's (1962) idea of 'performative utterances': sayings that produce what they refer to, such as the words 'I do' at a wedding. These are contrasted with 'constative' utterances that merely describe. Performative utterances are types of speech act that practically bring about some change in the world. Deepening this idea, Butler uses the term 'performativity' to refer to the way in which sexual identity is both contingent upon actions that bring it into being and, by consequence, also profoundly unstable and variable.

For Butler, individuals perform their gender identities in so far as they enact through bodily actions and gestures (ways of dressing, comporting themselves and talking) the style of gender that is then ascribed to them as 'natural'. Thus the everyday actions through which identity is outwardly expressed come to be seen as a consequence, rather than the cause, of an 'inner' character. In that way, universal norms of identity and behaviour are deemed natural and usually policed through expectations about dress and comportment. But, if identity is taken as the outcome of repeated performances and not as an essence, then gender and desire (which are traditionally assumed to flow from predetermined sexual dispositions) can be multiple and varied, with no fixed anchor in nature. Gender comes to be a kind of rhetorical performance that may be infinitely inflected in varying contexts. Butler's work on parody and 'drag', where the artifice of identity is explicitly on display, underscores the subversive politics she associates with performativity (for a discussion see Lloyd, 1999).

While it starts out as a deconstruction of sexual identity, Butler's analysis points to the political dimension underlying rhetorical delivery. For political action can also be understood as a kind of performance strategy by which outward gestures indicate 'essential' and 'authentic' qualities that are in fact contingently produced through performance. The voices and the bodies of political agents are not simply 'tools' for communicating preconceived ideas but also the medium through which ideas, arguments, aspirations and desires are given material embodiment. The agent of persuasion could be thought of as a subject that is created through the gestures and sounds that invoke an authentic point of view and the supposedly coherent identity that expresses it. Although many people can argue for the same conclusions, some manage to embody their arguments in such distinctive ways that it is difficult to separate the person and the ideas they transmit.

For example, Sir Winston Churchill was not always regarded as a great speaker and noble leader, but achieved those qualities in part by his oratorical performances as a wartime leader. His style of delivery succeeded in generating, in the circumstances of great national threat, a sense of ethos that particularly suited and helped shape the mood of his audience in the 1940s. Churchill-the-great-leader was, in a sense, a mythical fabrication, a character generated by means of oratorical performances in the House of Commons and on the radio. Interestingly, immediately after the war, Churchill's performances no longer succeeded in swaying the public and he was unceremoniously removed from office in the election of 1945.

Butler's notion of performativity underscores and greatly enhances some of the ideas already at work in the classical notion of delivery (and rhetoric more generally): speaking is a form of action that shapes *both* the speaker *and* the audience in specific contexts. For our purposes it is important to see how delivery is not simply about the routine politics of making an emphasis or appearing well. It also concerns the political dimension of persuasion: that is, the dependence of common principles and norms of behaviour upon contingent circumstances. Through voice and gestures, speakers embody their arguments, the motivations behind them and the qualities of the ideas they represent. Far from being pure abstractions or universally agreed truths, then, shared principles depend for their force upon repeatable performances that are often inflected by their association with, for example, sexual, racial or class-related qualities. These qualities invoke desires or identifications on the part of the audience that attract attention, stimulate feelings and help sway them. Thus we regularly see delivery styles that affirm ideas of sexual 'normality' (for example, politicians appearing on platforms with partners and children) or moral probity (clean-shaven, smartly but conventionally dressed). While we may like to think of arguments as essentially separate from the persons enunciating them, rhetorical inquiry reminds us that such things can be hard to distinguish.

Summary

Today, *style* and *delivery* are ubiquitous dimensions of political communications such that it is difficult not to define politics entirely in their terms: that is, in relation to highly stylized methods of communication, the fashioning of personalities and 'celebrity', image-friendly characters, soundbites and marketable phrases. As we shall see, it is often felt that modern media techniques have transformed politics into something like a marketing campaign.

But to reduce politics in that way is to risk emptying enquiry into rhetorical style and delivery of its political insights. If such things have become disproportionately evident in recent decades, nevertheless, we should not dismiss the obvious fact that humans can be deeply receptive to the sound and vision of public performance such that the mere inversion of words, their repetition or a simple gesture can alter the way in which we hear and understand speech. Of course, we are not all receptive in the same way and the use (or overuse) of such techniques can have negative as well as positive effects on the persuasive process. Indeed, to highlight style and delivery is not to discount the possibility that, as with all aspects of rhetorical communication, too much effort may be expended on such things. Florid, excessively verbose and exuberant orations still appear absurd and overstated, except at certain moments. This is what is often dismissively referred to as being 'too rhetorical'. When we notice such things it is because those aspects of speech immediately stand out, and the persuasive encounter will have already failed.

Like discovery and arrangement, the canons of style and delivery are elements of a whole process, rather than discrete parts. An effective oration needs a degree of coherence between these elements, a sense of continuity that ties them together, seamlessly linking arguments in a clear order with stylistic elements that affirm the point, all held together in a delivery that distributes emphases with gestures that match them. Undeniably, this is a tall order and rarely do most speech encounters reach such heights. But the classifications of ancient rhetoric do more than simply advise us of handy techniques for eloquent oratory. They point us towards the ways in which most speech and communication seeks to achieve control over a situation and an audience. Such efforts are never without a wider context of power relations. What remains for us to consider is how the ancient techniques of rhetoric can illuminate the type of interventions we encounter in contemporary political speech.

6 Rhetorical political analysis

How can rhetoric help us to understand modern politics? The categories and devices examined in the previous two chapters were originally designed as practical techniques for generating persuasive arguments. Because of this practicality, Plato dismissed rhetoric as having little significance for a genuinely theoretical knowledge of politics. That is to say, he believed the skills of persuasion could not account for the fundamental conditions that made political community possible. Rhetoric, argued Plato, only dealt with short-term manoeuvres and strategies, not the basic principles by which political order was structured. Since Plato, however, we have learned to appreciate that politics and basic principles are difficult to separate from each other. That view, formulated by figures such as Aristotle and Machiavelli, has only been reinforced by the emergence of the modern state and the development of democracy. Despite efforts to eliminate contingency from principles of political order, we are inclined now to regard the two as mutually intertwined. Politics and the political, as I claimed in Chapter 1, are inextricably linked. It is in practically mediating that link that rhetoric illuminates the character of politics today.

In this chapter I set out a rationale and a method for applying rhetoric to the study of politics. This is a form of what has been called 'rhetorical political analysis' (see Finlayson, 2007; Nelson, 1998). It involves employing rhetorical categories to explore how political actors make interventions to control or 'appropriate' particular situations. These interventions can be understood as strategic in that they are a means to negotiate the opportunities and constraints of any circumstance so as to achieve certain ends. They do this by deploying ideas – or, better, arguments – to reorient audiences in relation to the prevailing situation. Rhetoric helps us understand how political actors try to create agency by resituating an issue in time and space so as to realize their goals. Democratic politics, we could say, is awash with rhetorical strategies – not all of which succeed – competing to shape public perceptions of people, events and policies. In so doing, such strategies blend politics and the political – the struggles for advantage *and* the higher principles that govern spaces of conflict – through the medium of speech and argument. A rhetorical approach to politics allows us to disassemble these strategies and to identify how they work.

In what follows, I explore the character of rhetorical political analysis by contrast with other approaches in political science. What is at stake here is the question of political agency. Traditional approaches in political science have largely diminished the role of subjective agency in political explanation by treating individuals as maximizers of utility or bearers of fixed values. More recently, 'interpretive' approaches have sought to correct this tendency by incorporating into their explanations the values, perceptions and norms – or 'ideational factors' – that actors themselves use to understand and alter their environment. A rhetorical political analysis can be aligned with these interpretive incursions into political science. However, it also differs from them in important ways. Against a tendency among interpretivists to treat ideas and beliefs as stable 'cognitive frames' or normative dispositions – rather like tinted spectacles colouring the way we receive information – a rhetorical approach understands ideas as arguments, which are more akin to projectiles moving outwards in varying degrees, purposefully displacing the context around them. Rhetorical enquiry invites us to treat ideas as situated in specific moments and, moreover, as efforts to refigure situations by actively privileging particular interpretations and diminishing others. As we shall see, this view is compatible with so-called 'dialectical' accounts of structure and agency that emphasize the negotiation of constraints and opportunities. This discussion leads directly on to the formulation of a methodological schema for conducting a rhetorical analysis by drawing upon the toolbox of rhetorical techniques. I complete the latter discussion with a brief reflection on the example of President John F. Kennedy's famous inaugural address of 1961.

Political science, ideas and interpretation

Ideas enter into contemporary politics in a myriad of different ways: as preferences and attitudes shaping voters' choices; as party ideologies and doctrinal statements; as practical theories and paradigmatic policy frames; as 'live' public debate in deliberative chambers; as official statements, public addresses or remarks on contingent events; in political interviews, campaign advertisements and, more recently, in 'blogs' and Tweets. Such variety precludes any simple explanation of the role ideas play in politics. Variations in the form, intensity and breadth of impact make a full appreciation of the role of ideas difficult to gauge.

Partly because of this complexity, ideas have often been ignored in political science which, under the sway of positivism, has reduced human agency to narrow psychological operations such as rationally calculating utility or following routinized behavioural patterns (for a discussion, see Hay, 2002: 7–10). Rational choice theory (or 'public choice theory'), for example, 'explains' human behaviour on the basis of an abstract model of human reasoning drawn from economics. In short, human subjects are understood to be rational maximizers of utility, calculating in advance what course of action would benefit them best. This model of behaviour can be applied to politics, too, in so far as electoral democracy involves a process of exchange on a par with economic transactions. The most famous proponent of this approach to politics was Anthony Downs (1957) but it was prefigured by the work of the economist Joseph Schumpeter (1954). Generally speaking, individuals – be they politicians or electors – will make choices that enable transactions of mutual benefit to occur. Politicians, for instance, seek the advantages of office, while electors seek policies that advantage them (lower taxes, more welfare benefits and so on). For rational choice theory, what brings individuals to have these desires is not of concern. What matters is how to explain the choices they make in light of them. It is taken as axiomatic that individuals will calculate which options will benefit them most: electors vote for the candidates who offer policies of optimal advantage and politicians will offer the policies that will accrue the largest number of votes and so get them into power. In different scenarios the situation becomes more complicated but, in essence, rational choice theory works from this surprisingly simple model of human behaviour.

What is notable in this approach is that speech is regarded, if at all, as little more than an expression of a reasoning process that has already occurred. That is to say, individuals come to politics already largely persuaded of how they will judge the choices on offer. Uncertainty or doubt about how to reason is not a great obstacle. Parties and individuals may have to bargain with each other to work out the optimal choice in any given circumstance. That might involve ditching an unpopular policy or encouraging people to rank their preferences in a different order. If rhetorical speech is used at all, it is in order to manipulate rational choices to achieve certain outcomes (see McLean, 2001; Riker, 1996). But, generally speaking, persuasion is primarily a matter of clarifying or distorting the calculation, not of shaping judgements.

Rational choice theory works by applying axioms to certain scenarios, or dilemmas, where choices need to be made. Politics is conceived as a kind of game where competing parties and individuals take up predefined roles to win rewards. Like all games, however, it works best when everybody accepts the rules and calculates in a way that is not fundamentally challenged. That may reflect some features of democratic politics (its rules being like the predictable rules of a game, for example). But the approach has been widely criticized for holding to an impoverished view of human nature – deemed to be essentially self-interested – and distorts the experience of politics, which entails more than just hard-headed calculation of interests (see Hay, 2002: 37–40, 52–53). Above all, it is argued, people come to politics with a range of values and emotions that are often irreducible to calculations of utility – shared desires and ambitions, attachments to certain symbols and people – and with doubts and grievances that are yet to be clearly defined. The rational choice approach reduces these to one type of rationality and, in so doing, misses the depth and complexity of individuals' *social* encounters, both in elections and in politics generally.

The other dominant approach in political science is behaviouralism. Rather than approach politics from abstract premises, this model is based on the empirical (and supposedly 'neutral') observation of behaviour and the various measurable 'inputs' and 'outputs' that contribute to decision-making (Hay, 2002: 10, 41–45). The virtue of that approach, in contrast to rational choice theory, is it does not assume a universal rationality. We need not agree that people are rational actors at all. Their choices are made in accordance with a whole range of desires and feelings, calculative reason being only one. Behaviouralists are less attached to drawing conclusions from abstract premises than to observing what people do; they use actual behaviour to predict their future choices. For instance, it was widely noted in the post-war democracies that there was a strong correlation between voting intentions and social class (see Butler and Stokes, 1969). In the UK, for many years, voters appeared to identify with political parties (notably the Conservative and Labour parties) that represented stable clusters of values, experiences and aspirations. Thus people would vote for those parties, often despite the policies offered at any moment. Rather than adopting the outlook of a maximizer of utility, voters' judgements were governed, at least to some extent, by symbols shared among members of their class that would shape their preferences and guide their judgements. Voting was less like a marketplace and more like a demonstration of identity and tradition.

The 'party identification model' of politics started to break down from the 1960s and it became clear, as voters became more volatile in their choices and as traditionally dominant parties struggled to sustain their support, that it no longer effectively explained people's behaviour, if indeed it ever had (see Clarke *et al.*, 2004). Like rational choice theory, it suffered from an impoverished view of how people formed judgements. Rather than seeking utility, individuals were understood to be reasoning from collective identities and interests. But that was still to diminish the place of speech in shaping judgements. People remained already persuaded in advance, this time by their loyalty to a party associated with their class traditions and interests. What they did at election time was merely re-enact an established habit, rather than have it substantially challenged or changed.

Neither rational choice nor behaviouralism had much interest in practices of persuasion in politics. Human judgements were deemed predefined by virtue either of reason (conceived as self-interest) or habit. Inherent to both approaches were largely static conceptions of the human mind, which was not expected to change very much. It is no surprise that both approaches were eventually criticized for taking for granted the stability and durability of post-war politics in the West (Hay, 2002: 49–50). By the late 1960s and 70s it was clear that contrasting ideals, symbols and values were having a greater effect on people's behaviour, and in ways that neither politicians nor political scientists were able to predict or control (see Edelman, 1971; Bernstein, 1976: 55–114).

More recently, political scientists have incorporated insights from disciplines sensitive to the varied perspectives which individuals themselves bring to the world, such as cultural anthropology or cognitive psychology. These invite a richer understanding of the way in which behaviour is mediated by subjective outlooks, which the analyst must also interpret if behaviour is to be understood. They provide a nuanced picture of the attitudes and values actors bring to political problems and their judgements of how to act. Thus it is now increasingly common to find political scientists employing terms such as the 'ideational' or the 'discursive' to denote a field of subjectivity where individuals and groups construct their own relationship to the world (see Gofas and Hay, 2010; Blyth, 1997). For instance, Bevir and Rhodes favour what they call a 'narrative' form of explanation that reconstructs the 'stories' which agents tell to account for how they act (Bevir and Rhodes, 2003: 5, 20, 26). Here we are invited to understand behaviour by reference to the complex 'webs of belief' and ideological 'traditions' upon which individuals draw to frame their encounters. In the face of what are called 'dilemmas', the authors explain, narratives are transformed as actors meet new circumstances and adjust their frames (see, for example, Atkins, 2013). Alternatively, Vivien Schmidt champions an all-inclusive approach which she calls 'discursive institutionalism' that, like the work of Bevir and Rhodes, identifies the role of ideas and values in making institutions work (see Schmidt, 2008, 2010). She highlights a distinction between 'background ideational abilities', by means of which institutional practices are reproduced, and 'foreground discursive abilities' that permit actors to 'communicate' and 'coordinate' with other actors so as to innovate and extend institutions through the deployment of ideas.

These approaches have begun to incorporate subjectivity into the assessment of political and institutional change. They do so with considerable sophistication and with some appreciation of the dynamics of ideas as they shift from routine habits to active exchanges where new beliefs are formulated, articulated with other ideas and put into circulation. At the same time, however, the default position of such approaches has been to treat ideas as relatively stable cognitive frames by means of which actors follow rules (see Carstensen, 2011). Although Bevir, Rhodes and Schmidt refer to moments when new frames are formulated, the assumption is that, rather like the institutions they seek to interpret, ideas function primarily as coherent and stable outlooks that determine a consistent pattern of behaviour.

Another approach – one that captures more fully the dynamic aspect of ideas – can be found in rhetorical approaches to discourse that build upon the insights of interpretivism. The central premise of rhetoric, as social psychologist Michael Billig claims, is that 'our private thoughts have the structure of public arguments' (Billig, 1991: 48; 1996). That is to say, human thinking is more like public deliberation than the 'cognitive arranging and cataloguing of information according to procedural rules' underscored by cognitive psychology (ibid.: 41). Accordingly, adopting attitudes, endorsing theories or expressing opinions and beliefs is less like putting on mental spectacles and more like positioning ourselves within a controversy: by taking sides, adopting reasons, repressing alternatives and identifying antagonists (ibid.: 43). To 'believe something', Alan Finlayson argues, 'is to accept the (many kinds of) reasons that can be presented for so believing it' (2007: 551; see also Finlayson, 2004). That, I suggest, implies we also treat ideas as projectiles with 'expressive' qualities of force and direction, as well as settled narrative frames. To hold ideas, from that perspective, is not merely to perceive the world in a particular way, but to participate in a more or less hidden dispute. Viewed rhetorically, the world of subjectivity is less the smooth space of formulated beliefs and narratives and more a world contoured by uneven and constantly moving forces.

In assessing ideas and ideologies, Billig and Finlayson emphasize this outward activity of argumentation, where reasons and the conclusions they support are proffered and contested. They underscore the point that ideas are given force and direction in processes of public argumentation. Private attitudes and beliefs represent secondary outcomes in a wider, ongoing process where ideas are recruited to enhance some arguments and diminish others. To interpret that process involves a change of emphasis, switching focus from more or less stable and structured outlooks (coherent beliefs, attitudes and discourses and so on) – which appear to give actors and their institutions an enduring solidity – to argumentative practices that recharge, articulate and recirculate ideas (see Fairclough and Fairclough, 2012). Although that process is acknowledged by existing interpretive and discursive approaches, it is often set apart as one possibility in an otherwise stable and consistent set of institutional conditions. Yet revising narratives in the face of dilemmas (Bevir and Rhodes) or 'coordinating' with other discourses (Schmidt) necessarily involves choices and exclusions that have to be argumentatively expounded and defended.

By contrast, a rhetorical perspective interprets the way ideas are given charge in argumentative processes that unsettle, transform or simply reaffirm established narratives, often when their coherence might be in doubt. Rhetorical argument therefore admits various degrees of intensity and can be said to mediate the extent to which ideas remain in settled frames or approximate forceful projectiles that shift the terms of debate. Thus we find many uncontroversial forms of rhetoric that reinscribe new ideas or events in accepted frameworks – the ritual of the UK Queen's Speech in parliament or the rousing of the party faithful at Conference, for example – as well as more combative, declamatory forms of speech aimed at smashing accepted frames and projecting new ways of thinking and acting – the Rev. Martin Luther King's 'I Have a Dream' speech, for example, or President G.W. Bush's invocation of an 'axis of evil'. In most cases, however, rhetoric *combines* continuity with provocation, endorsing established ideas while simultaneously advancing new ones. It falls to the analyst to interpret the degree to which this is accomplished and with what consequences.

But how is that interpretive process undertaken? As we have seen, rhetoric was originally conceived as the art of persuasive communication or, in Aristotle's more precise terms, as 'the power to observe the persuasiveness of which any particular matter admits' (see Aristotle, 1991: 74). Here 'persuasion' entails forging a relationship between speaker and audience so as to shape the latter's judgement around an issue, not only to convey information. In Chapters 4 and 5 we looked at some of the key classifications for the linguistic and performative techniques involved in crafting that relationship, formulated often with a view to their subtle psychological effects. These can help to disassemble the various components, manoeuvres and layers of persuasive discourse designed to incite certain responses. Rhetoricians traditionally seek out the 'means of persuasion' by locating the argumentative forms of appeal (to reason, character or emotion), the ordering of the components of a discourse, the style of language and figures and any peculiarities of delivery (Lanham, 1991; Leith, 2011). Unlike linguistics and other approaches to discourse, rhetoric is not strictly about language: it describes a composite, multilayered performance embodied in communication. A speaker usually mobilizes language and emotion, personal authority and, if delivered 'live', bodily gestures and audible voice to make an argument work. These elements combine to give ideas a force that is often both affective and rational, and is impressed upon audiences to shape their judgements on any specific matter (see Clark, 2011; Cockcroft and Cockcroft, 2005).

Of course, as I noted in Chapter 1, the term 'rhetoric' has something of an equivocal reputation that has limited its appeal for scholars of politics. On the one hand, it is routinely disparaged as the distracting surface of political discourse, the superficial immediacy of utterances in the day-to-day competition for advantage, but not a useful guide to the deeper interests or intentions at work. This is what is regularly dismissed as 'mere rhetoric'. On the other hand, examples of political speech come to acquire iconic status in a virtual pantheon of significant utterances: what are often referred to as 'great speeches of our time' (see, for example, Safire, 2004). The latter category typically includes the oratory of Abraham Lincoln, Winston Churchill and other such notable communicators. Thus rhetoric tends either to be dismissed as having no genuine impact at all or lauded for having a self-evident, transformative effect. A rhetorical political analysis, however, needs to explain the impact, or not, of speech and argument, rather than presuppose it in one way or another. To do so, I claim in the next section, requires a conceptualization of the ways in which arguments are deployed strategically in relation to a prevailing situation.

Rhetorical situations and political strategies

'Rhetorical strategy' denotes the purposeful assemblage of arguments for a particular occasion and setting in light of its anticipated effects and by means of available techniques (see Rowland, 2002). The classical legacy – and particularly the work of Aristotle – has handed down the notion of rhetoric as speech fashioned to be as persuasive as possible to specific audiences, particularly those of the court (forensic rhetoric), the ceremony (epideictic rhetoric) or the citizen's assembly (political rhetoric). My claim in this section is that the concept of rhetorical strategy can be adapted to understand political action in contemporary settings. Its enduring virtue lies in registering how argument itself articulates time and space, thereby charging ideas with force and direction in order to orient audiences in their perception of a situation.

'Strategy' is an indispensable concept for political action and analysis. If politics names an endeavour that is neither randomly contingent nor totally static, then strategy generally describes the mediation of these extremes. Agents participate in political activity in so far as circumstances permit them some opportunity to intervene and control their environments. Yet such choices, opportunities and interventions are rarely wholly open-ended but are rather circumscribed by constraints in various degrees. To strategize, then, is to formulate a distinct set of judgements to achieve certain ends given (more or less) known constraints.

What is important to note here is that, in politics, strategy is the stuff of public engagement itself, and not simply a private, rational calculation made in advance of action. Political actors invite audiences to form judgements by weighing up alternatives, anticipating outcomes and selecting what seems the most appropriate option in light of their goals. Strategizing is thus a distinctively rhetorical activity: it entails formulating interpretations of a situation such that audiences are moved to respond in certain ways rather than others. Sometimes this is done in relatively closed, elite settings; very often it is much more public.

We saw in Chapter 3 how classical scholars and rhetoricians understood the strategic aspect as an intrinsic dimension and responsibility of the rhetorical arts. Rhetoric was designed not simply to achieve persuasion but to do so without radically disrupting the parameters of the community. Attention to the time and space (or *kairos* and *stasis*) of persuasion was thus an implicit component of civically responsible argument (see Carter, 1988). Today, however, it is less easy to identify a stable or common sense of time and space against which strategic choices might be made. Classical rhetoric can therefore seem anachronistic, because it assumes conditions for speech and its reception that now no longer hold (see Black, 1978). This issue – of how rhetoric relates to its social context – came to the fore in debates among rhetorical scholars in the 1960s and 70s. In a famous article, Lloyd F. Bitzer (1968) argued that rhetoric is called into being by a determinate situation fuelled by a problem – or what he called an 'exigence', such as a crisis, a disaster, or a policy failure – whose disruption to routine habits compels the speaker to provide a 'fitting' response through argument. The exigence obliges a persuasive intervention 'in the same sense that an answer comes into existence in response to a question, or a solution in response to a problem' (ibid.: 5). Thus the objective situation itself is thought to determine the intervention by an agent in order to resolve the dilemma. For example, we might say that the global financial crisis since 2008 has forced politicians to find new ways of explaining and resolving a situation whose destabilizing effects exceed any 'normal' narrative of events. In response to Bitzer, however, Richard E. Vatz (1973) defended the reverse point of view: situations don't determine rhetoric; rhetors (or speakers) themselves create situations with their rhetoric: 'No situation can have a nature independent of the perception of its interpreter or independent of the rhetoric with which he chooses to characterize it' (ibid.: 154). It is the creativity of rhetors that shapes reality by defining the situation through arguments by means of which traits are ascribed to certain events. Keeping with our example, we might say that the financial 'crisis' is largely the product of interpretations that emphasize uncertainty and risk for continued investment, rather than simply an objective fact to which politicians merely respond. On the one hand, then, the exigence circumscribes the parameters of rhetorical strategy; on the other, strategy consists in the intentions and skills of the rhetor.

The dispute was brought to an instructive resolution in a later article by Scott Consigny (1974), who returned the emphasis to a classical concern with argument as the medium of strategic action. For Consigny, rhetoric is indeed often a response to an exigence, but not exclusively so. The skills and creativity

96 *Rhetorical political analysis*

of the rhetor are also important in shaping the situation. Neither, however, is all-determining. If situations provide a stimulus for rhetorical intervention, the situation is nevertheless often 'an indeterminate context marked by a troublesome disorder which the rhetor must structure' (ibid.: 178). Agents are thus partially forced by situations to act, but how they do so depends upon their ability to formulate what is at stake in the situation. For Consigny, the rhetor's creative engagement with the situation makes all the difference:

> Through his actions the rhetor attains a 'disposition' of the situation, or a new way of seeing and acting in the situation. He discloses a new 'gestalt' for interpreting and acting in the situation, and thereby offers the audience a new perspective to view the situation.
>
> (Ibid.: 179)

The 'art' of rhetoric, according to Consigny, consists in identifying issues in indeterminate situations and finding a means of managing them. Doing that depends, fundamentally, on the selection of argument. In classical rhetoric, as we have already noted, the selection of argument is classified under the category of the 'topics': 'commonplace' or established argumentative structures, or formulae, that rhetors select. The topic was a device to help the rhetor ascertain the type of persuasion germane to the particularities of the situation (see Lanham, 1991: 152–53): for example, whether it concerned a problem of definition, of comparison or of relationship (for a full list, see Corbett and Connors, 1999: 87–130). For Consigny, as well as being a technical device, the topic also has what might be called an existential dimension as 'a realm in which the rhetor thinks and acts'. Deriving from *topos*, meaning place or site (hence 'situation'), a topic is itself a place from which to conceive the situation. Selecting the topic is thus about both responding to objective conditions *and* creatively resituating them in the words of the rhetor. This diminishes the distance between the speaker and situation and provides the audience a place from which to grasp the moment anew.

Consigny helps us to think about rhetorical strategy as the creative combination of established narrative frames with projectile-like ideas that shift perspectives on a situation. Accordingly, the task of persuasion is to reorient the audience in relation to an exigence by selectively re-appropriating the situation as an exemplification of a distinct type of issue, therefore making it amenable to a certain kind of management. In our example of the financial crisis, we could say that the situation has a variety of objective features, but some politicians have sought to define its dimensions by interpreting it as a 'crisis of debt' (to be resolved through a policy of 'austerity') rather than, say, a 'crisis of growth'. Here ideas amplify some aspects of the situation over others, generating associations that trigger particular reactions or introducing new terms that heighten the appeal of certain responses. As such, they construe the situation as a particular kind of event in, and of, time and space with a distinctive significance for the audience – the argument serving as a privileged location from which this new perspective is illuminated.

As another example, take Prime Minister Harold Macmillan's 'Winds of Change' speech to the South African parliament in 1960, in which he announced Britain's support for majority rule across Africa and an end to his government's acceptance of white domination. Macmillan responded to an objective situation of spreading demands for national independence across the continent by presenting these, metaphorically, as an inexorable, nature-like 'fact' to which whites urgently had to adapt by abandoning their vain aspiration for continued supremacy (Macmillan, 1960). That charged reconception of the situation was blended with an insistence that adaptation was the only way to ensure the continued influence of 'western civilization' in the face of growing communist influence (see Myers, 2000). Thus Macmillan boldly conveyed a controversial idea (radical policy change) by means of topics of definition (what something is) and circumstance (what is possible or impossible), supplemented with an established narrative of western cultural supremacy.

Structure, agency and rhetorical intervention

How might an understanding of rhetorical strategy be incorporated into the analysis of contemporary politics? Here, we should admit, arguments are developed and applied in environments defined by complex institutional practices that are rarely amenable to casual alteration. Moreover, institutions involve numerous formal and informal layers of custom and practice (for example, law, professional discourses, structures of authority and so on) that are never immediately visible in one glance. Such layers are resistant to change and typically orient institutions towards some modes of operation and outcomes rather than others. Rhetorical strategies are therefore better conceived as interventions designed to shape arguments and forge alliances *in and through* as well as against those constraining contexts.

The debates over rhetorical strategy noted earlier can be linked to the 'dialectical' approach to structure and agency developed by recent political sociologists (see Jessop, 2001 and 1990; Hay, 2002 and 1996). In that approach, social change is conceived as a process interweaving structure and agency. Accordingly, change involves the interaction of enduring practices and discourses, reproduced over time, and efforts by specific actors deliberately to alter those practices and discourses. In a dialectical approach, structure and agency are mutually constitutive, not ontologically distinct: structures offer resources by which actors function as particular kinds of empowered subjects with degrees of agency (for instance, political institutions supply legitimate leaders, with access to resources, who can then speak with authority and support their words with practical action) and actors are the medium through which structures are instituted as routinized practices. Thus agency emerges out of structures and structures emerge out of the actions of agents. It also follows that structures never totally structure and agents never fully master their environment; neither commands the field entirely. Structures provide opportunities for agents, which they may or may not take up, but also constrain them to act in accordance with established scripts and routines; and agents inherit rules and customs but nonetheless seek opportunities to impose their will and alter their constraints.

In this partially structured, partially agential environment, strategies are constantly formulated with imperfect knowledge and in contexts that are always already the outcome of earlier strategies. In the 'strategic-relational' approach to the state developed by Bob Jessop, for example, the state is conceived as strategically selective; as the 'condensation' of earlier strategies, it is readily amenable only to some types of action and agency over others (Jessop, 1990: 260–62). Only certain strategies will be realizable in the short term. Long-term, transformative strategies may be required in order to restructure state practices to make possible other types of action. But such efforts will also be open to delay, revision and failure, with certain opportunities being activated only at distinct temporal stages and phases.

Political sociologists also underscore the dimensions of time and space at work in strategic negotiation. For instance, Hay examines the diachronic pattern of 'punctuated evolution' in which periods of stability are interrupted by moments of state crisis and transformation (see Hay, 2002, 1996). Likewise, Jessop and others explore the co-present spatial 'scales' of state activity in globalizing capitalism, from local to national, international and global (see Brenner, 2004; Jessop, 2002). Strategic action is thus understood as 'adaptation to structural constraints and conjunctural opportunities' (Jessop, 1990: 266) in light of *multiple* and overlapping times and spaces that do not spontaneously cohere but require deliberate (re)alignment – for instance, the temporalities of government terms, economic cycles and the spaces of governance and political conflicts at both national and international levels.

Yet because these political sociologists are focused on macro-structural phenomena such as states and economic systems, strategic calculation is not usually explored from the perspective of agency. Consequently ideas and discourses are treated as relatively coherent rather than as tentative and provocative manoeuvres. But this is where a rhetorical approach can make an important contribution. The reappropriation of the situation can be conceived as the agential moment of strategic intervention where constraints and opportunities are given definition in argumentative form (see Opt and Gring, 2009). Such interventions aspire to mediate structure and agency by disclosing 'the truth' of the situation and determining the issues at stake. Actors use the structural resources at their disposal to rhetorically 'problematize' (see Turnbull, 2007) and so (re)fashion the parameters of choice and conflict so that a preferred kind of agency becomes both legitimate and urgent, often in the face of competing arguments. Of course, strategically selective contexts will make some arguments seem more plausible than others. Effective rhetoric then builds upon its own success by generating 'feedback loops', such that earlier interventions are the unquestioned premises of later ones (and are then available for generating enthymemes). What was once rhetoric later comes to be 'common-sense' premises to routine decisions; what began as an audacious intervention becomes a coherent discursive frame.

In modern political orders, rhetorical situations tend to emerge in the context of the routinized processes and behaviours of social and political systems. The scale of those situations will vary greatly: some will be small interruptions in fairly regularized processes that will not alter much of their overall functioning, while others will dart around and ricochet from one location to another, eventually bringing the survival of whole systems into doubt. If the model of the first is scandal or policy failure, the model for the second is corruption, a key resignation, war or economic crisis. Politics in complex multilayered systems unfolds simultaneously at various scales and temporalities, such that it is difficult to gauge fully the objective dimensions of the situation. Indeed, it is the task of rhetorical intervention itself to give definition to the exigence in order to control it, to pinpoint its limits and reinscribe it as much as possible within established terms or, where a risk is viewed as an opportunity, to utilize its disruption to impose a new grammar (see Hay, 1996: 86–7).

Furthermore, political regimes typically supply their own platforms for actors to make such interventions in a regulated manner that reduces the potential for uncontrolled disputation. Representative democratic systems, for example, distribute speaking functions in various ways that provide privileged times and places for intervention: in parliamentary debates, for example, at party conferences or in electoral campaigns, as well as via press conferences or political interviews (see Palonen, 2008). The effectiveness of strategy will partly depend, then, on how a speaker utilizes the prevailing conditions of any speech event (its conventions and audiences, for example) to maintain the exigence within the times and spaces of 'normal' governance (for example, within a term of office, using normal channels of political support and policy formation). Equally, it may be that a crisis prevents regular forms of communication from being effective and exceptional forms may be used (for example, De Gaulle's radio broadcasts to the French resistance during the Second World War).

The theoretical debates about structure and agency in political analysis can deepen the concept of rhetorical strategy developed in the previous section by alerting us to the wider, dynamic context to speech interventions. *Contra* classical rhetoricians, they suggest that the situations in which political actors intervene are often complex, layered intersections of space and time, substantially structured and so constrained by previous strategies. But it should also be noted that the dialectical perspective also benefits from a rhetorical approach to strategy, for two reasons: first because, like other interpretive approaches, it fills out the 'agency' side of the structure/agency dynamic by attending to actors' roles in producing ideas, namely through argumentative strategies in specific situations; and second because, *unlike* other interpretive approaches, it uniquely identifies rhetorical techniques as strategic manoeuvres in the recasting of structure.

Analysing rhetoric: a method and an example

What, then, might a rhetorical analysis (or interpretation) of political strategy look like? I have argued above that strategies comprise arguments situated at specific moments which they provocatively recast in order to orient audiences. The task of the analyst, then, is to interpret not just the internal coherence of a discourse but the way that speech is assembled in response to specific situations. Certainly, that may be achieved in any number of ways. A generic approach, however, will help us to identify some core features. Here I want to set out three moments and use these to explore, in brief, a well-known example of speech.

A method for rhetorical analysis

Rhetorical analysis should be concerned with three distinct moments of a speech intervention, each of which combines structure and agency in a particular way and hence serves as a separate area for interpretation: 1) the rhetorical context, 2) the rhetorical argument and 3) the rhetorical effects.

In what do these moments consist? The *rhetorical context* refers to the immediate conditions giving rise to a speech occasion. Interpreting a rhetorical context involves identifying the historical time and place of the intervention, the exigence(s) to which it is a response (a perceived problem) and any broader circumstances the intervention also seeks to shape (thus rhetoric is central to so-called 'contextualist' approaches to political ideas; see Skinner, 2002a). The local time and place of speech often involves its own degree of constraint and opportunity where a speaker is charged to deliver a particular type of discourse to a specific audience. Where classical rhetoric divided these into three, today it is reasonable to identify forms that combine generic elements of each, such as parliamentary speeches, press conferences, party conference speeches, political interviews and so on. Specifying the generic occasion helps to determine what is expected of the speaker and what conventions are typically upheld. An effective intervention is often elaborated according to recognized formulae that ensure its reception as a proper speech for the occasion. That accordance with convention constrains what can be said but also offers opportunities to speak legitimately. Party conference speeches, for example, use ceremony (with associations of goodwill and common feeling) in a way that speeches in formal assemblies cannot. The shaping of speech and argument to fit with the occasion, we have noted, is known as 'decorum'. Given the degree of disruption caused by an exigence, it is always possible for the genre conventions to be altered or challenged (as, for example, Tony Blair did in his 'farewell' speech in 2007; see Finlayson and Martin, 2008; Freedman and Medway, 1994).

The *rhetorical argument* concerns the situation configured in the language and performance of the speech itself, where constraint and opportunity are discursively reimagined. Here the traditional classifications of rhetoric permit us to interpret how discourse defines the situation and refigures perceived constraints to make an opening for effective agency. This is the moment that ideas are shaped into an argument for an audience (and often more than one audience). Rhetorical argument typically comprises the four classical canons explored in Chapters 4 and 5 – argumentative appeals, arrangement, style and delivery – shaped to maximize its effect and hence its persuasive force. While usually following the conventions of the occasion, the choice of topic, as discussed above, is the central, creative aspect of this strategic moment.

Finally, gauging *rhetorical effects* involves interpreting the alteration to the situation after the intervention – that is, noting whether any constraints have been overcome and certain kinds of action made possible. Such effects may be immediate (provoking a decision or a form of conduct) but also longer-term. An intervention may aim to supply the language by which other actors are constrained to interpret similar or related situations. To do so requires repeated efforts to build a vocabulary and arguments that may be redeployed later. In Chapter 5 I noted the importance of the term 'peace process' in Northern Ireland in the 1990s and 2000s, which exemplified the eventual success of a definition of the situation as a developmental transition open to erstwhile antagonists (see Shirlow and McGovern, 1998). Of course, the measurement of success is never easy, since rhetoric develops and alters over time as it is deployed in different circumstances. It is also true that some rhetoric becomes influential in ways that are quite different and even at odds with the original circumstances of its delivery. Nonetheless, the effects of a speech intervention can often be gauged if they appear to have enabled a speaker to enhance her capacity to act and speak in certain ways and constrain others to follow likewise. In that respect, we may reasonably infer that rhetorical strategy has contributed to defining the parameters of choice and conflict, compelling others to accept its terms of reference to the situation and positioning themselves accordingly.

Example

In the remainder of this section, I apply these three foci to a specific example of rhetorical strategy. President John F. Kennedy's inaugural address of 20 January 1961 (Kennedy, 1961) is a familiar, iconic speech and a much-admired example of liberal idealism at the height of the Cold War. It is not exemplary of every aspect of rhetoric but serves as a useful example of the strategic appropriation of a situation, deliberately moving its audience by combining established narratives with provocative rhetoric. What follows cannot be an exhaustive analysis (for which see Tofel, 2005) but, rather, a loose discussion of the type of investigation that could be undertaken. Let us proceed in the order of the three aspects of analysis.

Rhetorical context

Any analysis of the speech must begin from its status both as an inaugural address and as an intervention at a particular moment in the Cold War. The strategy of the speech is closely bound up with the constraints and opportunities supplied by those – partially structured – contexts. As an inaugural address, the speech fits a tradition in the life cycle of a presidential administration (every four years): it follows the swearing of the Oath of Office and is delivered publicly at the White House in Washington, DC in the January following the election of the previous November. As a ceremonial speech, it embellishes a ritual function of confirming the new president. This is signified in the affirmation of values that 'renew the covenant' connecting leader and citizens, and the invocation of the origins of that

102   Rhetorical political analysis

covenant in a common historical experience (namely, founding the Republic; see Campbell and Jamieson, 2008: ch. 2). The speech is therefore a safe opportunity to say little of overt controversy but, rather, to enhance the President's ethos – or character – by invoking larger themes, thus inscribing him within depoliticized expectations. As Campbell and Jamieson (2008) put it, the inaugural is a place to start 'creating' the Presidency through words (see also Tulis, 1987).

It would be wrong, however, to think of the inaugural as being entirely outside of domestic politics. Kennedy was aware that his personal authority had yet to be fully established, having emerged the winner of the 1960 campaign against Richard Nixon with only a small margin in the popular vote. He was not unequivocally the people's choice. Indeed, he was young, relatively inexperienced, a Catholic and regarded as something of a playboy (see Dallek, 2003: 225). Furthermore, he was conscious of a need for civic renewal in a society undergoing rapid economic growth but still shaped by defensive and paranoid attitudes from the war. So the inaugural provided a first opportunity to underscore Kennedy's substance and appropriateness for the post by presenting himself as a progressive, unifying leader of the US and the world.

The wider context of the Cold War, however, provides the dominant exigence for the speech's strategy. The hostilities between the two superpowers – the USSR and America – directly inform the sense of uncertainty and potential for violence that the speech addresses. The Cold War was in many respects an unavoidably rhetorical experience, in that its focus was rarely on actual 'hot' conflict but, rather, on the perceptions of threat, definitions of strategic interests and negotiations with the 'enemy' to avoid dangerous escalation. Designating a structured space both of rivalry *and* of forced co-operation, the Cold War was marked by a deep ambivalence that each rival sought to master (Scott, 1997: 4).

Kennedy therefore inherited a situation that had already been strategically framed. Under President Eisenhower the US had not only completed a war in Korea, but was also involved in continuing disputes with the Soviets over the status of Berlin and had observed the Chinese revolution and the stirrings of communist activity in Latin America and Cuba. Most importantly, the US military was convinced of its own inferiority in weapons in relation to the USSR. The arms race had begun in earnest and the capacity to send nuclear warheads on missiles across Europe was an urgent priority. Soviet superiority had already been demonstrated with its launch of the Sputnik satellites. Though Eisenhower had been (rightfully) suspicious of the degree of Soviet advances in weapons technology, a frantic, hawkish atmosphere pervaded US military and intelligence circles. Eisenhower had initiated a form of national mobilization – funding universities and research projects, as well as enhancing already massive military spending (see Walker, 1993: 115–17). The prevailing sense, among some at least, was that the USSR was on the offensive and could not simply be 'contained'. The US had to be prepared to defeat it.

In retrospect, if the structure of the Cold War remained relatively stable, at any moment it was never clear precisely what advantage either side had over the other, and that made for a constant sense of uncertainty. Moreover, underlying cracks and fissures were never entirely resolved or predictable (not least because each superpower had to rely on its partners, who pushed and pulled against it). So the parameters of international political action had regularly to be defined, if only to shape some foothold from which to proceed. Let us now look at how this was sought in the rhetorical argument of Kennedy's speech.

Rhetorical argument

Kennedy's speech sets out an indirectly political argument addressed primarily at an international audience. The arrangement and delivery follow a regular ceremonial format proper for a domestic audience, but the mode of argument and its stylistic elements subvert that format noticeably. Having just sworn the Oath of Office, his speech adopts a pattern of addressing named audiences in the world and making pledges to them, too. Thus his argument is not that of logical claims supported by evidence (an appeal to *logos*) but a series of personal pledges (*ethos*) in keeping with the decorum of an inaugural. That combination of ceremonial elements with wider themes allows him to set out ideas that, in projectile fashion, challenge the audiences' orientation to the prevailing situation and yet remain disguised within an apparently depoliticized frame. As we shall see, the argumentative topic is that of contraries – mutually incompatible positions (see Corbett and Connors, 1999: 105–6) – that are to be overcome by a sense of common endeavour.

As one scholar notes, the speech is unique as an inaugural by virtue of its 'address system' (Meyer, 1982). By tradition the inaugural is addressed to one, generalized national constituency, but here it is uniquely utilized to address a variety of audiences. Of the speech's twenty-seven short paragraphs, twenty-three contain a direct or indirect address to a specific addressee (Meyer, 1982: 247). For example:

> To those old allies [...]
> To those new states [...]
> To those people in the huts and villages of half the globe [...]
> To our sister republics [...].
>
> (Kennedy, 1961: 298–99)

Kennedy also appeals to the United Nations, to 'our enemies', to 'fellow Americans' and to 'citizens of the World'. The safety of the inaugural ceremony permits him to 'hail' his auditors as though he was renewing America's pledge to the world. By the end of the list it is also clear that his real focus is the Soviet Union. This is evident when he switches to his repeated pledges, all of which begin with 'Let both sides ...' (ibid.: 300). The many named audiences are now reduced to two hostile camps: a return to the dichotomous spatial logic of the Cold War (see Meyer, 1982: 247).

Stylistically, the speech is filled with dramatic contrasts and oppositions, as well as powerful imagery of conflict and reconciliation. These support the

104 *Rhetorical political analysis*

argumentative topic of the speech by signifying the risks of antagonism and potential rewards for cooperative behaviour between the superpowers. In one phrase, for example, Kennedy pledges 'the loyalty of faithful friends' taking up 'a host of cooperative ventures', but then warns of being 'divided' and 'split asunder'. He welcomes new states to the 'ranks of the free', but then alerts his audience to the threat of 'iron tyranny'. Almost every significant pledge is doubled up with a contrary sentiment that qualifies it. The device even becomes part of individual sentences focused on abstract principles (or aphorisms) that turn their original meaning around, such as:

> If a free society cannot help the many who are poor, it cannot save the few who are rich…
>
> Let us never negotiate out of fear, but let us never fear to negotiate.
>
> (Kennedy, 1961: 299, 300)

The effect of these paradoxes and oppositions is to present a series of quandaries that construct the international situation as an uncertain space of dilemmas, choices and dangers. Kennedy offers the implicit metaphor of an exhausted battleground, shaped by an extraordinarily costly and 'uncertain balance of terror' (in the form of nuclear weapons). From that image of entrenched and unwinnable warfare, however, comes a repeated invitation to reconciliation: 'Let both sides explore what problems unite us instead of belaboring those problems which divided us'.

Kennedy then uses the battlefield theme to call a truce – that is, to place both sides on the *same side* and to open the door to co-operation. He invites the imperious advance of 'mankind' (rather than states) not across national territories but into other parts of nature – space, the seas, the deserts, as well as the arts – and around 'the common enemies of man' – 'tyranny, poverty, disease and war itself'. A divided space of contraries now comes to be envisaged as a unified open space of mutual endeavour.

As for the temporality of this situation, Kennedy conjures doubled-up images of urgency and eternity. He talks of the 'Hour of maximum danger' and invites an anxiety about swift and violent responses from the US when he offers to oppose aggression anywhere in the Americas. The temporalities of conflict are then combined with the eternal promise of peace. He announces the 'trumpet summons' that calls him and his 'embattled' audience to a 'long twilight struggle'. So the twitchy anxiety of real warfare is superseded by the more assured horizon of eternal justice. The metaphorical 'torch' being 'passed to a new generation' illuminates for Kennedy a future space and time that transcends the present situation.

The paradoxical intertwining of present risk and future reward is also reflected in that most memorable example of patriotic antimetabole (the repetition of a phrase in reverse order) where the speech reaches its climax:

And so, my fellow Americans, ask not what your country can do for you; ask what you can do for your country.

(Kennedy, 1961: 301)

This famous line is emblematic of Kennedy's argument. Reversing the order of the first phrase performs the very inversion the audience(s) are challenged to make in their own minds: to reorient their own priorities such that public duty overcomes private desire. By this means Kennedy invokes an idealized audience to authorize him to negotiate the contradictory space and time the speech has imagined.

Rhetorical effects

How did Kennedy's various audiences react to his oration? The speech was well received by his domestic audience, with the press noting its eloquence and economy (it was one of the shortest inaugurals). Rhetorical scholars drew attention to its elegance and the patriotic theme that served the immediate purpose of strengthening the speaker's personal authority and providing healing after the divisions of election (see Corbett and Connors, 1999: 461–72). This was very much the reaction Kennedy hoped to have; later reports indicate that he wanted a memorable address to enhance his personal appeal and worked hard on the draft with his advisors, particularly Ted Sorenson, to achieve this (Dallek, 2003: 321–33, 324).

As a speech addressed to the international world, however, the reaction was less effusive. The Soviets, in particular, were baffled. As one commentator asks: 'were they being invited to an international coalition to give foreign aid to the poor, or to a nuclear war?' (Walker, 1993: 146). The contradictory signals in the speech – a battlefield scenario versus the forward march of mankind – did not permit an unambiguous reading of Kennedy's intentions. Furthermore, in retrospect Kennedy's administration did not achieve anything like the positive advances proclaimed in his inaugural. Alongside his successes in facing down the Soviets in Cuba might be set his failure to make advances elsewhere in Latin America, Africa or the Middle East; his unsuccessful summit with Khrushchev over Berlin, where East Germans were eventually walled in; to say nothing of Vietnam (see Graubard, 2009: 20–21). Any sober assessment of the effect of Kennedy's intervention will take these details into consideration. Arguably, his untimely death (in 1963) may have permitted his mediocrity as a president to be set aside and his early promise to be magnified as his enduring legacy.

A brief sketch suggests that Kennedy's inaugural sought to initiate an intervention in international affairs by rhetorically refiguring the Cold War situation. That he ultimately failed in this quest is not solely the fault of his rhetoric, either in this speech or others. But his rhetoric does give us a clue to his limitations. Kennedy, like other presidents after him, was unable to overcome the Cold War logic of rivalry. The conciliatory tones of the 1961 speech were intrinsically linked to those of censure – that is, to the demand that the enemy withdraw from overt hostility and antagonism. Despite the enduring humanitarianism of his rhetoric, his strategy did not succeed in reshaping ideas to become a new language of international co-operation.

Summary

In this chapter I have set out the rationale and a general method for rhetorical political analysis. In so doing I have claimed that speech is a dynamic medium for mobilizing ideas as a form of action. To explore such action requires that we interpret how speech both responds to and acts upon a situation, utilizing ideas both as relatively structured resources and as 'projectiles' that provoke reorientation among audiences. A rhetorical approach to politics provides a wealth of categories and terms for examining how arguments are deployed strategically – that is, in specific times and places and for particular audiences. Important in this account, however, is the claim that argumentative topics are a means to re-situate prevailing circumstances. That view is taken from debates in rhetorical theory, but is compatible with recent developments in political sociology that defend an interactive or dialectical account of structure and agency. Unlike classical rhetoric, a dialectical political sociology treats discourse within the complex and shifting terrain of modern states. Accordingly, a rhetorical response to a situation is an intervention at the intersection of overlapping times and spaces that are partially structured but also partially open to creative alteration. Finally, I have sketched the basis of a method to analyse speech this way, underscoring three moments of rhetorical significance: the context, the argument and the effects. The example of President Kennedy's inaugural was briefly employed to illustrate how such a method might be applied.

There is, of course, a wide variety of other ways to explore how ideas and arguments inform politics. A rhetorical approach can and should draw upon work in linguistics and the analysis of ideologies, discourses or culture, for example. These can illuminate many of the techniques of communication and the discursive resources upon which political actors regularly draw, as well as the constraints upon them when they utilize ideas. Rhetorical analysis is not incompatible with such approaches and shares much with them. But the distinct advantage of the rhetorical approach is its focus on speech itself as the locus of creative political action. This is an action not simply of asserting preconceived ideas or applying normative claims but, rather, of projecting these so as to reposition opponents and refresh the audience's perspective on the situation. As the Kennedy example indicates, these strategies do not always succeed. Nonetheless, examining rhetorical speech helps illuminate one of the vital means by which actors do politics with ideas.

7 Democracy, rhetoric and the emotions

Democratic politics is, undoubtedly, an emotional business. Designed, seemingly, to channel popular feelings into government but also to restrain them through debate, criticism and compromise, democracy regularly stages our, often contradictory, attitudes towards emotion. More often than not this plays out in a rhetorical register – that is, in controversies over who can say what, where they can say it, and how. Take, for example, the public dispute in October 2009 over the appearance of Nick Griffin MEP, the leader of the British National Party, on the BBC television show *Question Time*. A vocal constituency argued that a public broadcaster was an inappropriate host for someone with highly contentious views on immigration and who leads a party known for its fiercely prejudicial views on race. Letting him speak on a legitimate platform was morally wrong, they felt, because his opinions mobilized undemocratic sentiments. However, others claimed that an elected representative was in fact properly required to expose his views to criticism and should be permitted to appear, however objectionable those opinions. The BBC held firm and, despite physical protests outside the studios, Griffin took his place on the show's panel. In the end, it was the live audience that, with aplomb, took Griffin to task for the vacuity of his beliefs and opinions (see BBC News, 2009).

The Griffin case exemplifies the difficulty that contemporary democratic cultures often have in negotiating the tension between politics and the political – that is, between routine exchanges of opinion and deeper questions of principle. 'Normal' politics operates typically by minimizing controversy, sometimes by repressing intense, emotion-laden viewpoints in favour of a settled consensus or set of conventions that moderate what can be said, by whom and how. Doubtless that has the worthy effect of reducing unpleasant abuse, even harm or offence, and making agreement more likely. Yet consensus and convention can also be unduly restrictive, perhaps accentuating a sense of grievance felt by those whose (controversial, unpleasant or just plain odd) opinions cannot always get a hearing. At such moments, speech takes on a heightened importance – the words, styles and techniques of public argumentation mediate exchanges that may bristle with an underlying sense of fundamental disagreement over what is at stake. Here, despite the best intentions of many democrats, the issues of what one says, where and how carry an emotive force that, at times, imbues speech with a potential for danger, perhaps even violence. For that reason, as we saw in Chapter 2, political philosophers have sought regularly to diminish the function of rhetoric in politics (see Garsten, 2006).

How, then, are we to conceive of democracy as an environment in which matters of deep conviction or controversy might be raised and debated? In this chapter I explore the way democratic theorists connect emotions and democracy via the question of rhetoric. I begin by taking issue with efforts by so-called 'deliberative democrats' to eliminate or minimize rhetorical exchanges in public dialogue. As I shall argue, at work here is an unconvincing separation of reason and emotion and an impoverished conception of democratic space as a neutral realm of 'transparent' communication. I then sketch the insights of thinkers inspired by neuroscience and psychoanalysis, both of which understand cognitive judgement (or reason) as one moment in a wider, *affective* process. If 'emotions' are observable human responses with attendant feelings (such as anger or joy), 'affects' describe deeper, unconscious intensities and forces that provoke and stimulate emotion. Rather than distortions of reason, emotions are better conceived as conduits of affect that prompt feelings and shape cognition. Despite important differences in locating and defining emotions, scholars influenced by neuroscience and psychoanalysis foreground the dynamic network of connections moving across memories, feelings and cognitions that helps to orient individuals and position them in relation to their world and how they reason about it.

Emotions, then, are integral to the process – discussed in the previous chapter – of situating audiences. They are, moreover, intrinsically receptive to modification by techniques such as those found in rhetoric. Those techniques, which I go on to label 'affective rhetorical strategies', invite an alternative conception of democratic encounters as sites of competition for attention and allegiance, not reasoned argument alone. Such encounters require not the exclusion of rhetoric or emotion but, rather, an appreciation of how these may be negotiated and contested. Finally, I argue that a 'rhetorical democracy' – that is, a democracy attuned to the function of rhetoric in helping to situate citizens in relation to the issues that concern them – may well be one that is more deliberative in nature, but it will also accept the role of emotions, however hostile or benign, in generating and sustaining dialogue.

Deliberative democracy

The deliberative model of democracy came to prominence in Anglo-American democratic theory from the 1990s onwards. It is now a well-established framework taking a variety of directions, not all of which fully align (see Warren, 2002). Indeed, one commentator argues there are now at least three generations of deliberative democrats, each with their own preoccupations and distinguishing features (Elstub, 2010). In essence, the deliberative model promotes democratic practices in which citizens take an active part by exchanging views and informing and persuading each other *by giving reasons for their judgements* prior to any formal decision-making. In fact, not all deliberative democrats emphasize taking decisions. Some conceive deliberation as an end in itself, one that produces a dynamic and open 'public sphere' that generates informed opinion. Either way, the term 'deliberation' here denotes an inclusive process of discussion and dialogue where different judgements and reasons are elaborated, defended, criticized and revised. As Mark Warren summarizes: 'Deliberation induces individuals to give due consideration to their judgements, so that they know what they want, understand what others want, and can justify their judgements to others as well as to themselves' (Warren, 2002: 173). That emphasis on the process (rather than the outcome) of communication gives priority to the democratic *legitimation* of opinion, decisions or legislation by shared speaking, listening and the forming of mutual understanding (see Parkinson, 2003). Specific demands and claims achieve legitimacy through practical deliberation and not because they purport to be intrinsically rational, just or simply 'in tune' with common opinion.

The motivation for enhancing deliberation arose primarily from a sense of the limitations of prevailing models of electoral democracy and its alternatives. Deliberative democrats typically oppose themselves to the 'aggregative' model – that is, the model of mass franchise, but limited participation, electoral democracy now well established in Europe, the US and beyond. Goodin calls this 'minimalist democracy' (Goodin, 2008: 1), and we can see why. Liberal democracy consists primarily in an electoral system that sends representatives to legislatures on behalf of citizens. Citizens' votes are aggregated – simply added together – and governments with policy agendas are formed as a consequence of those accumulated choices. While parties and politicians may seek to shape voters' preferences, the vital moment in this type of democracy is when citizens vote.

Deliberative democrats view this as an impoverished conception of democracy, one that fails to grasp the vital importance of legitimacy in sustaining democratic government (see Young, 2000: 19–21). For them, a sense of trust in government is required to sustain our co-operation. If we lose, we must nevertheless feel as though we lost fairly and that the system still deserves our support. That legitimacy, they argue, is better achieved by our actively taking part in ways other than voting. Rather than remaining silent, we often prefer to voice our concerns, to promote particular issues and to persuade others to change their preferences or, indeed, invite them to change ours. That can be achieved only by offering opportunities for greater deliberation among the public than is supplied by electoral democracy. Crucially, the aggregative model refuses to treat preferences as changeable. Its proponents assume people come to political encounters already persuaded of their essential (self-) interest. For deliberative democrats, on the other hand, preferences are always revisable – open to critical interrogation and, subsequently, transformation in a process of dialogue.

How, then, is deliberation to occur? Proponents of deliberative democracy envisage a variety of scenarios at different scales and degrees of formality, from expanded 'town hall' style meetings, citizens' juries or revised legislative assemblies for regular and more inclusive discussion to specific issue-based arrangements for gathering opinion locally or on distinct matters of public policy (see Parkinson, 2006; Goodin, 2008; Fishkin, 2009). For some, deliberation can be added to existing institutions of electoral democracy; for others, they may substitute those institutions. We might also include the numerous efforts at negotiating agreement in community disputes or civil conflict peace talks such as those in Northern Ireland in the late 1990s. There are many different venues for employing deliberative methods where previously elite bargaining or secret talks was the norm.

What has preoccupied deliberative democrats, however, is how to conceive deliberation as a process of inclusive communication undertaken in conditions that permit participants to meet as equals. Thus early proponents devoted attention to specifying the ideal form, or 'normative preconditions', for deliberation itself. In short, it is claimed that arguments must conform to certain conditions or standards if they are to be considered valid contributions. As Warren summarizes it, these conditions are usually that such arguments appeal to common rather than sectarian interests, such that everyone can conceivably agree to them; that they involve factual and truthful claims rather than purely self-serving interpretations; and that participants are sincere in employing their arguments, rather than seeking to deceive others about their views or intentions (see Warren, 2002: 183).

How these normative conditions are defended varies from thinker to thinker. Jürgen Habermas, for instance, has famously argued that deliberative rules are implicit presuppositions contained in *any* communicative practice. To speak at all, he claims, we have to assume a certain 'ideal speech situation': 'anyone acting communicatively must, in performing any speech action, raise universal validity claims and suppose that they can be vindicated' (Habermas, 1996b: 119; see also the discussion in Chapter 3). That is, all moral demands imply certain standards of rationality and impartiality that can be redeemed in the procedures of democratic deliberation: namely, that the demands are universally understood, that they are sincere and that they are true. Democracy should, in Habermas's view, approximate that ideal by eliminating 'distortions' to communication and permitting moral claims to be collectively validated. Habermas's ideal informs his influential account of 'discourse ethics' (Habermas, 1996b: 180–95). Gutmann and Thompson (1996), on the other hand, defend the idea of 'reciprocity' as the root principle and precondition of deliberative encounters, along with notions of publicity and accountability. For them, reciprocity demands that 'a citizen offers reasons that can be accepted by others who are similarly motivated to find reasons that can be accepted by others' (ibid.: 53). Regardless of whether it can be presupposed of all communication, Gutmann and Thompson follow Habermas in seeking a standard by which moral argumentation takes place on an equal footing; where citizens can accept each other's reasons as valid without necessarily agreeing with their conclusions.

Central to deliberative democracy, then, is the claim that dialogue should be transparent and free of the distorting influence of interests or deception. Deliberation must be honestly motivated and not manipulative. If it is not proposed that participants free themselves entirely from 'outside' influences, nevertheless they must divest their arguments of any trace of strategy such that listeners might be deceived into accepting reasons whose motivations are not fully evident.

Encouraging others to do so is tantamount to changing preferences by coercion. As Dryzek (2000: 8) claims, there is only deliberation when 'domination via the exercise of power, manipulation, indoctrination, propaganda, deception, expressions of mere self-interest, threats, and the imposition of ideological conformity are all absent'. Presumably, then, that means not arguing from religious premises or readings of sacred texts not shared by others, unless these can be translated into more general claims. Equally, we must exclude overt expressions of ridicule, mockery, contempt, anger or sarcasm; we cannot quietly hint at the prospect of violence should others disagree, or flirt with and charm those who do agree.

It is for these reasons that many – though not all – proponents of deliberative democracy explicitly reject rhetoric. By 'rhetoric' they tend to mean direct appeals to emotion or to personal authority; what classical rhetoricians termed *pathos* and *ethos* respectively. Efforts to change the preferences of others in the process of deliberation must appeal solely to reason, or *logos*, which is deemed entirely separate from ethos and pathos. Only rational deliberation, it is claimed, can ensure transparent communication and common agreement. For arguments to be deemed rational they must conform to standards of universality, truthfulness and sincerity. Emotion, by contrast, is presumed to be manipulative in so far as it bypasses reason and invites participants to accept arguments on the basis of unexamined feelings and automatic responses to symbols that do not bear rational scrutiny. Likewise, appeals to personal authority are thought to ask participants to accept conclusions regardless of good reasons for doing so. In the words of Habermas, persuasion should be achieved only by 'the force of the better argument', not the deceptive tools of rhetoric.

Not all deliberative democrats take this hard line on rhetoric, however. Iris Marion Young (2000) and John Dryzek (2000), for example, are among those who explicitly invite different kinds of communicative style. Young, for example, rejects the notion of 'dispassionate, unsituated, neutral reason' as a 'fiction' with 'exclusionary implications' (Young, 2000: 63). While she endorses the 'basic outlines' of the deliberative model and even Habermas's account of communicative action (see ibid.: 26, 34), she prefers a less rigorous application of public reason. All communication is rhetorical, she insists, because it tries to produce effects on its listeners; meaning and effect (or 'locution' and 'perlocution' in the speech–act theory employed by Habermas) are in practice inseparable. The important distinction for her is not between reason and rhetoric but between 'communicative acts that aim to further understanding and cooperation and those that operate strategically as means of using others for one's own ends' (ibid.: 66).

Thus for Young, rhetoric can have affirmative uses for inclusive democratic communication, such as getting issues onto the agenda by introducing new topics, allowing people to speak in ways appropriate to their situation, using language in an idiom with which they feel comfortable and encouraging the formation of judgements in situations of uncertainty. She highlights the value of 'narrative' forms of communication that express local and culturally 'situated' forms of knowledge that might otherwise be excluded from ascetic versions of public reason (ibid.: 70–77). Of course, giving licence to non-rational forms of communication in order to 'enlarge' the conversation may introduce the possibility of deception and manipulation into the deliberative scenario. But for Young, only exposure to broad public criticism, not adherence to a rigid conception of reason, can eliminate or reduce such strategies. She remains convinced, perhaps optimistically, that the inclusive and deliberative ends of communication and mutual understanding can be achieved without interruption or distortion.

For Dryzek, too, rhetoric need not be exclusively a method of manipulation. He concurs with the spirit of Young's argument: namely, that rhetorical appeals are particularly effective in reaching out to a wide audience 'by framing points in a language that will move the audience in question' (Dryzek, 2000: 52). Being able to 'move' the audience's feelings provides an argument with greater thrust, helping it 'transmit' its rational core further than it otherwise would (see the discussion of the 'projectile' character of rhetoric in Chapter 6). Dryzek cites Rev. Martin Luther King's oratory and the US Declaration of Independence as examples of successful appeals that have supported rather than undermined rational judgements. The issue, then, is not to eliminate rhetoric entirely but, as he puts it elsewhere, to minimize 'categorically ugly rhetoric' in favour of rhetoric that has some positive 'systemic' effects – that is, that produces further rational deliberation (Dryzek, 2010: 333). He cites President George W. Bush's advocacy of a 'war on terror' as an example of ugly rhetoric because of the 'denigration directed at any actor not totally aligned with the Bush Administration's position' (ibid.). Ugly rhetoric inhibits further deliberation by closing down dissent or prejudging the opinions of others, thereby eliminating the need to engage them in dialogue. Yet at the same time, Dryzek also recognizes that some ugly rhetoric can contribute to expanding deliberation, perhaps despite its intentions. For example, the virulently opposed positions of the parties in the Northern Ireland peace talks later contributed to fruitful dialogue.

Although, as Dryzek goes on to claim, deliberative democrats are increasingly open to rhetorical appeals (that is, to ethos and pathos) as legitimate devices in deliberation, it is clear that for him, as for most others, reason remains both distinct and superior. As he reminds us, 'emotion can be coercive; which is why in the end it must answer to reason' (2000: 53). Yet his aesthetic distinction between ugly and positive rhetoric fails to provide a clear test to isolate negative speech because, as he admits itself, it can never be certain whether sectarian, violent or aggressive language eventually might lead to beneficial outcomes for deliberation. In the end, the effort to affirm some types of rhetoric over others merely exposes a prejudice that deliberation is, fundamentally, a rational process from which emotions can be eliminated. As with Young (who is, admittedly, much closer to Aristotle than is Dryzek), rhetoric's primary virtue for deliberative democrats prepared to endorse it is, as one commentator puts it, 'in prising open the doors of the deliberative forum and widening its agenda' (Parkinson, 2003: 184–85). It gets people heard, it expands the democratic community, it broadens our appreciation of difference; but it should never *replace* reasoned debate.

The trouble with the overt anti-rhetorical dimension of deliberative democratic arguments, as Young herself acknowledged, is that it threatens to reduce democracy to an arid forum that makes unrealistic demands on how participants communicate and effectively excludes those who cannot comply with its strictures. By emphasizing preconditions for legitimate speech deliberative democrats, to varying degrees, remove communication from the world of controversy, passionate disagreement, intense attachments to principle and the weight of personal experience – all dimensions that contribute to regular kinds of argument and strategies of persuasion (see Olson, 2011). Deliberation is thus imagined as a practice beyond the unevenness of power relations, a neutral and transparent space of encounters where the orderly temporal succession of argument, justification and eventual resolution are unforced by sensations of urgency, danger or risk.

In imagining democracy in that way, deliberative democrats effectively suppress the political dimension of politics – that is, the contingent and fundamentally contestable nature of any decision or judgement and their grounding in contexts circumscribed by differential relations of power. Doubtless that is connected to its overwhelming orientation towards achieving agreement or consensus (see Norval, 2007: 26). Having accepted in advance *how* they might be persuaded on any matter, deliberating citizens are in principle far more likely to reach consensus. Yet when its advocates do reintroduce 'real-world' situations into the deliberative scenario – including contingencies such as sectoral interests, partisan loyalties, 'situated' knowledge and local forms of expression, compromises and intense disagreements – the normative foundations of deliberation appear rather unrealistic, perhaps even utopian.

The affective unconscious: neuroscience and psychoanalysis

For many – if not all – deliberative democrats, rhetoric and reason are pitted against each other as more or less opposites. Informing that contrast is a suspicion about the role of emotions and emotional attachments in argumentative practices. But, as critics point out, even Aristotle did not object to the use of emotional appeals in his classic account of political deliberation (see Garsten, 2006: 135–39, 195–96). In the *Rhetoric*, Aristotle recognized the importance of emotions – such as anger or pity – in shaping and altering judgements by connecting reason to sensations of pleasure or pain (see Aristotle, 1991: 141). In legal disputes, where disinterested discussion of the facts was required, emotion may not be an appropriate proof. But for Aristotle, as Bernard Yack reminds us, political reasoning about the common good is 'more like a contest for attention and allegiance' than a forensic examination of truth claims (Yack, 2006: 427). Such a contest concerns not simply how we form judgements but, sometimes, that we should make them at all. For Aristotle, it was never possible to make deliberative judgements simply a matter of reason. 'Decisions about future action', continues Yack of the philosopher's conception of politics, 'draw on an inseparable mix of desire and intellect, emotion and reason' (ibid.: 432).

Unlike Aristotle, however, contemporary theorists of democracy are less confident that their polities can ever be motivated by a substantial sense of the common good. Of course, even Aristotle knew that politicians frequently had scurrilous intentions and were not always driven by a desire for the common good. But in the modern age we have grown culturally accustomed to suspecting the motives of others, instituting 'rights' to immunize individuals from each other (see Esposito, 2008). Liberals, in particular, are prone to viewing claims to the common good as a guise of fanaticism, often of a 'religious' variety, where sentiments are mobilized in order to impose moral claims partial to one group or another. On what basis today, then, might emotions be reconnected to reason?

Below I consider two contemporary approaches that insist on the inseparable nature of passions and the intellect; work inspired, respectively, by the fields of neuroscience and psychoanalysis. Although different and internally diverse, both fields examine unconscious, affective processes that support cognition. Such processes are deemed receptive to techniques of manipulation that activate memories and associations with varying intensity, consequently shaping our 'attention and allegiance' prior to – and in the process of – reasoning. Emotions are perceived by advocates of these approaches to be at the heart of public deliberation, and not a supplement or a distraction.

Neuroscience

In the western tradition of philosophy, emotions are typically conceived as antagonistic to reason: feelings and passions entail bias, an unreflective attachment towards certain objects or outcomes that overrides reason and threatens to subdue it; reason, on the other hand, involves the dispassionate use of logical, repeatable procedures that do not favour any specific object or outcome. Emotion is partial and reason is impartial or 'neutral'. Since Descartes, the association of emotion with unreasoned bodily instincts often accompanies this conception, while thought is associated with an independent domain of rational cognition (see de Sousa, 1987).

Neuroscientists, however, see this separation of two domains as untenable. Emotions are not irrational reactions but material, physiological processes necessary to perception and the preparation of conscious thought. Basic emotions such as anger, fear, dread, joy and so on form the outward manifestation of deeper, complex and otherwise unconscious processes that are constantly receptive to environmental stimuli in a way that cognitive processes cannot be. Laying down neural pathways and connecting different regions of the brain and body, emotions operate behind the scenes of the conscious mind to filter and evaluate perceptual information. 'Emotion systems' undertake specific tasks, monitoring and responding to sense experience prior to our conscious awareness and calling up appropriate dispositions in the form of sensations, such as 'moods' and feelings, before we actively deliberate (see Damasio, 1999; 1994).

The implications of neuroscientific research for understanding political behaviour have been explored by a number of scholars in political and social science. Drawing upon Damasio's notion of 'somatic markers', for example, George E. Marcus (2002) has sketched the way that different neural systems steady or provoke conscious reasoning. For example, our awareness of threats often arises *before* we have consciously thought through a situation. Indeed, we 'think through' a situation only because our 'fight/flight system' alerts us in advance and generates sensations of imminent danger. Alternatively, the 'disposition system' monitors the success of our learned behaviours and alerts us, with a sense of success or failure, when certain parts of a procedure are executed or are not. Finally, the 'surveillance system' is sensitive to the gap between our intentions and the actual performance of a procedure, reminding us with a sense of discomfort or surprise if something interrupts the action.

Far from intruding on reasoning, emotions describe a constant background activity between the body and the brain that triggers the appropriate dispositions for reasoning. Thus for Marcus, '[r]eason must rely on emotion' because the latter tap into our procedural memories, supplying responses to situations, focusing us on what is required at any moment and initiating processes that take too long if left to the conscious mind. Emotion is therefore the foundation of reason, the support system that makes 'strategic assessments' of the context and disposes us towards actions accordingly (Marcus, 2002: 76).

What implications does this view have for how we conceive of democratic deliberation? Marcus argues that far from disparaging the emotions, we should appreciate their role in political reasoning. He highlights two emotions in particular: 'enthusiasm' and 'anxiety'. These serve to affirm or to stall habits, respectively, creating conditions for deliberation. Enthusiasm – a variable sense of well-being based on the successful accomplishment of habitual behaviour, registered in the disposition system – is required not only if we are to promote causes but also to recognize the successful exchange of views in dialogue (ibid.: 83). Without that emotion indicating success or failure we would not recognize the accomplishment of persuasion. Democratic participation needs habitual forms of conduct whose performance must constantly and efficiently be monitored so that we know when to correct, repeat or revise our contribution and whether to reward others by affirming their success.

On the other hand, political engagement also prompts anxiety – that is, an emotional resource rooted in the surveillance system that halts our habitual behaviour and demands we think again. Anxiety interrupts habits and prompts us to 'reason things through' explicitly. The painful or unpleasant sensation that things are not what they ought to be inhibits thoughtless custom, focusing consciousness on the fine details of an issue or activity so as to relearn our habits. For Marcus, anxiety is the foundation of cognitive reason because anxious citizens are those who set aside lazy assumptions in order to reconstruct argumentative positions and practical choices (ibid.: 103–4). Reason arrives not because a neutral survey will allow facts to speak for themselves but because we are disposed (indeed, provoked) to revise our views: 'Anxious voters are willing to be persuaded; they are willing to learn; they can and do change the outcomes of elections; they are willing to adopt new and untried alternatives rather than insist on habitual commitments. They fit the characteristics of traditionally conceived democratic citizens' (ibid.: 106). His conclusion is rather striking: 'If we want everyone to be rational, the seemingly effective solution is to make everyone anxious' (ibid.: 108).

116 *Democracy, rhetoric and the emotions*

For Marcus, democratic politics is largely dominated by the contrasting emotions of enthusiasm and anxiety, of habitual practices and principles being affirmed and habits being contested. Pleasure and pain intermingle, not as a distraction from rational dialogue but as its very precondition. Emotion is triggered not just at a conscious level – the naming of feelings by words – but also implicitly, in the use of tone and style, arguments that confirm certain outlooks and the use of metaphors and analogies that picture certain images for us. All these devices assist in enveloping arguments emotionally, heightening levels of enthusiasm, confirming our habitual understandings or (perhaps even at the same time) raising anxieties by alerting us to their limits and shaking us from sedimented habits.

Similar conclusions are drawn by the cognitive psychologist George Lakoff, whose work on metaphors in American politics draws attention to the ways in which electoral campaigns involve competing 'framing devices' that activate deep-seated and largely unconscious associations and values related to notions of family. Lakoff distinguishes the 'strict father' and 'nurturing parent' moralities that, he argues, structure political discourse, but which are also rooted, via 'neural binding', in the minds of most Americans (Lakoff, 2002; 2008). Here, images of government modelled on contrasting feelings about the family are believed to influence the way that public debate is polarized between authoritarian exhortations to self-responsibility or, alternatively, liberal assertions of the value of social solidarity (see also Westen, 2007).

Marcus affirms the need for 'political activists to create the circumstances that invite the public to see and willingly reinterpret what it has seen many times in a new way, with new eyes' (Marcus, 2002: 140) – and that task, he admits, is one that falls, at least in part, to practices of rhetoric (ibid.: 147). Only a lively, conflictual public sphere, he concludes, where enthusiasms and anxieties are brought into play – along with institutions that channel them effectively – can supply deliberation with the energy to keep democracy working well. For him, 'emotional politics is also a rational politics' (ibid.: 148). Likewise, Lakoff and Westen openly promote the application of neuroscientific findings to generate effective Democratic party campaigns so as to match the powerful, emotive appeal of conservative ideology in the US. Creating convincing political arguments, they suggest, is primarily, if not exclusively, about persuading by means of a positive emotional story.

Alternatively, the radical pluralist thinker, William E. Connolly, explores how neuroscientific research supports a democratic politics attuned to difference and creativity rather than mainstream party politics (see Connolly, 2002a). Drawing upon Nietzschean and Deleuzean philosophies, Connolly traces the affective dimension of pre-conscious perception in order to foreground the possibility for alternative, 'fugitive' experiences that escape the coding inscribed in dominant cultural norms. The receptivity of the affective unconscious to various techniques, prior to the formation of judgement, opens the way to experimental forms of thinking that enable memory and feeling to find new kinds of 'composition' that cannot be grasped if we focus on language and cognition alone. Neuroscience, he argues, brings to our attention the myriad, microscopic speeds and delays, hesitations and hiccups, intensities and variations that underscore conscious thinking; it shows how 'the composition of thinking and judgement is indissolubly bound to complex relays between an intersubjective world and body/brain processes' (ibid.: 92–93). Humans are embodied subjects but are also diverse in their embodiments and receptive to 'experimental tactics of intervention' (ibid.: 86). Such insights, he argues, can support a radical pluralist politics of difference, transgression and new kinds of solidarity.

Psychoanalysis

The psychoanalytical approach to emotions offers a less materialist outlook than that of neuroscience, though the two are not incompatible. Both share the views that reason and emotion are interlinked and that consciousness is shaped by processes outside of its immediate purview. As a discipline, however, psychoanalysis tends less to causal processes (such as the micro-signals and triggers in the brain) and more to interpreting symptoms and their symbolic formation. It is therefore a 'hermeneutic' form of enquiry that explores how meanings are constructed and come to wield power within the psyche (see Craib, 2001: 9–10). For that reason it, too, lends itself to a rhetorical approach to politics.

To be brief, psychoanalysis, founded by Sigmund Freud and now consisting of numerous and diverse schools of thought, argues that human psyches are constructed around an unconscious core of drives and repressed desires that persistently irrupt into consciousness. The formation of the Ego in human development typically entails subduing and disciplining those forces, which for Freud were fundamentally sexual (or libidinal, stemming from the drives of the 'libido'). Repressed forces are then experienced as intense feelings of, for example, anxiety, desire, anger, lust and attachment underlying our everyday behaviour. The cultivation of 'civilized' subjects able to communicate and co-operate in society requires that we control such feelings. But they can never be wholly disciplined and regularly evade the defences of the Ego and rise to the surface, often with pathological consequences. For Freud, social and cultural phenomena, such as war and fanatical political movements, were evidence of how psychic instability operates in the social world (Freud, 1991).

In this understanding of the psyche, reason and emotion are inseparable because the subject is constituted through its affective relation to other objects (see Rustin, 2009). In that respect, emotions aren't purely physiological reactions; they frame the self as a coherent subject equipped with intentions and attitudes. Our emotional dispositions – the precarious balance of desire and self-control achieved to varying degrees – orient us *towards* the world, not only in reaction to it (see Frosh, 2011). As Marcia Cavell puts it, from a psychoanalytic perspective, emotions provide 'framing attitudes' or 'background conditions for [...] our perceptual dispositions', investing the world with a distinct tincture: 'As orientations toward the world, emotions have intentionality. A feeling of melancholy, or joy, is *about* the world, the world conceived in a particular way, *as* empty, *as* full of promise, or *as* sad' (Cavell, 2006: 133). A 'feeling toward', she continues, is not something that can be simply 'tacked on' to a belief; it shapes the belief itself (ibid.: 136).

The advantage of psychoanalysis over neuroscience lies in the rich palette of socially operative emotional dispositions it describes. Anxiety, depression, paranoia, narcissism and so on comprise a variety of common affective states that psychoanalytical therapy diagnoses as unconscious forces shaping rational judgement. Moreover, the therapeutic dimension indicates that emotions are both communicable and revisable. For some, therapy itself (the so-called 'talking cure') is a form of persuasion open to the application of rhetorical techniques (see Frank and Frank, 1991). Emotions are not just private and subjective, but shape and are shaped by our social interactions and, both via therapy and in the course of life generally, can be transformed and channelled (Cavell, 2006: 134–36; see also Gross, 2006). The self that is formed through its emotions can be reconstituted differently by giving shape to new channels for desire and identification.

Various contemporary political thinkers make use of psychoanalytical concepts to explore how public arguments are framed through emotional orientations. Judith Butler, for example, has examined reactions to the 9/11 terror attacks in the US through the conceptualization of 'mourning' (Butler, 2004). Butler draws on Freud's claim in *Mourning and Melancholia* (Freud, 2005) that the process of mourning involves grieving the loss of an attachment to someone or something. After a while, the pain of loss diminishes and feelings are directed to a new object. Yet if that process is not successful, a 'melancholic' disorder arises by which the subject cannot 'let go' of the image and seeks forcefully to maintain it.

For Butler, the loss for many in the US after 9/11 (both personal and symbolic) played out as a public feeling that some lives were grievable and others not. That produced a 'generalized melancholia' – that is, a pathological mourning that lashed out aggressively at others (2004: 37). But the government and media did not regard the losses of those hurt by American foreign policy as worthy of the same sense of grief. Indeed, in some instances, public grief for anyone other than American civilians and soldiers was tantamount to support for terrorism. Although, as Butler claims, 'nations are not psyches', disavowal and even prohibition of grief in that way entailed a collective subject being invoked to represent the nation:

> In recent months, a subject has been instated at the national level, a sovereign and extra legal subject, a violent and self-centred subject; its actions constitute the building of a subject that seeks to restore and maintain its mastery through the systematic destruction of its multilateral relations, its ties to the international community. It shores itself up, seeks to reconstitute its imagined wholeness, but only at the price of denying its own vulnerability, its dependency, its exposure, where it exploits those very features in others, thereby making those features 'other' to itself.
>
> (Ibid.: 41)

What Butler describes is not a series of rational propositions isolated from emotions but an affective structure that defines an argumentative stance. Here, emotions shape the arguments, at least in so far as they validate specific objects and distribute recognition. Using a psychoanalytical framework, Butler explores an affective rhetorical strategy in which a collective self (the 'nation' in grief) is given form. This resembles Sara Ahmed's description – also 'borrowing' from psychoanalysis – of the way that emotions work socially, rather than privately, to create 'surfaces of bodies and worlds' by 'sticking figures together' and connecting the self to an imagined collective body (see Ahmed, 2004).

Similar psychoanalytical readings of events can be found in the many writings of philosopher Slavoj Žižek. Drawing upon his reading of the Lacanian school of psychoanalysis, Žižek regularly examines the workings of 'ideological fantasy' in people's behaviour (see Žižek, 1989). Fantasy refers to the unconscious images and desires that frame our reality, often regardless of what we consciously claim to know is 'really' going on. Such fantasies include the image of the free market, the unified nation or a world of ecological harmony where all organisms co-exist in peace. Each fantasy scenario promises the fulfilment of selfhood, an impossible but alluring ideal of completeness that focuses our libidinal investments and invokes a whole register of affects. But this process occurs unconsciously, structuring our thoughts and reasonings around a desire to overcome an intrinsic 'lack', or absence of completion, in our psyches.

Žižek underscores the importance of 'enjoyment' as a factor at work in political fantasy (see Žižek, 2008b). In his view, people get a perverse pleasure from the perceived threat to the realization of their fantasies, a sense of enjoyment invoked by identifying enemies who have 'stolen' the object of desire: foreigners, bankers, religious fanatics and so on (see Daly, 1999). The identified enemy simultaneously helps to account for the failure of the fantasy to be realized and also sharpens the desire for it. Žižek insists that this affective structure is what really motivates us, not our professed beliefs. We act according to unconscious fantasies that drive us and give meaning to our world by investing it with purpose and the promise of fulfilment.

These examples of psychoanalytical approaches to emotion explore the way that public selves are constructed by channelling powerful psychic energies into identification and abjection. Importantly, the affective dispositions described are socially constructed, not merely instinctual processes. Practices of mourning or fantasizing are fabricated ways of channelling feelings, calling up deep memories and reactivating traumatic experiences. To that extent, we might say they are rhetorically crafted: they are, in part, assembled by actors seeking to direct public discourse in particular ways by manipulating symbols for persuasive effect. But that is not a rhetoric generated through reason alone, and sometimes it is not generated through reason at all. Reason and emotions interweave in arguments that inscribe subjects in emotionally structured frames, invoking anxieties, resentments and pleasures in ways that rational discourse alone cannot.

The psychoanalytic approach presents a picture of emotional politics as unwieldy and always potentially violent. This constrasts with the picture presented by many influenced by neuroscience, who tend to see a fit between emotional politics and etablished institutions and forms of democratic leadership. For Marcus these can prevent extreme emotions, such as 'loathing', from spiralling out of control and threatening the orderly regulation of democratic demands. For radical democrats, who are often influenced by psychoanalysis, however, such careful steering is neither likely nor entirely desirable.

Chantal Mouffe's democratic theory, for example, explicitly builds upon a psychoanalytical conception of subjectivity (see Mouffe, 2000). Not unlike Connolly, she underscores the possibility of a radical pluralism that emphasizes diversity. For her, however, pluralism entails conflict: without the rationalist assumption that desire can be quelled in favour of reason, democracy opens up the prospect of 'adversarial' disputes among hostile, passionate differences of principle, rather than the fetishization of consensus which she detects in deliberative theories. For Mouffe, post-Lacanian psychoanalysis supports an ethics in which multiple and contrasting forms of affective identification are acknowledged as part of the democratic game, but none can legitimately claim pre-eminence over all others (ibid.: 129–40). Democracy, in that vision, is a constant and ongoing contest to 'hegemonize' identities by recruiting them to different overarching projects. That 'agonistic' contest inevitably has rhetorical aspects, involving efforts to domesticate identities by arguing for 'common-sense' principles.

Affective strategies and emotional orientation

What, then, do the insights of thinkers drawing upon neuroscience and psychoanalysis bring to our understanding of the relationship between rhetoric, emotions and democracy? In this section I want to suggest that, despite their differences, the two approaches point us towards what I have called 'affective rhetorical strategies' in democratic politics. Far from being a necessarily pernicious force that blocks or interrupts transparent communication, emotions are productive of political subjectivity, inciting citizens' attention and allegiance to particular issues and ideals and, in so doing, shaping the spaces and forms of democratic engagement. Although they locate them differently (in the brain and in the psychosocial world, respectively), in both approaches emotions serve to *situate* subjects in relation to their world, orienting them towards its objects with degrees of proximity and urgency, sympathy and concern, aversion or hostility. These emotional orientations are never fixed or complete but are open to contestation and negotiation, mediated often (though not exclusively) by rhetorical argument. As I shall claim in the next section, however mainstream or 'radical' we might prefer it to be, a rhetorical democracy – that is, a democracy inclined to endorse rhetorical engagement – is one that recognizes and enhances the prospects for affective strategies to unfold.

As we saw earlier, deliberative democrats typically dispute the value of emotions because they are thought to disrupt the transparency of communicative exchanges, urging participants to adopt positions despite their rational judgement. That worry is not dissimilar to the hostility to Griffin's television appearance noted at the start of this chapter. There, too, we find concerns over the neutrality of debating space being tarnished by unjustified or inflammatory arguments that mobilize harmful and disruptive feelings. Calling into question who is or is not entitled to be a citizen via forms of 'hate speech' (see Butler, 1997), ridicule or (in the case of President Obama's disputed nationality and religion, for example) campaigns of misinformation is often to exert a pernicious force that invites allegiance without reflection. To that we might add highly partial media messages attuned primarily to scandal and outrage, professional media 'spin' and negative campaigning in elections and generally manipulative forms of propaganda and 'political marketing'. Mankind may be born with a capacity for emotion, but everywhere emotion seems to place it in chains. No wonder deliberative democrats suspect its value for reasoned dialogue.

Yet it is the very idea of a neutral space of dialogue, one that sweeps away the distracting clutter of feelings, that research into emotions and affects calls into question. Democratic encounters, it suggests, unfold at the intersection of numerous strategies and power relations, not outside them. Inevitably, democratic subjects are formed in and through these uneven relations and encounters. Although they differ in important ways, neuroscience and psychoanalysis invite us to think of subjectivity in terms of complex networks of layers and circuits, with distinct temporal dynamics and patterns of connection in which interventions are constantly being made. The focus in neuroscience is the circuits between the brain and the body, while psychoanalysis attends to circuits connecting the psyche to language and social relations. Yet each identifies affective processes that connect memories to cognition and charge conscious thought with associations and emotional density. In both approaches, emotions function like movements behind and across consciousness, remapping the perceptual field, distributing degrees of intensity and ordering its orientations and cognitive responses to the wider world. Rather than spontaneously rational psyches interacting in neutral space, subjects are more like lost tourists trying to work out which way round the map should be, whereabouts they are 'on' it and how they can get to where they want to go. The space around them alters as they respond to different clues, revolving the map to place themselves where they think they might be. As they do, some landmarks get closer and more urgent, others further away. Persuasion, like a kindly intervention by a tour guide, acts upon this fragile (dis)orientation. Interestingly, both Connolly and Mouffe conceive such interventions as being akin more to 'conversion' – transformations that work on judgement affectively – than rational argument alone (Connolly, 2002a: 44–45 and 2002b; Mouffe, 2000: 102). It might be better to say that conversion is the first step towards speaking (and listening) differently.

So neuroscience and psychoanalysis support the view that emotions work to orient individuals in time and space. This connects to the idea of the rhetorical situation discussed in the previous chapter. In operating affectively, rhetorical strategies work on our subjectivity, triggering perceptual responses, invoking symbols and fantasies that pull us unconsciously and often stimulate emotional excess and intensity around certain objects so that we reason in specific ways.

Like the tour guide in the illustration above, such strategies are rarely creating something entirely new but, rather, lead us to new places via those which we already know how to feel about.

Take, for example, former Prime Minister Tony Blair's remarkable response to the death of Diana, Princess of Wales, on 31 August 1997. Blair's eulogy – performed in an apparently extemporaneous discourse before the media and in a 'sincere' manner of pained, hesitating speech – exemplifies a rhetorical strategy based around ethos and pathos (see Blair, 1997b). Diana's death in a car crash in Paris was a shocking and tragic end for a celebrated personality who had, in equal measure, enthralled and infuriated the public for some years. The object of much admiration (for her work for charity) as well as censure (for her public separation from her husband, Prince Charles), Diana's passing brought a huge outpouring of emotion in the UK and around the world. Blair's two-minute speech in the immediate aftermath of the news acknowledges the initial shock and confusion, channelling it towards a process of shared remembrance. His speech seeks to appropriate a situation of loss and shock by defining it as a bereavement for her immediate family but also for the world more generally. Blair names the appropriate feelings attached to the news (pathos) – 'we are today a nation ... in Britain ... in a state of shock ... in mourning ... in grief' – but also alliteratively redefines Diana as a part of public identity (ethos) – 'she was the people's princess ... and that's how she will remain ... in our hearts and in our memories'. Playing on the fantasy image of the princess as an idealized figure of desire, Blair restores the lost Diana as a public object, emotionally orienting the audience away from shock and horror towards a sense of itself in mourning.

Blair's was not the only speech about Diana in the aftermath of her death (see Montgomery, 1999). But unlike others, it worked affectively to channel the intensities of the moment into legitimate feelings of grief – rather than, say, anger or resentment. Here pathos helped frame the public's perception about what Diana's death meant. This is a common role for political leaders in response to tragic events that put affects into circulation (see, for example, Bill Clinton's speech in response to the Oklahoma bombing). At such moments, emotions are often guided towards key symbols, such as the family, through performances whose delivery and style seek to trigger a sense of appropriateness for the feelings on show. Of course, such interventions do not prevent people from reasoning critically about the situation, but they do help to prioritize what people (and the media) reason about.

But are affective rhetorical strategies and emotional orientation, as I have described them here, not simply crude forms of manipulation and control? Sometimes, no doubt, they can be. Equally, there is a degree of ambiguity here: what is a moving expression of sentiment for some might, for others, be a distracting and mawkish display of crass sentimentality that favours certain groups in society over others. How can we possibly tell the difference? There is no absolute, objective answer but a rhetorical approach involves asking, further, how the public display of emotions situates its audience in relation to the wider circumstance. Does it help them reason it through in a new or more satisfactory way?

Does it illuminate a fresh perspective on the situation or enable people to speak where once they could not? Can difficult issues be spoken of in a way that they could not have been before? To approach such questions requires us not to dismiss emotions in advance as dangerous forms of power but to think of them as ways that can help or hinder (and perhaps both) how audiences view themselves and the situations they face.

Research into neuroscience and psychoanalysis invites us to think of subjectivity as a negotiated boundary between its inside and outside, with affects and emotions as forces and mechanisms that position that boundary and colour experience in different ways. Subjectivity is not simply an interior state; rather, its layers, speeds and connections persistently link to bodies within wider social and material contexts. The velocities and motions, directions and interconnections of selfhood mesh with and ricochet against the overlapping times and spaces of nature and society. Emotions are therefore physiological/psychic relays in the wider movement of affects, which can be viewed as 'transindividual' movements that disperse across the landscape of social relations (see Massumi, 1995; Protevi, 2009; Williams, 2010). Nigel Thrift (2007: 171–97) argues, for example, that cities have a distinctive character as sites of layered, sometimes clashing, affective networks where different subjectivities are calibrated and co-ordinated (for example, sites of pleasure, work, rest, danger, and the flows between them). In this, urban spaces mirror what neuroscience and psychoanalysis, in their different ways, tell us about subjectivity.

Rather than a negative force blocking free movement, emotions can be conceived as productive processes, supplying channels and connections for thought and experience that enable responses to the wider pressures of social space and time. Of course, that is not to say that emotions cannot be manipulated or 'get out of hand', exceeding the situation and laying down traces that inhibit further, perhaps more effective, reorientation. Emotions are always doing this, for sure. But so too, in its ways, does reason (for example, bureaucracy can create infuriating confusion and delay in the name of efficiency and order). The problem here is not power but, as Foucault once argued, domination. Power, in his view, is coextensive with society and the 'strategies by which individuals try to direct and control the conduct of others' (Foucault, 1997: 298); we are permanently caught up in efforts to shape each other's conduct and there are no spaces of liberty outside power relations. However, domination occurs when the mobility of power is constrained, when further strategies to modify it are blocked (ibid.: 283). Foucault's distinction can help separate persuasion from insidious forms of manipulation such as propaganda or techniques of political marketing; but there is no absolute difference here. Persuasion offers us prompts and grounds to believe or act, although we may contest them; propaganda deliberately disguises its own contestability (see Jowett and O'Donnell, 2006). We might argue, then, that democratic encounters are constrained when affective strategies are locked in place, when it is barely possible to challenge emotional appeals or recirculate feelings and further transform them. In such situations it is difficult to think and feel otherwise, to resist the clamour for agreement, to invoke ambiguity and doubt over dominant emotions and the arguments they support, perhaps to take seriously what is otherwise treated with ridicule. The point here is not to eradicate emotions, but to work with them more inventively. How might we imagine a democracy like this?

A rhetorical democracy?

Instead of viewing democracy as a space from which emotions need to be evacuated, it may be better to think of it as an uneven network constantly (re)generated in and through affective strategies that assemble and reshape communicative practices by working on popular attentions and allegiances. Those strategies, as we have seen, are deployed 'to direct and control the conduct of others' by mobilizing metaphors and imagery, invoking memories and shaping perceptions or reactivating traumas and the promise of resolution. Whether we prefer a more rhetorically vibrant representative democracy (as with Marcus or Lakoff), where existing parties confront each other more or less equally, or a pluralist democracy (as with Connolly or Mouffe), where potentially hostile differences co-exist and clash creatively, we need to think of emotions as the forces that position subjects for such engagement. A rhetorical democracy, however restricted or diverse, is one where emotions are brought to the fore, not held back, so that they are productively contested and challenged through argumentative controversy.

Despite their philosophical differences, both the deliberative and radical pluralist accounts of democracy have something to offer here. Where the deliberative model seeks to achieve greater participation by circumscribing the way citizens exchange their views in order to reach an understanding on the basis of equality, the radical model seeks no such constraints and emphasizes the contestation of common understandings and the very terms of equality. In that respect, radical democrats more readily acknowledge and engage the dimension of the political. That is, they highlight the contingency of shared principles and their foundation in decisions that are always open to critique and transformation. For that reason, radical democrats of a postmodern bent tend to be more sensitive than liberals to the way language and power operate rhetorically.

Yet, as Bryan Garsten points out, it is also perfectly possible to imagine a type of deliberation that endorses rather than excises rhetoric. Here deliberation can be conceived as a matter more of persuasion than of justification. It invites individuals to make considered judgements not on the basis of renouncing their own partisan feelings, emotional dispositions and personal commitments, but by asking them to reflect upon them (Garsten, 2006: 191–96). That kind of deliberation can allow for varying degrees of private motivation (rather than wholesale public transparency) and will require an element of respect for (but not necessarily agreement with) others (ibid.: 196–99). For Garsten, such principles are not founded in universal reason but are merely intuitive, pragmatic ways of sharing a discussion by accepting certain grounds as a starting point. They require us to show some degree of self-restraint, although they cannot rule out the potential for manipulation or demagoguery. 'The politics of persuasion is a risky enterprise', he rightly reminds us (ibid.: 199). In rhetorical deliberation, we need not submit our judgements to the sovereignty of reason, but only take responsibility for them and allow them to be tested.

Likewise, Aletta Norval (2007) offers a conception of democratic argumentation that accepts both the virtues of deliberation and the disruptive effects of certain rhetorical strategies. In her view, we need to overcome 'the false dichotomy between consensus and contestation' offered to us when the deliberative and radical models are contrasted (ibid.: 55). Democratic dialogue entails a permanent negotiation between established forms of reasoning and struggles to contest and transform consensus. It is possible, however, to reconceptualize democratic participation, not exclusively in terms of ways of following procedures or of challenging consensus, but in a manner of steering 'a path between radical rupture and continuity' (ibid.: 117). Procedures of deliberation are important, argues Norval, if democracy is to become a regularized way of displacing violence, but they will only work if they are open to innovation and challenge via diverse rhetorical styles. Like Mouffe, she underscores the importance of an encompassing democratic 'ethos' favourable to dissent, passion and criticism, rather than one specific type of regime; for these are ways to keep returning participants to the very idea of what it means to be a democratic subject alongside others (ibid.: 185–86).

A rhetorical democracy, then, is one that offers ways of forming public judgements through numerous practices of persuasion and, in so doing, exposes politics to the uncertainty and riskiness of the dimension of the political. That may entail a wide variety of institutional forms, including those suggested by deliberative democrats, but also the non-formal and controversial types of intervention including protest and dissent that polemically challenge social and political customs. Whether it is directed at producing agreement or cultivating and sharpening areas of disagreement, rhetorical persuasion involves mobilizing both reason and emotions, in order to constantly renew the terms of our allegiance to democracy.

Summary

I have argued that, like rhetoric, emotions are an integral part of democratic communication because they help to situate us in relation to matters of controversy. Anxiety, joy, fear, anger, contrition, love, as well as ambivalence, hatred and desire are better conceived as prompts and devices for orienting citizens than simply as distractions from serious debate. It is for this reason that emotions have always been important to rhetoric and its idea of persuasion based on the combination of ethos, pathos and logos. Recent work drawing upon neuroscience and psychoanalysis, I have claimed, further affirms this view by underscoring a view of the human subject as part of a wider network of affects. Far from separating reason and emotion, these fields demonstrate how unconscious forces that emotionally orient them in their reasoning constantly shape individuals and society. Rhetorical political strategies work upon such forces to encourage people to reason about particular objects in specific ways.

The tradition of deliberative democracy is wrong, then, to be so suspicious of emotion and the rhetoric that appeals to it. Although there are signs that such suspicion is diminishing, an obsession with the ideals of rational justification, transparency and inclusivity cannot help to tame controversy. Undoubtedly there are moments when uncontrolled and violent feelings are best subdued, when allegiances are more productively reflected upon than uncritically endorsed. But the alternative to eradicating power and emotion from democratic discourse is to do democracy differently. That may mean a number of things: developing a greater awareness of the way rhetorical strategies work, of how specific spaces are organized affectively; formulating a vocabulary of affects that operate in public life, learning how to argue through emotions yet without the excess and intellectual silence that so often accompanies thoughtless outbursts; developing affective strategies that support new and difficult encounters rather than relying on habit and custom. In short, it means constantly innovating in democratic speech to find new and more productive ways of negotiating controversy.

8 Media rhetoric
Speaking for the public

How do contemporary 'mass' media influence practices of persuasion? This question has surely been at the heart of social and political debate for over a century. While there is still little agreement as to the precise effects on its audience of media such as the press, radio and television, there is wide acknowledgement that they have profoundly altered the ways politics is communicated. Today democratic representation is so deeply interwoven with mass media that it is difficult to make a clear distinction between the two – when events occur, they often seem designed to have an impact in and through media. Political news and information, the activities of governments, leaders' speeches, party announcements and political commentary, cultural values and aspirations, debate and scandal, are all now regularly communicated via the technologies and organizations of mass media. Not surprisingly, perhaps, politicians cultivate close relations with newspaper editors and journalists, they have media advisors, they hire PR companies to market their policies and they offer themselves as celebrities and pundits to court publicity as well as sell their policies.

Moreover, the proliferation and expansion of mediatic forms in recent decades has created a vast network of channels and platforms reaching across the globe, disseminating information at astounding speeds such that it is impossible to know what is going on in world politics without them. Media shows and reports are accessed from TVs, newspapers, radios, computers and on hand-held devices and phones from almost anywhere in the world, increasingly inviting consumers to participate by sharing their opinions. 'Media', then, no longer names just one set of activities among others but, rather, a vital system of social representation itself. Contemporary politics takes place *inside*, not merely alongside, a 'media culture' (Kellner, 1995; Thompson, 1995; Street, 2001).

In this chapter I discuss some of the ways in which mass media influence the practice of rhetoric. That requires us to think of media as a range of sites through which particular strategies of persuasion are enacted but also, more generally, as shapers of what it is that can be communicated, by whom and how. In keeping with the focus in Chapters 6 and 7, we can say that mass media contribute significantly to the way that rhetorical situations are appropriated. Media do not merely disseminate public discourse, they influence the manner and means by which such discourse unfolds, if at all. In that respect, media undertake a political role in shaping what is said and sayable in public – that is, in determining how communicative space is constructed and how citizens might position themselves within it.

Certain kinds of persuasive strategy are therefore enhanced by media techniques, and others diminished. For many critics that entails the trivialization of public culture, an excessive emphasis on 'style' over matters of 'substance'. In rhetorical terms, we would call this a preponderance of appeals to ethos and pathos – character and emotion – rather than logos, or reason. Media help fashion rhetorical situations by amplifying personalities and heightening sensation to make events seem directly relevant to us. At the same time, the mass mediation of public life disconnects speech from specific contexts and resituates it in a virtual world fabricated by the voices, characters and styles of the media. Mediated rhetoric encourages strategies that conform to techniques designed to grab people's attention and secure their allegiance, above all, *to specific forms of media themselves*. Yet, although media compete to recruit and retain audiences, they obscure their rhetorical features by trying to minimize the gap between rhetor and audience, claiming to speak, authentically, 'on behalf of' the public. Therein, I want to suggest, lies the media's distinctive rhetorical power.

In what follows, I sketch the way a mediated public domain shapes rhetorical strategies around what constitutes 'the public'. It is this ambivalent concept that lies at the heart of media's appropriation of situations and which invites communicative styles by political actors that for some resemble marketing strategies and for others are more like show business. I go on to sketch the kind of rhetoric that media often produce by drawing upon the distinctions and categories set out in Chapters 4 and 5, using the example of TV news. Finally, I briefly question the possibilities for alternative forms of media to stimulate 'counterpublic' rhetoric to resist the purported trivialization of politics in public life.

Mediating the public domain

It has been the common fate of rhetoric and modern mass media to be regarded as vital ingredients of democratic life and, simultaneously, its absolute scourge. On the one hand, it is difficult to think of modern democracies without a 'free press' through which to exercise the other freedoms of speech and expression and to hold governments (and other powers) to account. An independent media, political theorists have argued for centuries, is the cornerstone of a free society (see Keane, 1991). How else would we get news of political corruption, such as President Nixon's deceit in the Watergate affair, if not for the investigations of journalists such as Woodward and Bernstein? Yet, on the other hand, no part of democratic life has been subject to so much critical interrogation for its negative impact on politics and society. The 2012 Leveson Enquiry into the ethics of the press in the UK – following revelations of widespread illegal phone hacking and other callous intrusions into individuals' private lives – demonstrated how some journalism exceeds the boundaries of civil conduct. The media, like rhetoric in its day, treads a fine line between the ideal of a robust, transparent public life and the reality of a vapid and tawdry obsession with scandal and celebrity.

For radical critics in the 1960s a popular, if perhaps exaggerated, critique of media was as forms of authoritarian conditioning designed to 'manufacture consent' among citizens (see Herman and Chomsky, 1995). It is certainly the case that in the course of the twentieth century, politicians and governments have found it opportune to make direct use of mass media (see Davis, 2007). A myriad of examples support this view: from the recruitment of the newspaper magnate, Lord Beaverbrook, to the UK Ministry of Information during the First World War, to the more insidious 'ministry of propaganda' run by Joseph Goebbels in Nazi Germany or the dissemination of pro-western views by Radio Free America during the Cold War. Today, however, the idea of media as part of an authoritarian system imposing itself on society is less convincing. Although structures of media vary from country to country – some pluralistic and others more closely linked to the state (see Davis, 2010: 7–9) – the sheer diversity of media suggests that, if powerful and unaccountable interests are undoubtedly at work, there is no one organizing centre and rarely one point of view. If democratic states once (and occasionally still) used mass media purposefully to disseminate preferred messages, it is important to remember the difference between 'propaganda' and persuasion, noted in the last chapter. Whereas propaganda typically works by promoting one, entirely unassailable point of view, persuasion assumes a degree of choice; the receiver of the message is required, to some degree, to make up her own mind (see Jowett and O'Donnell, 2006). As opportunities have multiplied in the global marketplace, media have had to compete to make consumers choose among them. That does not mean that they do not serve very powerful interests with a consequent bias in the messages they disseminate, only that there is no one overarching interest or authority they serve.

Instead of trying to understand the power of media exclusively by reference to interests and organizations operating behind the scenes, a rhetorical approach ought to reflect on the practice of communication itself. In the terms established in previous chapters, we can think in terms of the way media help construct situations. Here it is important to think about the idea of the 'public' to which both media and politics claim to be subservient. As Michael Higgins (2008) points out, the notion of the public and qualities of 'publicness' are enormously significant in liberal democracies: the public, conceived as a more or less unified subject, is a source of authority that confers legitimacy and significance on judgements made in its name. Notions of 'public good', 'public service' or 'public interest' are rhetorically powerful because they invite automatic assent and a setting aside of what is deemed private or particular. To be able to speak 'in the name of' the public is therefore to command attention and allegiance.

The term 'public' has both formal political and informal cultural sources. The formal political representation of the public comes as an ensemble of distinct 'publics' and as a unified public body in the parliaments, legislatures and executives of democratic government. In societies with extensive mass media, however, the 'public domain' in which this privilege is exercised extends beyond the formal powers of the state, into the wider society and its informal means of cultural self-representation. In some countries a public broadcaster – such as the BBC in the UK – may assume a primary role in laying claim to represent public values. But as channels of information and opinion, *all* media take on informal public roles in so far as they transmit the views of leaders, comment on politics and events and convey popular opinion back to political representatives, as well as entertaining audiences around boundaries of public taste.

'The public' therefore functions as the primary rhetorical figure – one of ethos – by which a democratic society imagines itself and legitimates its own self-governance. Yet it is also an ambivalent notion in that it names both the object and the frame through which objects are perceived. What is classed as public is usually something under examination (opinion, policy, the behaviour of politicians, the actions of other states and so on), but also an aperture *through which* to do the examining (debating 'in public', inviting the glare of 'publicity', public scrutiny and so on). Invoking the public is a matter of deciding both what needs to be discussed (objects) and also whether it is discussed at all, and how (frames). Very often objects become public simply by virtue of their capacity to be put into the public gaze. To take up a public perspective, then, is another distinctively rhetorical activity, one of situating issues for the purpose of judgement for or by the community by bringing those issues into view. Parliaments and legislatures serve as exemplary, formal means to do this while, on the other hand, artists, academics and mass media provide a largely informal means. The rhetorical power of the media, I shall argue later, consists less in making specific judgements (supportive of vested interests, for example) and more in their capacity to influence whether, what and how issues are situated 'before the public'.

For all the moral force of the term, the parameters of 'the public' are rather flexible, dependent upon the means that brings them into view. As is well known, media technologies (such as TV and the internet) have persistently expanded the public gaze and increased the velocity of information transmission such that formal political conventions for collecting and deliberating issues are subsequently diminished. Publicness has consequently accrued a number of contradictory meanings and accents. On the one side, the traditional qualities of publicness include hierarchical values such as transparency, accountability, bureaucracy, formality, 'high-brow' cultural distinction, duty and elitism – qualities that elevate public over private. On the other, they increasingly include levelling qualities such as anti-elitism, informality, popularity, cultural unification, popular participation and pleasure – qualities that reconnect publicness to aspects of the 'private' realm. With the advent of mass democracy, the formal, political qualities of the public, where citizens are defined by their *separation* from and deference to political power, are increasingly confronted with less formal, 'cultural' senses of the public that accentuate *connection* with audiences, 'authenticity', immediacy, participation and pleasure.

Speaking 'for' *the* public, then, has become increasingly problematic. On the one hand, as a marker of authority, what is public retains its distinction and to speak for it remains highly prized. But on the other, political institutions and democratic representatives can no longer assume automatic or exclusive access to that authority. Media such as TV and the press also claim to speak for the public. The high degrees of audience participation that media can mobilize in, for example, 'reality' TV shows or press campaigns suggests they have a strong claim to represent the public and 'its' values, too (albeit without the trappings of formal elections). But this is a public that has become ever more indistinct from qualities previously attributed to the private realm. As Michael Warner (2002: 417–19) argues, mediated public discourse is peculiar in that (unlike formal public procedures) it is simultaneously intimate and rather impersonal, addressing its numerous audiences as individuals but also as members of the wider group. A 'virtual' sense of community connecting the private individual with others is being perpetually fabricated through media, for instance in its presentation of political news and information deemed important enough to concern us, or its repertoire of sport and entertainment designed to meet our personal tastes. Constantly at stake here are values and desires that purportedly connect us to each other and join our personal preferences with wider norms and expectations, placing what is private in public and treating what is public as something private to be uniquely 'revealed'. Thus the public represented in and through the media is – unlike the virtuous and sober citizens often imagined in a democracy – a citizenry often characterized by intense feelings and attachments of which politicians (ever weary of declining voter turnout and increasing apathy) can only dream. But, as John Hartley (1992) points out, these citizens are strangely 'fictional' rather than directly present before offices of power. They are inclined to view the world in terms of images rather than complex arguments, but they are also difficult to distinguish from the very media that claim to be on their side and voicing their views.

A mediated public domain blurs the distinction between the formal and informal senses of the public and, consequently, what and how issues should be situated before it. By consequence, media of different types (but particularly press and TV) have become sites for competing strategies to control what comes into view and how. This competition takes organizational and, as we shall see, rhetorical forms. In terms of organization, most media are formally independent of the state, although subordinate to the rule of law. But as platforms for publicity, they articulate and shape the norms of public life to which democracies are accountable and upon which governments are ultimately dependent. That places media in an ambivalent position in relation to politics: they are both a subordinate and, at the same time, extremely valuable source through which legitimacy is sought. Politicians need the media to promote and justify their policies and arguments, but the media need politicians to provide them access to the stories and comment that sustain their market share of the audience. The relationship is a fraught one of simultaneous dependence and competition over the limits of the public and who can properly speak to and for it. How, then, does a mediated public domain influence the actual communication of political rhetoric?

Public sphere, marketing or showbusiness?

It has long been acknowledged that the development of modern mass media has created the space for a certain kind of rhetorical agency. Media make possible independent comment upon the activities of the state such that strategies

132 Media rhetoric

of speech and argument might counterbalance its power. We can appreciate how, on the back of the expansion of literacy and the technologies of printing in the sixteenth century, media became integral to generating a common awareness of place and responsibility. In Benedict Anderson's terms, by these means the nation was constituted as an 'imagined community' where once distant and dispersed events were experienced as occurring within a common, 'national' horizon (see Anderson, 2006; Thompson, 1995: ch. 2). Media overcame barriers of space and time by assembling many and distant matters of concern in one place at regular moments, thereby generating a virtual space for speakers to communicate as if directly with an audience. From that perspective, the mediation of public life through diverse and critical media institutions allows for the flow of information and opinion between governments and citizens, helping to represent and shape the common interest.

Yet the communicative space generated through mass media is also perceivable not as an open channel of unhindered communication but, rather, as an unequally structured set of relations, with some interests dominating over others. Here, in fact, public life becomes 'mediatized', or taken over by the demands and preoccupations of private media interests and values. The space of publicity is thus 'colonized' by the expectations, pressures and techniques of commercial media. Media present themselves, *ad nauseam*, as a wholesome and noble part of a democratic order, the 'fourth estate' speaking truth to power. Yet their practices regularly demonstrate a cynical preoccupation with maximizing audience share and safeguarding the interests of their owners, seemingly at the expense of factual truth (see Hobsbawm, 2006; Sparks and Tulloch, 2000). Often that entails minimizing substantive critical content and openness to deliberation in favour of populist spectacle and, frequently, a conservative politics that effectively narrows citizens' critical participation in public life (Kellner, 2005; Edelman, 1988). Too often, mainstream media seem willing to limit their critical potential to the intrigues of regular politics, leaving aside deeper questions of political principle and controversy. This is particularly noticeable during wars and military ventures, where mainstream media regularly appear willingly complicit in sustaining official interpretations of events (see Thussu and Freedman, 2003; Taylor, 1998).

Furthermore, we might note the deleterious effect of mass media on political speeches and speech-giving since the media's expansion in the twentieth century. Kathleen Hall Jamieson (1988), for example, highlights the substantial shortening of speeches in the age of television and the reduction of time devoted to political debate. The 'compression of political discourse', she argues, has the consequence that citizens are not able to hear all the nuances of an issue and so cannot evaluate arguments in sufficient depth (ibid.: 13). Politicians then try to simplify their arguments by using short phrases and soundbites, employing hyperbole rather than subtle argument and relying upon the logic of 'association' rather than evidence and well-crafted enthymemes that draw upon a deeply held common knowledge. Furthermore, she continues, the proliferation of hired speechwriters has resulted in 'the sundering of thinking from speaking' (ibid.: 27); public speech becomes heavily formulaic rather than an expression of a speaker's personal views or stock of knowledge and experience. Regularly, politicians do not know in detail their own arguments, because they never thought them up in the first place, nor did they participate in crafting the speeches they deliver – a situation that can have serious consequences for a politician's credibility when called to account (see ibid.: 218–19).

Of course, the contrasting perceptions of media are not mutually exclusive: one might hold to the ideal of unrestricted communication that mass media promise but be nonetheless conscious that the reality falls somewhat short. In the work of thinkers such as Habermas and other followers of deliberative ideals, the media constitutes a potentially vital mechanism in the emergence of freely formed public opinion (see Habermas, 1989; Garnham, 1992). In his account of the emergence of the 'public sphere' in Europe from the eighteenth century onwards, Habermas underscores the vital role of 'men of letters' in the development of critical opinion that can subject the state to rational critique. Yet Habermas also notes the 'decline' of the public sphere with the emergence of modern mass media, which are concerned more with advertising and appealing to what is 'popular' to service its commercial interests, so restricting the capacity to deliberate (Habermas, 1989: 181–222). That concern is reinforced by recent research suggesting that, although current media platforms regularly appeal to the public and claim to disseminate its views, increasingly they diminish the actual demonstration of citizen deliberation. Letters pages in newspapers are disappearing, television broadcasts limit their conversations with members of the public to short *vox pops* rather than to debate and discussion with politicians has assumed a rather cynical, interrogatory style that automatically assumes the likelihood of wrongdoing on their part (see Wahl-Jorgensen, 2001; Lewis, Wahl-Jorgensen and Inthorn, 2004). Thus proponents of deliberative democracy underscore the importance, in principle, of the media to a pluralistic and robust exchange of opinions. But in order to approximate a more rational deliberation where opinions can be expressed and evaluated, the media need, in their view, to undertake serious structural change. Such a view informs much progressive opinion: to mediate public life effectively, mass media must create more opportunities for different opinions to be expressed, cease functioning as the mouthpiece of corporate interests and reduce their obsession with sustaining (rather than challenging) popular prejudices (see Chambers and Costain, 2000; Butsch, 2007). In short, effective democratic rhetoric requires media that cultivate genuinely autonomous public spheres.

An alternative, less idealized way of looking at the mediation of public spheres, however, is to view politics as irremediably bound up with media, its forms of representation and the interests and powers that support them. That does not rule out giving greater space and more seriousness to deliberation. But that can only happen with and through a media culture, not by juxtaposing that culture to the ideal of free communication. This is where we can see a greater role for rhetoric and a rhetorical understanding of politics. For a mediated public sphere need not be condemned outright as a distortion of communication, based on the dubious assumption that if we remove that distortion, communication will flow freely; instead, it can be conceived as a strategic field where politics and media interact and compete to define what and how issues are made public. The question here is not whether the media should be restrained in order to live up to an ideal, but what the media actually supplies that enables some communicative strategies to work rather than others.

One way that we might characterize the rhetorical relationship between politics and the media is in terms of *marketing*. As organizations attuned fundamentally to winning audiences, media outlets provide an extensive means of contact with citizens that politicians themselves crave (see Davis, 2010: 36–9). It is no surprise, then, to find that democratic parties and campaigning organizations have adopted the 'professionalized' techniques and strategies of commercial media. Indeed, the platforms and personnel of media are, increasingly, an integral part of formal democratic politics (see Negrine *et al.*, 2007). Media advisors (frequently former journalists and press editors: often referred to as 'spin doctors'), professional pollsters and advertising and marketing experts are now integral members of party campaign teams. Close relations with journalists and press barons have long been part of liberal democratic politics, but now it is common to find such people working full-time for the parties and closely with political leaders. Accordingly, the manner of political communications has come to resemble that of the private media more generally: simplified styles of writing and communicating, the use of popular idioms and imagery in political advertising, the deliberate provision of soundbites for quick circulation through media, the employment of anecdotes to suggest contact with genuine people and experiences (see Atkins and Finlayson, 2013), targeting of key voter segments and the 'market testing' of policies on an identified audience demographic prior to campaigning (see Lees-Marshment, 2009). In short, a mediated politics is a 'packaged' politics where messages and modes of appeal are fashioned to be as popular as possible so as not to alienate key constituencies. Winning an election is now like winning over a TV audience.

The marketing model of political communication directs attention to the myriad techniques that are now commonplace in democratic politics (see Lees-Marshment, 2008; Davis, 2010: ch. 3). The recent successes of the Democrats in the US or the Labour party in the UK (packaged as 'New Labour'; see Negrine, 2007), for example, were built upon extensive and sophisticated use of polling data, high quality advertising and often vacuous but easily digestible political messages that invoke sensation more than practical goals (for example, President Obama's tagline, 'Change we can believe in'). The language of professional politicians is increasingly disciplined by media advisors who ensure that they stay 'on message' (that is, do not diverge from the official line of argument), that the primary message remains uppermost in their own discourse when interviewed and that a turn of phrase or epithet is persistently recalled to help define the situation. These techniques ensure consistency and simplicity in a media environment that all too readily exposes inconsistency and dismisses complexity.

The picture of the relationship between politics and media provided by the political marketing model is not one that would please deliberative democrats. Indeed, it broadly converges with models of economic rationality favoured by political scientists in the 1950s, noted in Chapter 6. Here the voter is conceived essentially as a consumer seeking satisfaction in the political marketplace and political parties act like firms to meet that demand by competitively marketing their products (policies and leaders). Political rhetoric is thus reduced to a good 'sales pitch' and good communication reduced to success in maintaining popularity. But if that model undoubtedly illuminates the style of campaign speeches delivered by parties, nonetheless its conception of human motivation and the way politicians respond to it is rather restricted and unrealistic. Indeed, for some, it treats citizens as fundamentally passive and even weakens democracy (see Hamelink, 2007). If we understand citizens' motivations to be more complex than ranking preferences, then we might also consider how a mediated rhetoric extends beyond salesmanship.

That is precisely what John Street argues in his alternative to the political marketing model. A mediated politics, for him, functions more like *showbusiness* than sales and marketing (see Street, 2003; 2004). Politicians, claims Street, are not simply selling policies. In adapting to media techniques they also change the ways in which they address citizens and the kind of arguments that appeal to them. Above all, they are marketing themselves as personalities. As evidence Street points, in particular, to the emergence of the 'celebrity' politician. This refers not to entertainment celebrities who participate in politics, but to politicians who adopt a communicative repertoire that owes more to the techniques of showbusiness than to the marketing of commodities. According to Street, politicians do not sell objects of use whose value can be compared and calculated. They are selling themselves and their own performances. As he points out, amplifying sensation is similar to political marketing, but the public celebrity strategy is less instrumental and more cultural or 'expressive'. That is, it involves promoting images and ideals with which citizens can personally identify, rather than material objects for consumption (Street, 2003: 90–91).

Politicians increasingly act like public celebrities by hiring media consultants, controlling access to themselves by managing interviews and photo opportunities, associating themselves with other celebrities and attending celebrity events, modelling clothes or appearing on entertainment shows on television (Street, 2004). The aim here, claims Street, is to cultivate and manage their symbolic status through the manipulation of style (2003: 94). Mass media have therefore enabled not simply the branding of parties and politicians for electoral market advantage, but also accentuation of celebrity status so that politicians may fashion themselves as distinct personalities, making associations with images, ideals and activities such as music, film or art that are deemed 'authentic' or outside the cold rationality of official party politics.

A notorious example of this celebrity model is former Italian Prime Minister Silvio Berlusconi, who achieved considerable electoral success in the 1990s and early 2000s. Berlusconi, a media magnate who owns a vast proportion of private media in Italy but had previously had no direct experience of politics, originally modelled his party, *Forza Italia*! ('Go, Italy!'), on a football supporters' club; that is, as a vehicle to promote its leader (himself, with the help of his vast television network). Despite achieving little in terms of public policy, Berlusconi's 'personalized' politics came to dominate Italy for many years. His success was built upon an amplified image of himself as a dynamic businessman with a 'can-do' approach to politics, authentically in touch with the aspirations of ordinary people and yet also with good looks and a 'star' quality reminiscent of 1950s movie actors – features that distinguished him from regular party politicians (see Ginsborg, 2005; Fabbrini, 2012). The effort to present oneself as authentic but fascinating can be seen in other celebrity politicians who accentuate their personalities for the purpose of media consumption, such as the Conservative Mayor of London Boris Johnson, former French President Nicholas Sarkozy or even US President Barack Obama.

In rhetorical terms, we can understand the phenomenon of the celebrity politician as, once more, an accentuation of the dimensions of ethos and pathos. Mass media, particularly television, permit politicians to fashion personalized authority and a sentimental connection with their electorate, allowing them to speak as a type of stylized character. In that way, the politician's dislocation from context is overcome by fitting with existing cultural commonplaces. In this, the affective rather than purely rational aspect of communication plays an enormous part, encouraging the public to associate politicians with the world of feelings and performance more proper to the artiste than to the salesman (for further discussion, see Davis, 2010: ch. 6; BJPIR, 2012).

Does the emergence of celebrity politicians diminish the role of critical deliberation in politics? Are citizens being communicated with simply as passive admirers and star-struck fans? For Street, celebrity politics should not always be dismissed as empty populism. Indeed, he argues that it accentuates the aesthetic nature of representation in the modern age underscored by Ankersmit (discussed in Chapter 3). Communicating through style has always been a part of politics, but it is now increasingly visible. The celebrity politician responds to the media's enormous receptivity to such characters and to a thirst among electorates to see representatives in tune with their own tastes. While many aspects of style and celebrity are highly fabricated and relatively flimsy (on occasion the public mask drops), the need to catch people's attention and to hold their allegiance is paramount in democratic politics, especially in an age when other distractions are increasingly available. These may well be the first step in connecting people to issues, arguments and forms of deliberation that they would otherwise miss. At the same time, we may remain suspicious that a stylized politics is one that obscures the mediatic frame through which it operates – that is, the way in which it positions audiences as recipients of entertainment. By accommodating a mediatized public sphere, celebrity politics diminishes other ways of doing politics that, for example, demand attention to detail, precise argument and judgement over fine distinctions. Celebrity rhetoric thus exhorts from a stage where elites strut and perform for their publics but do not always invite greater critical attention.

Media rhetoric: the example of TV news

I claimed that mass media stage contests over the dimensions and qualities of the public and publicness. If politicians' own media strategies constitute a vital dimension of this contest, it is in the ubiquitous discourse of the media itself that it is most evident. In the course of recent decades, a vast amount of critical attention has been paid to the form and content of media output. Much of this attention has been highly critical, noting its peculiar biases and purported accommodation to establishment values (see Glasgow University Media Group, 1995). Whole traditions of analysis – such as media and cultural studies – have also emerged to explore the way the press and, especially, TV broadcasts work 'ideologically' to reproduce dominant norms and values, as well as sometimes to challenge them (see Bell and Garrett, 1998; Berger, 2005; Edelman, 1988). From studies of press and TV news coverage to analyses of 'soap operas' and sci-fi shows, the links between media and power relations in the wider society are regularly sought in the content of media output that produces, 'encodes' and recirculates dominant meanings (see Turner, 2011; Corner, 1998; Finlayson and Martin, 1997).

Much of this work on media discourse is highly relevant to rhetorical enquiry, particularly its concern with language and its effects on the wider public (see Matheson, 2005; Talbot, 2007; Fairclough, 1995). But what is distinctive to rhetorical political enquiry is not only whether or how discourse reinforces power relations located elsewhere but, as already noted, how it responds to and reappropriates situations, thereby shaping the kinds of intervention that might be made. Here it is important to underline the partially disembedded or 'de-situated' nature of media discourse: the medium of print or television broadcasting draws us to specific events and issues but also seems, itself, to have no fixed location in time and space (Thompson, 1995: 31–7). Media reportage on events is usually after the fact but presented as up-to-date, last-minute or 'live'. Improbable gaps in time are overcome, presenting situations that may have happened or are even yet to happen. Equally, media outputs are received spatially in very intimate surroundings, in the workplace and domestic environments where people read, listen and watch. So media discourse addresses audiences by collapsing the normal parameters of space and time and yet is experienced as deeply intimate, right in front of them, often at regular intervals. By consequence, public events are strangely doubled, occurring somewhere specific in the world but also 'in' the paper or 'on' TV (see Scannell, 1996: 76; Couldry and McCarthy, 2004).

What are the consequences of this peculiar circumstance? One is that media are constantly recruiting audiences *into their own space* by presenting themselves as privileged portals for grasping situations. In this, media are themselves rhetorical devices. They must simultaneously hail their audiences by getting their attention – ensuring their allegiance as readers, listeners or viewers – and successfully deliver the information they promise. As Robert C. Allen puts it in the case of television, it 'constantly addresses, appeals, implores, demands, wheedles, urges, and attempts to seduce the viewer' (Allen, 1992: 102). Form and content work together so that the distance between rhetor (the media form) and audience (viewers, listeners or readers) is reduced and media can appear to function as direct windows on events. This is partly a consequence of the fact that most media is commercially funded and each medium has to recruit audiences for its advertising. But it is also because, unlike literature or cinema (where consumers give themselves over to the medium), mass media such as television and newspapers cannot assume that audiences will stay attentive. The impact of these circumstances on the way media discourse works are profound. As Allen argues, television (but we can extend this to the press and radio as well, to an extent) is compelled to adopt what he calls a 'rhetorical mode of address' – that is, a simulated face-to-face encounter where a voice constantly speaks as though directly to the audience. That mode of address seeks to make audiences feel like participants in a 'communication transaction', persistently provoking them to respond, invoking an implied 'contract' (Allen, 1992: 117–19). Media are constantly calling out to potential audiences to pull them into the situations which they tell them, ideally, that they already want, amplifying issues and defining situations in familiar formats and packages, such as 'Friday evening's viewing', a celebrity-led campaign appeal on behalf of war veterans or a 'major debate' among politicians. As linguist Mary Talbot underlines, media discourse is not uni-directional speech. It is highly interactive, forever engaging its audiences in interpersonal exchanges to make them complicit with it (Talbot, 2007: 9–10, 14–16). If this form of address is so prominent, then might we also use rhetorical categories to explore how it works?

Let us set aside entertainment and leisure, which dominates media output (see Brummett, 2011), and think for a moment of TV news. It is here that much of what is understood as routine politics and argument is consumed (but see Couldry, Livingstone and Markham, 2010). Although news media present themselves as disinterested and authoritative gateways to the truth, we can find regular techniques that demonstrate rhetorical choices in accordance with the mode of address noted above (see Neuman, Just and Crigler, 1992; Edelman, 1988). These techniques align closely with the categories of rhetoric enumerated in Chapters 4 and 5, namely discovery of argument, arrangement, style and delivery.

Discovery of argument

Although formats vary, most TV news consists of a series of reports on selected items of social and political significance. The rhetor in this instance is typically a newsreader or 'anchor' who, in addition to short items by different reporters, speaks in various voices – as personable representative of the corporation, as authoritative narrator reading a script or as interlocutor speaking on behalf of the public or for different sides of a debate to illuminate their opposition. The anchor fulfils the role of rhetorical mode of address by acting as an identifiable individual seemingly talking directly to, and acting for, the audience.

The presentation of TV news items frequently takes the form of a summarized narrative description of events: who was involved, what happened and with what consequence. While such reports profess to be objective and factual descriptions, nonetheless they consist of certain kinds of argument. Inevitably, editorial choices are made and rules followed regarding how to present reports in a way that amplifies their newsworthiness, adopting the different voices expected by viewers. For news broadcasts are premised on the argument that what is to be delivered counts as 'news' for an audience rather than simply routine events. Already, news programmes are rhetorically structured by answering an implicit question: 'what is the news today'? The news addresses its audiences as viewers hungry for knowledge about what is deemed important for them. It is the job of news reporters and editors, then, to filter out items of news from routine or normal day-to-day business. As Meyer (2002) argues, news journalists typically seek out certain kinds of 'events' that disrupt or diverge from this supposed normality. Events that cannot be so categorized are unlikely to make it to the news or even to the news desk. Meyer lists some further characteristics that make for news events:

> Certain important factors of reportage enhance the newsworthiness of the events to be described: whatever has happened should have a short time-span and if at all possible have an already concluded episode; it should stand in close proximity to the observer, spatially, politically, and culturally; the information should have surprise value in terms of themes already introduced to and known by the audience; the events should involve conflict; and, finally, feature serious harm to somebody, or else great successes or achievements.
>
> (Meyer, 2002: 30)

These features help to dramatize the news item as an event outside normal life but in proximity to something familiar, allowing the reporter to redescribe it in terms that accentuate its distinctiveness. In short, they present us with a situation defined by what Bitzer called an exigence (Bitzer, 1968). The exigence may be a controversial public statement or speech, an election result, a scandal (see Thompson, 2000), a policy debate, a natural disaster, etc. Its status as news is defined by its actual or implied controversy within the horizons of a presumed, or 'ideal', audience (see Black, 1999). The narrative style of argument, as we noted in Chapter 4, usually allows for a coded redescription of the event in terms that reveal certain key 'facts': the sequences that led up to the event, the various moments or factors relevant to it and the actual or possible result. Although journalists typically refrain from assigning overt moral responsibility to human subjects, it is common to talk about news events via topics such as 'cause and effect' or 'consequences'. In these 'objective' redescriptions, as many critical analysts of the media argue, lies the potential for a wide variety of subtle prejudices or biases to operate.

Arrangement

Narratives provide a recognizable structure that influences the rhetorical arrangement of the news. What counts as 'news' has to be formatted to fit the space and time of the broadcast and the descriptive format of the items under discussion. News reports will typically be produced in short segments of a certain length, perhaps just a few minutes at most, that permit them to be inserted in the 'magazine' format of news programming. That means reporters and editors must condense their information in a way that, overall, resembles the telling of a short story. As Kozloff points out, television stories employ relatively formulaic structures that insert situations into a recognizable time frame, often in which an initial equilibrium is perceived to have broken and, later, may be (or have been) restored (see Kozloff, 1992: 69–77).

Within this story 'arc', a number of variations are possible. For instance, Meyer talks of the importance of personification. The story is usually about people who take up dispositions towards situations or other people, rather than about abstract systems or processes. That allows the story to unfold as a tale of human subjects with choices, grievances or demands that personalize the event in ways with which audiences can identify. Thus the story might be about a dictator who is clinging on to power, a dispute between political parties represented by specific people or an earthquake that has destroyed the lives of 'ordinary people'. Likewise, Meyer mentions the importance of drama to the narrative. Stories tend to dwell on conflicts between individuals, on the 'winners' and 'losers' in a situation, allowing the story to focus on the different 'sides' of an issue of contentious debate and the possibility of eventual reconciliation. Elections, for instance, provide a ready-made structure of conflict and resolution that can be easily packaged. Furthermore, in the telling of news stories we often find the recurrence of classic archetypes: mothers and fathers, friends and enemies, innocent victims and powerful wrongdoers, and so on. Archetypes permit the personified characters of narratives to resonate with the audience's already held understanding of social and moral conflict. Finally, Meyer points out the importance of verbal duels between the characters in the story. For the conflict to resonate and keep our attention, it helps to have concrete evidence of opposed characters arguing either with each other or to camera. If the individuals concerned cannot be viewed, then others might be brought into the studio in support of each side. Thus we regularly bear witness to fabricated 'heated debates' between political leaders or representatives of certain social groups. Again, this playing out of a conflict gives momentum to the story, inviting the audience to anticipate an outcome (perhaps even a 'winner') and permitting the reporter to present the story at a distance, as an objective observer. Equally, if there is no actual antagonist, by switching voice the anchor/reporter might offer up points of view on behalf of 'the public' or another absent constituency to which interviewees may respond as though in a debate.

Style

Rhetorical style, as we have seen, originally referred to spoken language. In TV news we tend to hear language that is concise, uncomplicated and descriptive rather than openly evaluative. News reportage tends to be in the third person rather than a direct address from the perspective of the newsreader (which contrasts with the 'demotic' speech of tabloid newspapers, which regularly speak as if voicing the popular conscience), although sometimes reporters on location will talk to the anchor of what they witnessed or have been told by witnesses.

Expert commentators (such as reporters on economics) may even summarize their own opinion of an event. But for the most part, narration takes a loosely formal style that is accessible and simple, purposefully making clear the issue for an audience presumed not to have expert knowledge. That is often evident in the brief headline statements that announce the items to be discussed, but it continues in the language of narration. Anchors may ask rhetorical questions on behalf of the audience, which are then subsequently answered in the report (see Kozloff, 1992: 80). Regular use is made of metaphors or similes to help convey the issues in a nutshell: thus political elections are usually described as 'races'. Indeed, the metaphor of competitive sport is common in narrating various kinds of domestic and international conflict, because it imposes a clear structure: disputes become intelligible as purposeful, ultimately resolvable situations (with different sides seeking to become the winner) and the reporter adopts an observer role, keeping the audience 'updated' as the competition unfolds.

In addition to the reportage, the news anchor – who functions like a chairperson to direct and order the segments of news – will often adopt a speaking style that helps retain the audience's sympathy and a tone that will prepare the audience for what follows. For instance, that might include the welcoming address at the opening of the broadcast, the humorous quip between segments of news, or the 'sincere' parting remarks. Very often male, mature and with a deep voice, the anchor speaks as a (gendered) source of authority indicating the professionalism of the whole programme and its entitlement to deliver news – all of which are markers of ethos.

Delivery

Finally, as regards delivery, it is clear that television is itself a peculiar combination of sound and vision. Television is known for the constancy of voices that can be heard (see Kozloff, 1992): most programming involves a high degree of spoken narration to guide the viewer through the schedule. TV news is no less dominated by the presence of voice. When there is no voice, there is sometimes music. The opening credits, for instance, play a peculiar type of musical announcement – drums or a herald fanfare – to draw attention to the broadcast and hail the viewer.

But if voices are a fundamental part of the delivery, so too are visual images. From the insignia of the opening credits, to the summary footage of reports announced at the start, through to the reports themselves and the linking segments in the studio, TV news unfolds a constant stream of visual information to which the spoken narrative is an accompaniment. On television, images are expected to be arresting but also informative, exciting our interest (perhaps by showing footage of the event in question) but also guiding us through elements of action. When delivering reports, it is important for us to identify the story with the images – a possibility enhanced by the 'live' shot outside of the studio, where the reporter speaks from the site of the event itself. At the same time, the news screen can contain a whole variety of textual information related to the event under examination (the summary headline), and also other news (for instance, in scrolling news 'ticker' at the bottom of the screen). Likewise, visual simplification in the form of photos, graphs and iconography permits complex data to be communicated accessibly and in keeping with the need to flow through a narrative.

Finally, in addition to the sound and vision of the programme itself, the scheduling of the programme influences delivery (see Kozloff, 1992: 89–94). In order to maximize its audience, news has to be delivered at a time that coincides with viewers turning on their televisions and making themselves available as viewers, although the advent of 24-hour news channels has enabled audiences to choose for themselves when they might be viewers. Nonetheless, news programmes still come in different lengths at key moments of the day: short bulletins on the hour, a longer lunchtime news summary and a more 'serious' evening news just as viewers settle down to watch the evening schedule or before they go to bed. The timing of the news also influences the way the narrative arguments unfold; in commercial TV, especially, segments must fit around the necessity for advertisement breaks. The latter are often incorporated into the broadcast by advance warning of upcoming items before a break in order to heighten (and retain) audience interest.

This, admittedly brief, account of how TV news communicates its content demonstrates a particular form of rhetorical stance common in contemporary broadcasting. TV news might be said to constitute a rhetorical 'genre' in which distinctive techniques of argument, arrangement, style and delivery are combined to create a portal through which situations can be appropriated as news events for its audiences (see Street, 2001: 44–46). Often these techniques are so familiar as to go largely unrecognized as a rhetorical strategy – we hear the message and do not always grasp its peculiar form. As we have seen, politicians and campaigners adapt their own arguments and interventions so as to coincide with the news genre by tactically timing the release of statements, supplying their own facts and figures for narration, simplifying issues and identifying areas of conflict, in a language that directly contrasts with other points of view.

There are, of course, other genres of TV broadcasting concerned with news and public controversy that present alternative ways to engage politics and argument. The political interview, for example, is a genre that lends itself to the 'confessional' nature of television (putting private thoughts into public) and the testing of personal ethos. The interaction of two personalities offers a potentially adversarial scenario, a species of deliberative combat that is often tantalizing and sometimes openly confrontational. As Higgins reminds us, at stake in this scenario are often the meanings we properly attach to the public (Higgins, 2008: 39–44). Politicians and interviewers wrestle, via their arguments, to speak 'truthfully' for the public: the politician through her defence of policy and the journalist in her role as democratic 'advocate', holding the politician to account. In some instances, this struggle is a type of rhetorical jousting, with a series of questions serving as techniques to expose inconsistency and answers as efforts to evade exposure.

Other genres include the documentary broadcast, an extended report that may combine forensic narrative with one-to-one interviews, as well as audio-visual footage such as fabricated re-enactments of events. Instead of the brief report, the documentary affords opportunities to look in more depth at social issues and weigh up different points of view in greater complexity. In some instances, however, the documentary may be a dramatized account of an event (with actors) or even be hosted by a popular celebrity. The latter represent 'hybrid' forms of media discourse that combine elements of entertainment with serious deliberation (Talbot, 2007: 29–33). While to some this may seem to diverge from the factual purposes of news broadcasting, it may still be said to follow the rhetorical convention of 'revealing' the truth of an event (see Corner and Rosenthal, 2005). In media discourse, as we have seen, ethos, pathos and logos are rarely easy to separate.

Counterpublic rhetoric

The picture sketched in the previous sections suggests that a mediated rhetoric is, typically, a rather conservative force. Conventional political strategies that work with mass media adjust their arguments to align with the format that effectively delivers the message. That means working within the time scales of media production and the values and symbols demanded by them. While popular tastes and participation may be incorporated into these strategies – and there are periodic struggles between politicians and media that seek to redress the balance between the two – mediated public domains offer little opportunity for critical engagement with their form, nor do they provide for alternative modes of speech and address. To many critics, a mediated politics constitutes a deceptive 'spectacle' that obscures rather than reveals the workings of power, numbs us to genuine controversy and distracts us from the issues we should be talking about (see Edelman, 1988; Postman, 2005). This is (and has long been) the view of many scholars of media, not without good reason. The question arises, then, as to whether media might ever furnish opportunities for rhetorical strategies that resist, perhaps even transform, dominant discourses.

It might help to think about this question in terms of what Warner (2002: 423–24) calls 'counterpublic' discourse. That term describes modes of address that are self-consciously directed *against* dominant accounts of the public and what constitutes publicness. There is an implicit subversiveness to counterpublic discourse in so far as it resists the assumed universalism of dominant media forms and norms, perhaps by addressing a distinctive constituency and broaching topics thought improper in public. Thus we could say that lesbian and gay magazines in the 1970s and 80s helped cultivate a counterpublic sphere by addressing groups who were typically marginalized in institutionalized media discourse. Such magazines discussed topics such as same-sex relations and sexual practices that, elsewhere, were not counted as worthy of debate. Moreover, this discourse helped prepare a progressive understanding of how to respond to HIV and AIDS in the wider public domain in the 1980s.

That example is useful in reminding us that counterpublic rhetoric is not simply the practice of servicing a minority. Rather, it takes issue with the dominant values that frame the public domain at any particular moment and, eventually, may even transform that domain by providing a new means to address citizens and talk about situations. Counterpublic rhetoric, then, emerges through controversies over the nature of situations, which political actors seek to appropriate in new ways. We might reasonably hypothesize that any public sphere consists of dominant and marginal media that compete to represent publicness, with the latter occasionally threatening to displace the former as authentic portals on events. With this hypothesis in mind, I want briefly to consider two areas: first, initiatives in traditional media and second, the emergence of so-called 'new media' as sites of democratic engagement. In both, there is thought to be a greater possibility of addressing publics as critical citizens, and not simply as consumers of entertainment, than is the case in mainstream media. Regarding initiatives in traditional media, 'public service' channels on various regional or national television networks, for example, offer broadcasts concerning social activities that address audiences in various ways, often as 'concerned citizens' or as seekers of information and critical questioning of dominant social norms. Likewise, local newspapers seek to maintain a close connection with specific audiences, providing them with information and advice concerning their locality. Like public service broadcasters, these papers usually have a relatively small audience and are under pressure to give way to the more powerful national newspapers or the increasing use of internet services. Nonetheless, they often permit individuals to speak for themselves and in their own idiom, to address others with similar concerns and to provide examples of local, self-organized public encounters that differ from the highly managed conventions of 'national' debate.

Public service broadcasters and local newspapers are perhaps unlikely sources for mobilizing effective counterpublic rhetoric, since they are often underfunded or, in the case of local newspapers, still dependent upon commercial revenues. A more significant example, however, might be *Al-Jazeera*, an originally Arab-based news channel that reports on the Middle East and its politics, explicitly presenting itself as an alternative to western news services. *Al-Jazeera* has news channels all over the world and in many respects presents itself in a similar format to that used in mainstream news delivery (as discussed above). Yet its explicit effort to report on events that get missed or ignored by western media and, in particular, its incorporation of reportage from citizens involved in such events set it apart from mainstream news. Particularly after the Al Qaeda attacks in 2001, *Al-Jazeera* developed a reputation for journalism from warring regions of the Middle East and for openly adopting a critical perspective on western reporting itself. The latter, it has been argued, are often too accepting of their governments' official statements and unduly prone to ignore the experiences of people displaced by their government's actions. Notably, *Al-Jazeera* journalists collaborate with citizens of the countries on which they report in order to broaden their coverage, and they regularly invite citizens to comment on their programmes (see Miles, 2005).

What these alternative media provide, then, is a focus on the particular and the marginal, as opposed to the universal and western national scales that dominate mainstream media. Addressing audiences as citizens and as participants in the events they cover, being concerned with their locality or interested in specific social identities, they refuse the homogenization of the public domain that mainstream western media generate. They offer an emphasis on publicness more in terms of particularity than universality. As such, they provide points of resistance to the output of mainstream media and offer alternative ways of addressing audiences and different kinds of argumentative stance.

In contrast to alternative forms of traditional media, which are often expensive to fund and require specialist expertise, the internet and digital communications technology has provided relatively cheap and massively participatory access to media. Indeed, the internet has aroused spectacular excitement as a potentially revolutionary form of communication by virtue of its global extension and minimal costs. The question arises, then, as to whether it can enhance democratic citizenship (see Dahlgren, 2009). The use of digital media platforms, such as Facebook, Youtube and Twitter, during the Arab Spring in 2010/11 sparked a great deal of interest in the possibility of such media offering a radically new sense of the public domain, especially for social movements (see Donk *et al.*, 2004).

The very idea of communication in 'cyberspace' is sustained by a powerful sense of unconstrained movement and non-hierarchical (or 'horizontal') opportunities to speak about whatever and to whomever one wants. Unlike traditional media, which require one or more fixed locations to site technology (TV studios, radio broadcasters, newspaper printing and so on) and experts to operate the equipment, the internet operates in a uniquely mobile context where messages can be relayed to and from an infinite set of locations by almost anyone. It also permits a high degree of interaction, unlike traditional types of media. Social media applications, for instance, permit members to stay permanently in touch with each other and also to make new contacts across the world. Meanwhile, a vast number of websites allow almost any groups or individuals to publicize themselves or their ideas, often with minimal interference from public authorities. The flow of information across the internet is on a scale that is utterly unthinkable for traditional media.

But it has been easy for the internet and digital technologies to have their potential for reviving political engagement vastly overstated. Precisely because they offer such a high degree of participation, states and private companies struggle to retain control over their use. Indeed, there is strong interest among authorities for such media to remain an extension of entertainment industries rather than challenging the political public domain. It is also evident that social media and web applications enable increased communication, but not always with rhetorical dexterity. For all its evident abundance, the web is not a uniformly effective medium to routinely transform judgements or formulate inventive ways of arguing, since it is largely insensitive to the diverse situations and character of its audiences. Likewise, 'social media' provide a further means for public confession of private opinion, but they do so with a notorious inability to help participants judge decorum. They offer an intimate and immediate sense of direct participation in events, but in privileging a politics of personal gratification they cannot of themselves sustain either the commitment or the argumentative repertoires necessary to advance political movements (see Nusselder, 2013). Certainly, social media permit expression and circulation of opinions and observations that might be informative and provocative. They can help recruit and coordinate communities of resistance to states and other powerful organizations, as events such as the Arab Spring and the 'Occupy' protests demonstrate. But, as sober commentators increasingly observe, social media are not in themselves intrinsically radical or revolutionary (see Hindman, 2008). At their most effective they have helped 'choreograph' assemblies of activists by employing the peculiar public intimacy of media to provide an 'emotional narration' to concrete events (Gerbaudo, 2012). As such, they may contribute to rhetorically re-appropriating situations (such as dissent and protest) that might otherwise be hidden from the view of mainstream media or neutralized by prevailing institutions. In this they help to build audiences and enable incipient forms of popular representation to emerge, at least temporarily, outside traditional parliaments and assemblies (if these exist at all). But sustaining that appropriation is still dependent on other, material modes of organization and assembly (such as, for example, camps and occupations) that physically transform public spaces and bring people into actual (rather than merely virtual) proximity with each other.

Digital communications and social media have provided important new ways to develop counterpublic discourse. They offer a means to bypass conservative political and media institutions and to initiate rhetorical interventions that provoke citizens to think again about the situations they face. In this they contribute to expanding the struggle, undertaken by all media platforms, to determine the nature and dimensions of what is public. But that is not a struggle that, in and of itself, always results in the successful transformation of public discourse. We should beware, as Jodi Dean (2002) argues, that the promise of publicity in what she calls 'communicative capitalism' can be itself deeply illusory, a veneer of ever expanding transparency that obscures our complicity with elites in power.

Summary

I suggested earlier that there are similarities between our attitudes to the media and to rhetoric. Both provide for the discursive representation of the world and involve the purposeful selection of communicative techniques to present situations to audiences. As a consequence, both receive regular praise and blame for how they shape – and perhaps manipulate or distort – the ways in which we understand what is going on in the world. Yet the media is also a vast and powerful set of organizations and practices and its reach extends far beyond the limited judicial, ceremonial and political spaces of persuasion for which rhetoric was originally developed. Dominated by a relatively small number of wealthy corporations, media can do what rhetorical instruction never could: that is, supply vast communities with representations of themselves far beyond the constraints of local times, spaces and political authorities. Democratic representation is now defined more by the techniques of mass mediation than by the arts of practical deliberation and persuasion. Indeed, we might say that media platforms and their techniques have replaced classical rhetoric as the repository of knowledge and instruction in public communication.

As we have seen, the consequences of mass media expansion for democratic politics are ambivalent for those who cherish reasoned debate. Political marketing and the cultivation of public celebrity are well-established responses by politicians that prioritize appeals to ethos and pathos more than to logos. Media can certainly provide space for *some* arguments and for rigorous political debate but, as we noted in relation to TV news, the rhetoric of media discourse tends to appropriate situations with strategies that suit its own medium. As a consequence, mainstream output conforms overwhelmingly to standardized dramatic narratives, clichéd modes of presentation and simplified forms of argument and debate. These are designed, above all else, to persuade individuals to become and remain audiences by regurgitating commonplace values and affirming a limited set of expectations. But if this can make contemporary media seem like an improbable environment for developing particularly radical or critical arguments, the contest to speak 'for the public' is itself a rhetorical dispute that can never be absolutely resolved.

9 Embodied speech
Rhetoric and the politics of gender

It could hardly have escaped anyone's attention that throughout most of the history of rhetorical enquiry, public speech has been imagined as an activity of men. Aristotle's deliberating citizens, Cicero's eloquent orators, even Rousseau's guiding legislator – all were assumed, naturally, to be male. It is, of course, men who have been associated with the capacity to reason, judge and debate with such skill and consistency that only they could deliberate the serious matters of public life. Women, on the other hand, have been characterized by a different sort of speech: typically, 'emotional' speech – a way of communicating that is thought to be excessive, uncontrolled and drenched in sentiment, easily swayed or prone to misunderstanding. More often than not, women's talk is dismissed as the chatter of the household, the nagging domestic matriarch, the stern overseer of child's play or the gentle singer of lullabies. Politics, it seems, is thought to be a man's business, suited to those with aggressively competitive but also sharply rational qualities (see Jamieson, 1988: 78–81).

Women's relegation to speakers in the private realm and the denigration of how they speak in public marks out another, fundamental way in which rhetoric connects to the dimension of the political. The basic questions of who speaks, how and what can be said are closely bound up with the gendered allocation of social roles and capacities. In democratic cultures, the formal public realm is almost universally coded 'male', while private life is 'female'. When these, often unconscious, principles are flouted – when private speech enters into public, for example, such as when intimate or personal matters are openly discussed or 'domestic speech' is employed to talk about political issues – there arises a sense of transgression. Yet despite continued efforts to make the private/public division map on to a male/female dichotomy, from the perspective of rhetoric, such efforts seem rather futile. For persuasion implies a softening of rigid distinctions and hardened oppositions, if not their complete dissolution – that is why rhetoric is often defined as 'seductive' speech, a term that implies stimulating bodily arousal and desire. If not all efforts at persuasion are obviously sexual, nonetheless rhetorical speech retains a sense of enticing an audience to relinquish barriers to agreement, to soften their principles or extend them in unanticipated ways, perhaps to give themselves up to the judgement of another. Politics may well be a competition for power, but it is also about making friends, building coalitions and bringing people 'on side'. The 'masculine' quest for control runs alongside a 'feminine' need to sustain relationships. Thus television, as a modern arena for personal self-disclosure and narrative, is thought to be more suited to a feminine style of communication (ibid.: 82–89). The fluid gendering of persuasion that occurs within public life, then, complicates the purportedly firm divisions and hierarchies that support it.

In this chapter I explore the relationship between gender and rhetoric. I begin by reconsidering how rhetoric is traditionally conceived as being embodied in the performance of a speaker, usually thought to be male. The way that gestures and voice – as well as argument – are inflected in public performances reminds us that gender has always been a dimension of the rhetorical arts, albeit one that is unacknowledged, and hence a feature of how interventions are made to shape situations. I then discuss the vital importance of feminism in critically illuminating the strategic dimension of a politics of gender by exploring power and oppression, the nature of male rhetorical domination and the ways it might be transformed – insights that, often, involve an explicit and critical awareness of rhetoric. While there is no single feminist position on how to conceive or resolve male domination, feminism has nonetheless been crucial to illuminating the ways in which conceptions of masculinity and femininity structure politics and communication. Finally, I use the insights of feminism and gender theory to interpret political rhetoric by taking examples of speech about British nationality in which the peculiar ambivalence of gender is played out.

Situating gender

Men and women are commonly believed to have distinct types of voice. Based on natural differences that produce physiological changes during puberty, men (with their larger larynx) are expected to speak with a deep voice (at about 120Hz) and women with a higher-pitched voice (about 225Hz) (see Karpf, 2006: 154). The deeper and louder sound common to men may once have supported their role as hunting animals able to scare away predators and protect the group, while women's voices lent themselves to comforting and nurturing children. This supposedly 'natural' distinction is perhaps mythical, but it underscores much of the way in which societies continue to distinguish men and women as speakers. Public speech is regularly associated with a masculine propensity to battle verbally with others, while private and domestic speech involves care and intimacy. Men are typically expected to do the first, women the second.

The idea that public speech is a distinctly 'manly' activity is found in the classical literature on rhetoric (see Brody, 1993). As I noted in Chapter 3, citizens of ancient societies (who were always and only men) were often expected to combine the skills of speech and physical combat as integral parts of active political membership. It is no surprise, then, that the one and the other are closely associated: prowess in persuasion is akin to a form of combat where the audience comes under the mastery of a dominant male. Ancient rhetoric, scholars point out, is rooted in an agonistic tradition of 'verbal duels' and 'fighting words' between adversaries (see Worman, 2009). There is, by consequence, a long history of misogyny in classical commentary on rhetoric that proscribes the vice of effeminacy in favour of the virtue of manliness. Rarely are women's voices heard as authoritative in ancient literature, except perhaps as idealized singing Muses or, as in Homer's *Odyssey*, the lethal Sirens who lure sailors to their deaths with irresistible harmonies (see Homer, 2003: 158; Cavarero, 2005: 95–116). Thus in his *Institutio Oratoria* Quintilian recommended a 'manly form of eloquence' that eschewed excessive ornamentation in style (see Brody, 1993: 14). The latter, in his view, was effeminate because it made a man seem, unnaturally, like a woman. 'Effeminate eloquence', however pleasing or alluring to the audience, was, like the Sirens, deceitful and not to be recommended in the education of the citizen. Quintilian compared ornamental speech to a eunuch being dressed by a slave dealer to make him more attractive: essentially without virility, yet with a bodily appearance fashioned to please. As Brody points out, Quintilian's reference to the eunuch's deception was 'a metaphor for all deceitful language. Cloaking the orator's spurious purpose in ornamentation, such discourse was always hollow and vicious' (ibid.: 20). Such language ceased to be truthful and honest – qualities associated with the virtuous (male) citizen – and undermined clarity in the orator's representation of the world.

Quintilian's admonishment of the effeminacy of ornamentation had a lasting impact on later generations of rhetoricians, particularly during the Renaissance and the Enlightenment. Instruction in the arts of speech and persuasion remained primarily directed at the education of young gentlemen for their participation in public life. For most rhetoricians in the Renaissance and after, women were simply expected to be silent. By consequence, the overwhelming denigration of femininity as an alluring deception to be contrasted with clarity and reason also remained at the heart of rhetorical instruction. The arrival of the Enlightenment in the seventeenth and eighteenth centuries did little to challenge this view, despite its appeal to reasoned thought and empirical evidence as the basis of judgement – indeed, it tended to reinforce it with arguments based on the authority of science. Men came to be associated with culture – 'rising above' natural attributes by dint of their reason – while women, partly because of their capacity for childbirth, were associated with nature and emotions, which were seen to be an obstacle to cool, independent thought. Although Enlightenment thinkers often took gender-neutral 'man' as the source of the universal authority of reason, that figure obscured the general tendency to assume a male as its original model. Hence even the French revolutionary appeal to the 'universal rights of man and citizen' imagined the citizen as a man and not as a woman (see Landes, 1988).

Although a great deal has changed in the intervening centuries, it remains the case today that men's voices are the most heard and valued, even in democracies. Of course, women have made tremendous progress in getting heard, not least as a consequence of the feminist movement in the twentieth century. Increasingly, political and public roles are undertaken by women and legislatures are less and less the self-evident 'men's clubs' they once were. Figures such as Indira Ghandi, Margaret Thatcher, Benazir Bhutto and Angela Merkel – to name just a few – have been powerful and vocal politicians in their respective countries. Yet those notable examples stand out partly because democratic politics still distributes speaking and leading roles primarily to men. Even as women participate in democratic politics in ever greater numbers and with ever more success, the nature of public speech and communication continues to be defined to a great extent as masculine (see Cameron, 2006). The well-known example of British Prime Minister Margaret Thatcher deliberately deepening her voice in order to sound more like a 'statesman' underscores this point well. Even as women enter more frequently into public life, it seems, politics remains predominantly a masculine business.

At this point, we should underline the important distinction between 'sex' and 'gender', for the emergence of greater sexual equality does not automatically translate into a gender-neutral environment. Whereas sex denotes the physical differences between 'male' and 'female', gender refers to the social and cultural expression of that difference, often as 'masculine' and 'feminine' respectively. Sex differences are typically thought to be biologically determined and so largely invariant, while gender differences are understood as social, hence conventional, historically variable and possibly more diverse than just two given differences. We will return to this illuminating but troubled distinction shortly, but for now it is reasonable to say that an increased appearance of people sexed as women in the public domain need not automatically result in a de-gendering of that domain. Public life can, conceivably, be gendered in ways that do not immediately reflect the sex of the people who comprise it. Thus party politics in representative democracies continues to be coded by traditional masculine values and behaviours such as an aggressively competitive style of communicating and responding to adversaries, expectations about loyalty and hierarchy, modes of dissent and strategies for dealing with disagreement (see Shaw, 2006). If, now, men are not always the actors in politics, masculine values and assumptions nevertheless pervade political life such that it is hard for any politician (professional or otherwise) to avoid reproducing them in their own speech and behaviour.

Reflecting on gender rather than sex alone brings us back to the political dimension discussed in Chapter 1. Gender is a primary means of characterizing the horizon of values and principles that render legitimate or illegitimate certain kinds of speech and behaviour. How does it do this? Gender, as Judith Squires points out, refers us to an ontological realm – that is, to the fundamental being of individuals and their basic relationships to each other (see Squires, 1999: 5–6). Gender describes not simply abstract qualities but, moreover, ways in which the body and desire are practically organized and displayed in society so as to demonstrate those qualities, how that display fits with normative values and what counts as a transgression of those norms. In that respect, to express gender entails adopting conventions in deploying physical attributes, movement, dress, visual appearance and voice. Established gender roles prescribe various, culturally specific ways in which bodies and desire are made present both in private and in public, as well as prohibit those that should not be present. Usually such roles conform to clusters of established (though still variable) ideas about masculinity and femininity which offer a repertoire of gestures and mannerisms deemed 'appropriate' to certain sexes. These include informal rules about women wearing skirts and men wearing suits, for example, or how each walks, sits or speaks (see Young, 2005). Women, for instance, are often assumed generally to be more polite than men – that is, prepared to speak publicly in a more formal register than men (see Talbot, 2010; Mills, 2003). As the denigration of women and femininity implies, such roles, repertoires and assumptions articulate wider power relations in society that diminish so-called female qualities and validate those of men (see Connell, 1987). Men, for instance, are regularly portrayed in the media as active subjects in public life – virtuous citizens pursuing civic causes – while women are objectified and defined by their physical appearance. Yet these culturally specific and unequal gender roles are treated as though they were based on the invariant foundation of sex – consequences of nature rather than fabrications of social convention.

The field of gender, then, is political in the sense that what counts as a legitimate citizen with rights and freedoms is conceived in and through varying moral and cultural norms that inscribe themselves upon human bodies and their behaviours. As many feminists have made clear, gender is not incidental to the formation of modern states and societies. On the contrary, it forms an integral, if usually unacknowledged, role in the modern separation of the state from society by defining the formal public domain in masculine terms (Squires, 1999: 24–32). The citizen is regularly imagined to be a creature that reasons about his self-interest by setting aside emotion, intimacy and responsibility to others (such as family and, particularly, children). The 'domestic' and emotional aspects of individuality are effaced in the modern idea of citizenship and relegated to the private realm, where they are ascribed to women, who are thought to be less instrumentally rational, more susceptible to emotion (conceived as excess) and naturally oriented towards intimacy and the care of others (see Prokhovnik, 2002; Litosseliti, 2006). The formation of liberal states organized around the principle of protecting individual liberty, then, is premised on the exclusion of women and the eradication of femininity from the citizenry and public affairs (see Pateman, 1988; Landes, 1988). That women are now enfranchised as citizens does little in itself to alter this gendered construal of the citizen and politics. Others even argue that the sovereignty of the state – with its claim to wield a monopoly of legitimate violence – expresses an intrinsically masculine ideal of power and control that genders all politics from the start (see Hoffman, 2001).

The gendering of modern politics is not always expressed through legal prescriptions or official directives but, instead, forms part of taken-for-granted assumptions about social identity and the proper organization of society. Setting aside the frequent examples of lewd behaviour or outright misogyny still displayed in public life, more or less silent assumptions about gender are a routine part of democratic politics and supply some of the commonplace assumptions that make it a meaningful and successful activity – for instance, the absence of children and child care arrangements from the legislatures, the time required to be spent away from home by politicians or the inappropriateness or sensitivity of certain topics of debate. But when these assumptions are brought into question, when they are discussed *as* cultural norms that might be altered in some way, then the political dimension comes to the fore. In disputes over women in politics, breastfeeding in public, how people treat each other at work or debates over 'gay marriage', to name some examples, the political gendering of politics often explodes into clamorous debate, exposing the contestability, perhaps even instability, of identities and arrangements otherwise thought to be set out by nature.

If gender relations structure modern democratic politics, then what is their impact on rhetoric? Again, it will help to think about this in terms of the rhetorical situation discussed earlier in the book. Gender forms an integral part of how situations are defined through practices of persuasion and how speakers perform rhetorical interventions. Gender roles provide ready-made platforms to craft agency in ways that affirm structured conventions and expectations, even as they limit that agency to certain kinds of script; but such roles are not wholly predetermined and can also be subverted. Our focus of attention here, however, is not only on argument conceived as a string of ideas (or logos) *about* the situation, but also, and rather, on the body as a locus *through which* situations are 'appropriated' in gendered performances. The embodiment of gender has been a focus in recent social and political theory and focuses on the ways in which social identity is performed, regulated and subverted through the lived experience of the body (see Howson, 2005; Butler, 1999; Bourdieu, 1990). While embodied aspects of gender are frequently non-linguistic (Uhlmann and Uhlmann, 2005), nonetheless they do contribute to shaping discourse. Rhetorical speech can be said to be embodied in two important ways: first, in the voice of a distinct physical body addressing other bodies – what is sometimes called 'embodied discourse' (see Poynton and Lee, 2011) – and second, in the representation of the 'body politic', or discourse about the common body. In both these respects, rhetoric articulates ideas of gender to shape the way that situations are defined and to orient the audience. Here, once more, ethos and pathos are of distinct importance, for gendered ideas about who can speak, about what and how, involve issues both of authority and identity (ethos) and allegiance and attachment (pathos). Let us look at each in turn.

As regards embodied discourse, it is common for many political speakers to ensure their bodies conform to commonly understood gender conventions concerning appearance, sound and general comportment in delivery. In the case of women, in particular, questions of dress and appearance are often critical points of reference in the public reception of their authority to speak. This is not so much a decisive issue for men; only women, it seems, have their credibility damaged if they are regarded as dressing badly or appearing poorly in public. Likewise, the expression in public of deep personal emotions that, for example, induce tears is something that is more acceptable for women than it is for men. Moreover, politicians often present themselves as idealized or fantasy versions of the people who (they think) their constituents admire: the sharp-suited executive types, the flirtatious heterosexual, the respectable 'family man' or chaste and supportive wife. Paradoxically, most mainstream politicians live quite unconventional lives, separated from their families or unavailable for the kind of committed relationships which they themselves endorse. Nonetheless, politicians speaking and looking *as if* they embodied gender ideals is a regular part of the rhetoric of politics and counts a great deal for how seriously they may be taken as speakers.

Representations of the body politic (or society) are also structured around assumptions about bodies and their relationship to each other. As we will see later on, metaphors of community are regularly invoked in gendered terms in political arguments. Politicians offer up idealized representations of what society is or needs in order to be properly itself. Such images usually contain gender-related claims about what kind of collectivity society is and how it calls upon our allegiance, perhaps identifying a social constituency that best expresses its essence: for example, patriotic soldiers, hard-working families, sporting heroes or industrious entrepreneurs. Images of productive masculinity, athletic androgyny or harmonious heterosexuality supply authoritative metaphors with which audiences can easily identify. Other kinds of idealized image include those of moral authority, often used implicitly in arguments about what the state or government should do (and hence what society should expect). George Lakoff's (2002) distinction – discussed in Chapter 7 – between 'nurturing parent' and 'strict father' morality in US political debates is a good example here. Each of Lakoff's metaphors invokes a gendered image of how citizens should relate to authority: one as an intervening (maternal) parent that actively provides resources for its children to learn and grow, the other as a distant, stern figure that promotes citizens' self-responsibility by refusing to intervene. For Lakoff, images of the family are deeply rooted in US culture and political thinking. They function not simply as isolated images but as frameworks that structure and connect a series of moral arguments about how individuals relate to each other as though the social body were a family. Even outside contemporary US politics, the metaphor of the community as a family has long been a powerful resource, not least because both in ancient times and now, familial connections provide ready-made cognitive maps by which to discern individual qualities or to invoke mutual obligations.

These representations of the speaking self and the wider community provide a repertoire of gendered rhetorical references to help define situations and the ways audiences might be persuaded in them. We could say, then, that *gender helps situate speakers and their auditors*, supplying a powerful means to achieve persuasion. Even when gender is not itself the direct object of speech or communication, nonetheless it helps position us affectively towards the issues at hand and so permits us to form judgements about them. But that is not to say that gender provides a neutral or uncontested terrain for rhetorical persuasion. On the contrary, it is precisely because gender relations have been exposed as unequal power relations and contested by feminism that we now understand them as political. It is to feminism's insistence on a politics of gender that we turn next.

Feminism and rhetoric

Feminism has had an enormous part to play in our understanding of the relationship between language, gender and power. Arguing that male domination is achieved, at least in part, through control over who can say what, where and how, feminism has expanded a rhetorical understanding of politics. Our appreciation of the marginalization of women's voices and their continued subordination to those of men is a consequence of feminist interventions across the last century (see Whelehan, 1995). More than most socio-political movements, feminism has drawn attention to language itself as a medium of domination and has encouraged profound shifts in the vocabularies we use in public life (see Talbot, 2010). More than that, however, feminism promotes the greater inclusion of women in politics and, hence, the opportunity for women to speak and be heard as equal citizens. In this, distinct attention is given to the 'situatedness' of speech in order to hear and see women in places – such as the home or the workplace – where they are not given equal recognition. Feminism's impact on public speech has been enormous, even if it is still contested and, in some instances, resented. In both theory and practice, then, feminism has helped define the stakes in a rhetorical politics of gender.

It would be wrong, however, to imagine that feminism constitutes a homogeneous and unified political or intellectual outlook. While many feminists identify obstacles to women's equality in the persistence of male-dominated institutions and practices and seek to redress these in order to enhance the opportunities for women, there is considerable disagreement about what that domination ultimately consists in and how women's lives may be improved. In this section I want to survey some of these differences, not to sketch the length and breadth of feminism but because these differences highlight a range of ways in which rhetoric relates to gender. Some of the key disagreements over a politics of gender (and the place of rhetoric in it) stem from the distinction between sex and gender, noted in the previous section, which posits male and female social roles as conventional. While the distinction has enabled feminists' general opposition to biological determinism, there are important differences over how it is conceived and with what social and political implications.

Squires (1999: 3–5) usefully identifies three separate types of political strategy associated with feminism that stem from differences over the sex/gender distinction. She calls these the strategies of 'inclusion', 'reversal' and 'displacement'. While there are many overlaps and complexities within and among these positions, each helpfully describes a distinct cluster of arguments about the politics of gender that, as I will show, has implications for how we understand rhetoric. Let us look at each in turn.

Strategies of inclusion

Strategies of inclusion involve efforts to identify ways in which women are excluded from public and political life in order then to get them included. That approach is often associated with reformist or liberal forms of feminism in the nineteenth and early twentieth centuries, such as the suffragette movement, which argued for women's political inclusion in democratic representation. Here the sex/gender distinction addresses the way that women's exclusion from full citizenship is based on conceptions of their purported intellectual inferiority and material dependence on fathers and husbands. As Squires points out, in such arguments sex remains a natural foundation for distinguishing men and women (Squires, 1999: 59), and the early feminist responses relied primarily on contesting conventions built upon sexual difference in the established spaces of formal politics. Early feminists such as Mary Wollstonecraft, for example, disputed the claim that women were less capable of reason than were men (see Wollstonecraft, 2008). It was women's enforced lack of education and confinement to the domestic sphere, she argued in 1792, that limited their opportunities to participate in public life. Wollstonecraft rubbished the picture of women as delicate, sensual creatures concerned with frivolity and appearance. Such qualities were the consequence of their exclusion from public deliberation and not reasons for it. Women should, therefore, be permitted equal rights to participate in public life as men.

The objective of strategies of inclusion, then, is to enable women to participate on an equal footing as men in the public domain, to include them where they have been excluded rather than to contest the character of public life as such. Because sex remains an accepted category (upon which 'false' beliefs are then constructed), early feminism did little to challenge the ways that speech and argument were conceived and delivered. The central issue was to get women recognized as intellectual equals by removing what were conceived as artificial barriers (social conventions and irrational beliefs) to their participation. The underlying assumption was that women and men were fundamentally the same as regards their abilities and modes of speech. Doubtless women's participation was expected to bring greater sensitivity to issues of concern to them and to diminish the discriminatory habits of some men. But the full integration of women into public life was not understood as a wholesale transformation of politics and society as such. Indeed, if anything, inclusion would be the fulfilment of modern liberal society's potential to enable rational deliberation over matters of common concern.

Strategies of reversal

The achievements of early, or 'first-wave', feminism should not be diminished. By the end of the Second World War, most democratic countries had granted women full political citizenship. The so-called 'second wave' of feminism, however, developed more profound critiques of gender conventions by locating them in the deep structures of society more widely, particularly in the realms of culture, the family and work (Whelehan, 1995). The kinds of radical feminism that emerged after the Second World War were concerned not simply with encouraging women to participate in existing institutions, but more with reversing the way those institutions had been monopolized by men, with masculine norms taken for granted at the expense of any other gender qualities. So-called strategies of reversal are based on a more thoroughgoing critique of gender conventions in society with the goal not of reuniting men and women in a gender-free realm but, rather, of highlighting their distinct contributions and advocating greater autonomy for women to cultivate their differences, often separately from men.

Central to many feminist strategies of reversal is a critique of the public/private distinction. Where strategies of inclusion tended to accept the idea that the public domain could permit a gender-neutral politics, second-wave feminists have largely regarded that distinction as part of the problem. For them, public life is inherently masculine: the separation of private from public realms involves an implicit denigration of the private/domestic as an inferior realm. That means that family life, domestic labour, the care of children and even personal intimacy, are all marginalized as non-political and unworthy topics of debate or sources of dispute. Even though these form a central precondition for public life (both the life of civil society generally and the formal political domain), they are treated as at best, secondary dimensions of existence or at worst, irrelevancies that amount to private matters for individuals. Not only women as persons, then, but also all the realms and activities associated with their daily lives are silenced. Post-war feminists therefore drew critical attention to the often absurd and inaccurate portrayal of women as creatures of the home and domestic comforts. These were images that represented men's preferred view of (harmless) female qualities and (limited) aspirations. Missing from such images were women's authentic voices and arguments about private and public issues (see Friedan, 1963).

Feminists were not looking simply to challenge the picture of domesticity that post-war consumer culture had foisted on them, but to assert their rights to define what was public in their own way. The oft-repeated phrase 'the personal is political', associated with feminism of the 1960s and 70s, highlights the view that what men consider political excludes the power relations that exist in the home. Private life was neutralized and rendered invisible and inaudible from the public domain. The feminist challenge, then, was to reverse the masculine hierarchies and standards that shaped all aspects of society to the detriment of women. For many, that also involved identifying and valuing what was distinctive about women's own contribution to society.

For instance, feminists such as psychologist Nancy Chodorow affirmed the uniquely 'relational' psychology of women – that is, the ability to relate to and care for others (see Chodorow, 1989: ch. 2). This was not a natural capacity endowed by sex but a consequence of early gender development and unconscious, pre-Oedipal identity formation. Girls, she claimed, were less individuated as a consequence of close relationships with their mothers, which ensured that female 'ego boundaries' were weaker than men's. Boys, on the other hand, learn to separate from their mothers and, as a result, grow to disavow attachment to and responsibility for others – values that are then expounded in public life as the norm. If female psychology is more attuned to care and to valuing relationships, then women's capacity for judgement is also different from the masculine ideal. Women might be said to judge non-instrumentally, with less focus on ego and with greater concern for the wider effects of their choices. Yet modern society denigrated feminine capacities and orientations in favour of the masculine. In the work of Carol Gilligan, the focus on feminine psychological traits was developed into a theory of the ways in which women speak and make moral judgements (see Gilligan, 1982). For Gilligan, women possess a unique capacity to speak with attention to others, to take into account other points of view and to listen. That contrasts with masculine modes of speech and communication, which, as we saw earlier, are often perceived as aggressive and competitive, designed to subdue opponents rather than accommodate them.

The argument of feminists such as Chodorow or Gilligan is that women's gendered identities and capacities can be valued in themselves and used for the better. That chimes with the general orientation of second-wave strategies of reversal that sought not simply to have women accommodated in male-dominated structures of power, but to reverse the polarity that made female subordinate to male. Public and private domains had to be transformed, and not simply repopulated with more women. The impact of those strategies on how we speak and listen today have been enormous. There is now not only increased awareness of the presence of women in public life, but also a greater concern with how people speak to and about women (in ways that recognize their equality), that women themselves are given opportunities to speak and, moreover, that the language used in public does not ridicule women or denigrate femininity.

But if those strategies have altered much of official public discourse, they remain nonetheless attached to a conception of gender that is still tied to sexual difference, presuming 'a stable category of sex upon which gendered identities are constructed' (Squires, 1999: 59). Sexual difference is still regarded as the organizing centre of gender, dividing gender into either masculine or feminine orientations. The problem with this retention of sexual difference is that, as a political strategy, it has the tendency to universalize certain qualities as though they pertained to *all* women. As many feminists came to argue, however, gender conventions are not uniform but vary in relation to other social differences, such as class and race (see Nicholson, 1999: ch. 4). Not all women share the same propensities to relate and care, or do so in the same way. To identify certain qualities as feminine, rather than masculine, was to reduce attention to the ways in which femininity could be differently experienced, subverted or not present at all. The limitation of strategies of reversal, then, is that the sex binary remains implicit and imposes conceptual and ethical barriers on the reception of women who do not conform to the qualities associated with women. If they lend support to an appreciation of the different ways that women might speak and argue as autonomous subjects, such strategies are nevertheless less receptive to the multiplicity of ways that gendered subjects can be cast.

Strategies of displacement

Differences and disagreements over feminist strategies of reversal opened the way to new claims about gender and its politics. Strategies of displacement describe the orientations of so-called postmodernist and 'queer' theorists who dispute altogether the idea that gender has any necessary relationship to sex. That is not to say that there is no difference between male and female sexes but, rather, whatever physiological differences there are cannot be treated as uniform or as 'foundational' to gender. Bodies fall under the sway of cultural interpretation, too, and are therefore 'mobile' (Squires, 1999: 64–72). As a consequence, gender cannot be said to rest upon stable sex differences and hence need not therefore be binary: what counts as masculine and feminine are themselves complex and varied. It might be possible to conceive gender not exclusively as 'heteronormative' – that is, as constructions of male or female – but, rather, as contingent 'performances' that include shades in between: butch, camp or asexual, for example (see Butler, 1999). Of course, society is still dominated by ideals of masculinity and femininity and these are typically treated as extensions of natural sexual differences. But alongside such conventions are a whole range of accents and composites that make for a much more complex picture.

So instead of seeking to reverse the male and female binary, postmodern feminists and queer theorists have sought to displace the dominance of a narrow framing of gender around two, mutually exclusive poles. The primacy of one version of gender (masculine) cannot be undone simply by prioritizing the other (feminine). Rather, the dichotomy itself is brought into question so as to legitimate a range of gender variations. In practice, that implies strategies to eliminate discrimination not only against women, but against lesbians, gay men, transsexuals and intersex individuals, too. For example, the legalization of marriage or child adoption for same-sex couples has been hugely controversial because it takes a social institution (the family) that has for centuries been dominated by heteronormative culture. Debates over marriage have brought into the public realm moral arguments, often of a religious nature, about the 'proper' sources of partnerships and the socially acceptable types of personal relationship. Given that marriage is an arrangement that has considerable financial and personal consequences (regarding insurance, mortgages, administering medical treatment and wills, for example) these debates are not purely moral, but are arguments over the nature of democratic citizenship (see Chambers, 2003: ch. 6).

Strategies of displacement have an important rhetorical element in as much as they dislodge the primacy of the feminine/masculine binary divide in public discourse and explore the complex ways in which gender is assembled, both in argument and in behaviour generally. Certainly, the emphasis on gender as multiple has problematized the feminist emphasis on women as a singular and identifiable category. Many feminists have found this difficult to square with a coherent resistance to patriarchy. But the gain has been to bring into view the stylization and performance of genders that can vary widely. Masculinity, for example, need not be conceived as exclusively the dominant other of femininity, but instead as a complex composite of varying qualities encoded bodily, not all of which are necessarily threatening to women or exclusive of feminine (or, indeed, non-gendered) elements (see Squires, 1999: 74–77; Connell, 2005). The 'hegemonic' male figure that dominates western domestic and international politics is usually treated as gender-neutral but, on reflection, can be said to articulate a masculinity that is complex, varied (Carver, 1996), and dismissive of other, more feminized masculinities (Hooper, 2001; Dudnik, Hagemann and Tosh, 2004).

The three types of feminist strategy sketched above need not be viewed as mutually exclusive, nor need we make a choice among them. But they do illuminate the different degrees to which a politics of gender may contest patriarchal relations of power. In rhetorical terms, they draw attention to different ways that speech mediates the dimension of the political: namely, by excluding women and their voices (strategies of inclusion), denigrating the distinct qualities and experiences they may bring to public life (strategies of reversal), and forcing both men and women to communicate according to narrow and constraining cultural stereotypes that refuse the multiplicity of human identity (strategies of displacement). While all are relevant to rhetorical analysis, the latter, in particular, invites us to see how persuasion can involve a complicated, sometimes ambivalent, articulation of elements that combine both in embodied discourse and in figures of the collective body. Let us now explore some examples of how political rhetoric works in and through representations of gender.

Gender and the nation

One of the most common sources of gendered political arguments is the idea of the nation, which informs much of modern political speech at both domestic and international levels (see Yuval-Davis, 1997). Stemming from the Latin root, *natio*, 'nation' shares its origins with words such as 'birth' and 'nature'. As a term for political community, 'nation' therefore links to ideas of reproduction, family and naturalized identity. It has powerful connotations as a figure in political argument because it can command automatic allegiance to notions of collective unity and cultural distinctiveness. One need only talk of 'national qualities' or the 'needs and interests of the nation' to set these ideas in motion. In so doing, the nation functions as a key argumentative device, a metaphor blending together various ideas and ideologies by simultaneously naturalizing the connections it makes. The nation itself can be coded in both masculine and feminine ways depending on what case is being made. This is clear in references either to the 'fatherland' or to the 'motherland', the first as a source of pride, status or legitimacy, the second as a source of nurturance and belonging. In the latter case, arguments for the nation invite us to identify with the gendered idea of a maternal body (from which we were born) that unifies us and serves as a source of identification. Moreover, however they are coded, appeals to the nation or national identity articulate ideas about gender roles for individuals, if only implicitly, by conceiving the nation as the family writ large.

We can see these connections between the nation and gender if we look at speeches concerned with Britain and Britishness. Britishness is a complex concept. Formally, 'Britain' refers to Great Britain, the union of England, Scotland and Wales under a single parliament and crown. The entire territory of the state is, officially, the 'United Kingdom of Great Britain and Northern Ireland' (the latter lying outside the formal union). Moreover, there is often a tendency to regard the British state as simply England. Part of the confusion here lies in the historical dominance of England over other nations of the UK, a cultural, political and economic dominance that means British politicians are often English and British institutions (such as parliament, the Church of England and public schools) are typically located there. Of course, in the recent past Britain was also an Empire with connections across the world and cultural influence flowing in and out of the state from all parts of the globe. Britishness, then, refers less to a single, homogeneous and territorially circumscribed state than to a complex, historically changeable, culturally diverse and politically uneven administrative structure. Making some kind of 'imagined community' out of the British state has always been a controversial exercise, since for several centuries much of what was supposedly British lay outside national territory.

In the late nineteenth century, for example, national identity in Britain was strongly inflected by ideas about the English middle classes, the Victorian idea of family that supported that class and Empire. The English middle classes came to be seen as the leading agent of British modernity, with its purported independence of mind and industrious spirit. The Victorian idea of family upon which this middle class was built tended to divide gender roles starkly: the home was the place of feminine domesticity and intimacy, while public life was the domain of the competitive, entrepreneurial male. The ideology of Empire provided the key frame within which national sentiment could combine these elements of class and gender. Britain's imperial domination provided both an image of outward adventure for young men (idealized in popular stories featuring figures such as Robert Scott) and, as Rutherford (1997: 2–23) argues, an actual escape route from the cloying femininity of the home. Young, white, middle-class men were encouraged to view the Empire as a place to relinquish domesticity and achieve manhood alongside other men. Imperial manliness was thus defined by emotional separation from women and the home, a no-nonsense 'stiff-upper-lip' disavowal of sentiment and a sense of adventure through friendships with other men (prefigured in sport and games at school). This was a conception of masculine national identity reinforced through public schools and the institutions of the British establishment, all populated by men. Thus the Imperial nation set in play distinct ideas of class and gender, mobilizing a sense of belonging to a symbolic maternal authority (with Queen Victoria as the Empress) that reinforced male dominance by separating women and men.

The decline of the British Empire across the twentieth century, however, entailed a strange loss of status for the British middle class and the gender roles imagined through it. The rise of working-class politics, the enfranchisement of women and the settlement of non-white communities in the UK all contributed to a growing sense of decline of British supremacy, compounded by relative economic decline and the resistance of colonial independence movements. As post-war politicians dealt with the pluralization of British society, it became important to try to reassert and redefine a new sense of nation as the backdrop to specific situations that comprised day-to-day politics. As Britain has changed, a variety of rhetorical strategies have been adopted to address the theme of the nation as the ultimate backdrop of social change and future progress. Each has been characterized by a notable rhetorical gendering figured both in the argument of the speech but also through the distinctive styles of the speakers. Let us look at some examples in the speeches of three key politicians.

Conservative Member of Parliament Enoch Powell was one of the first and most striking speakers on the right wing of his party to articulate distinctive ideas of nationhood and national identity in the post-Imperial age. His notorious 'Rivers of Blood' speech of April 1968 (see Powell, 1968), in which he predicted social unrest and catastrophic national decline as a consequence of continued immigration to the UK from overseas, expressed a populist nationalism that attacked the paternalism of Conservative party policy and the post-war liberal establishment generally (Rutherford, 1997: 113). Once a romantic supporter of Empire, Powell had come to accept the end of British supremacy only by adopting an insular and bitter nationalism obsessed with a racial threat to the purity of his homeland.

A scholar of Greek and Latin and a poet, Powell was uniquely aware of the importance of rhetoric in giving form to a sense of collective identity, and he cultivated a particular style of statesmanship to achieve this. As Rutherford points out, his distinctive, eloquent manner of speech – 'his meticulous attention to detail, his carefully chosen sentences and exacting syntax, the precision of his diction and the pre-eminence he gives to logic' (1997: 116) – expressed a type of masculinity that disavowed open emotion and softness. Thus his argument in the 1968 speech is ostensibly one of logos, delivered not in overtly emotional terms but as an intellectual forewarning of future 'peril' by reference, at one remove from his own experience, to a series of reports on statistics and anecdotes from concerned constituents. His reference to Virgil's prophecy of the river Tiber 'foaming with much blood' is a sign of both his learning and the detached manner with which he approaches his topic.

Powell's underlying message is nevertheless deeply emotional and evocative of the gendered dimensions of nationhood. His attack on immigration is expressed as a lament for a national mother-figure under threat of fragmentation by the influx of black and Asian immigrants, whose arrival has made native Britons 'strangers in their own country', unable to nurture their children and safeguard their neighbourhoods (Powell, 1968: 388). Powell gives expression to a subdued outrage 'among ordinary English people' due to 'the sense of being a persecuted minority' (ibid.: 389). This message is supported by his rhetorical use of an anecdote, again given as a report, from an unnamed constituent who writes of an old lady – 'who lost her husband and both sons in the war' – under attack for refusing to permit 'Negroes' into her boarding house. The old lady (whose actual existence is uncertain) functions as a metaphor for the nation – namely, as a vulnerable woman under attack by foreign bodies.

Powell's speech brings into play a racialized as well as gendered approach to nationhood. In its hostility to immigration, its attack on liberal policy and its appeal to working people's experiences, it construes the national community (still labelled as English) as a threatened integrity requiring 'resolute and urgent action' via the forced repatriation of immigrants. That view endorsed the sentiments of many lower middle and working-class voters in the late 1960s, increasingly concerned about their prospects in a period of stagnant economic growth. Not overtly racist in its language, the speech was nonetheless incendiary and viewed by many as a provocative attack on the post-war political consensus, giving legitimacy to racist opinion. Powell was sacked from his shadow cabinet post in the Conservative party and was marginalized in British politics thereafter.

Margaret Thatcher is often regarded as having inherited Powell's populist critique of Britain's liberal establishment, but without the racialized overtones that destroyed his career. Thatcher is, of course, recognized as one of the most significant and successful post-war Conservative politicians, having won three general elections and served as Prime Minister for twelve years. To that distinction is added her ideological success in challenging and transforming the post-war consensus concerning the social democratic welfare state. Her branch of neo-liberal conservative ideology came to be known as 'Thatcherism' and extolled the virtues of free enterprise and individual self-reliance alongside a conservative defence of the family and law and order, and unrelenting hostility towards socialism (see Gamble, 1988; Hall, 1988).

What is also important about Thatcher as a figure is the obvious fact that she is a woman. Although no feminist, Thatcher is still the only woman to lead her party and serve as UK Prime Minister. As a woman in a world dominated by men and masculine competitiveness in politics, Thatcher cultivated a sense of her own intransigence and robustness as a right-wing 'conviction' politician with a style of speech characterized by stark oppositions and simplified, populist language (see Charteris-Black, 2005: ch. 4). Adopting the epithet given to her in the Soviet Union, the 'Iron Lady', Thatcher combined masculine and feminine qualities in ways that at times dazzled and confused both her supporters and critics. At times, she spoke as the hectoring, upper middle-class nanny, scolding those who disagreed with her (particularly her cabinet ministers, known as 'wets'); at other times as the aggressive, petty bourgeois ideologue, promoter of domestic values such as hard work and thrift; but also, elsewhere, as a sympathetic maternal figure. In short, Thatcher defied a singular gender role and often confused those who saw the world through such roles. This eclecticism often worked in her favour, permitting her to be viewed, as one commentator puts it, as an object of fantasy (see Nunn, 2002): attractive yet inaccessible, potentially excessive but politically committed, simultaneously deploying feminine qualities and combining these with sometimes bellicose, masculine traits. For both friend and foe alike, Thatcher's evident, rather conventional femininity (her pristine hair, skirt-suits and handbag) jarred with the virulence of her opinions and the radicalness of her policies. This made her a singularly distinctive politician, the object of intense allegiance or hatred.

Thatcher's curiosity as a female political leader with overt masculine qualities gave her a position of strength from which to address the idea of the nation. In speeches on a variety of topics, she often extolled a bullish idea of national qualities, imagined in the form of the entrepreneur in a competitive world. As early as 1975, in her first conference speech as party leader, Thatcher presented a classic 'vision' of the British middle class as industrious and inventive, principled and independent:

> Let me give you my vision: a man's right to work as he will, to spend what he earns, to own property, to have the State as servant and not as master – these are the British inheritance. They are the essence of a free economy and on that freedom all our other freedoms depend.
>
> (Thatcher, 1975: 412)

Here, in the form of a parallelism linking related virtues and the threefold repetition, in different forms, of the symbolic term 'free', Thatcher offers an image of Britishness that revolves around the male head of household, defined by work, property and economic liberty. That concept of 'economic man' – the entrepreneurial individual separate from the household and independent of responsibility for anyone – was central to her politics throughout her career, especially later as Prime Minister. To that, however, should be added a notoriously combative dimension, especially following the divisions brought by her policies and by international events. For example, in military ventures such as the defence of the Falkland Islands in 1982 or against 'enemies within' such as trade unions (for instance, during the year-long miners' strike in 1984), Thatcher evoked a sense of Britishness as a libertarian refusal to surrender interests or power to any version of collectivism. With echoes of Churchill's war speeches, she proclaimed in the aftermath of the victory in the South Atlantic, 'When the demands of war and the dangers to our own people call us to arms – then we British are as we have always been – competent, courageous and resolute' (Thatcher, 1982: 435). These military qualities, she pointed out, offered 'a lesson which we must apply to peace just as we have learned it in war'.

In one notable, but also controversial, speech – the 'Bruges speech' of September 1988 (see Thatcher, 1988) – Thatcher speaks directly to the idea of Britain as an economically and politically independent state. Arguing against what she infers is the dilution of sovereignty through membership of the European Community (now the European Union), she again points to Britain's record as a 'sanctuary from tyranny' during world wars, prepared to do battle to defend freedom (ibid.: 465–66). While she affirms the country's fellowship with the other European states, she also warns of the dangers of suppressing national independence through a 'European super-State'. Here, again, is the appeal to Britishness in combat mode, defined by its resistance to collectivism and any incursions on economic sovereignty. Thatcher's aggressive nationalism was never racially posed. Rather, it mobilized a masculine view of market economics, sturdy independence and hostility to threats to the 'strong state'. Ironically, Thatcher was eventually deposed by her own party (nearly all men) while in office, in part because of her utter intransigence on the question of Europe.

Finally, Tony Blair's speeches offer a fascinating insight into the legacy of the Thatcher governments. Although Blair was the new leader of the Labour Party which had opposed Thatcher for nearly twenty years, his innovation was to rebrand Labour as 'New Labour' – that is, as a party that accepted much of Thatcher's restructuring of the British economy around free-market principles (see Driver and Martell, 1998). Importantly, however, New Labour supplemented the Conservatives' emphasis on family and personal responsibility with a social democratic conception of the state as an 'enabler' to society, actively helping get people to work or retraining them for a global economy. In this, its vision was less divisive and more inclusive and socially liberal than that of the Conservatives. New Labour developed a communications strategy to connect progressive social democratic goals to a hyper-competitive market economy. It did this by appealing to a sense of Britishness as entrepreneurial, youthful and 'modernizing', but also morally inspired – not to punish those who can't adjust to the economy so much as constantly to assist and include them in the community (see Atkins, 2011).

Blair's distinctive style of speech and argument has been much examined, often in relation to his transformation of Labour Party policy in favour of markets (see Fairclough, 2000; Finlayson, 2003; Bastow and Martin, 2003; Charteris-Black, 2005: ch. 6). But his success as a politician (up until his support for the Iraq war) was premised greatly on his personal ethos, which he viewed as the lynchpin of Labour's success (see Finlayson and Martin, 2008). Blair offered a softer, younger than usual image of a politician that chimed with voters less inclined to support parties out of habit than was the case in the past. In his halting speech, glottal stops (the informal non-pronunciation of 'tt') and broad smile, Blair appeared the modern man: open to his feelings, comfortable with modern society and popular culture, undogmatic but earnestly authentic. He was an archetype of the feminized man who relinquishes overt formality and speaks not to self-aggrandise or to crush the opponent, but to illuminate ordinary experience and sympathize with others. Blair therefore embodied an erotic image of youth and aspiration with which he wanted the electorate directly to identify.

In his first speech to conference following his landslide election win in 1997, Blair's populism and modernizing zeal was given expression as a celebration of national values and a renewed sense of unity (see Blair, 1997a). His 'thanks' to the 'British people' construed Britishness not as hostile to the outside world, fearfully protective of tradition, but as embracing of change and welcoming of risk: 'The British don't fear change. We are one of the great innovative peoples' (ibid.: 513). He goes on to list the technological achievements of the British, underscoring the national character as adventurous, creative and pioneering, a 'beacon to the world' for the twenty-first century. But in addition to this entrepreneurial spirit, fit for a dynamic global economy, Blair emphasizes British 'compassion', the importance of community and a sense of duty to others. His task, he claims, is to restore family life and to provide a suitable and supportive environment for rearing children and caring for the elderly. Synthesizing his modernizing programme with a sense of compassion and openness to difference, Blair issues a challenge to the nation with missionary zeal:

> Help us make Britain that beacon shining throughout the world. Unite behind our mission to modernize our country for all our people. For there is a place for all the people in new Britain, and there is a role for all the people in its creation. Believe in us as much as we believe in you.
>
> (Ibid.: 517)

Here terms such as 'mission', 'creation' and 'believe', the metaphor of a 'beacon' and the repeated phrase 'all the people' give his argument about modernization the form of a religious sermon, addressing the audience as a guide and protector on a spiritual journey. Like the figure he seeks to embody, Blair's rhetorical nation is a mixture of masculine entrepreneurialism and maternal warmth, creative and competitive but compassionate and yielding. New Labour's strategy to reconcile a market economy with social democratic goals was a similarly novel, perhaps improbable, combination and, in order to work, required popular faith and belief in Blair himself. Following the Iraq war and disagreements within the party, however, that faith gradually dissipated and Blair's premiership came to an ignominious end.

The three examples surveyed here demonstrate how, in different ways, the idea of the nation functions as a rhetorical device to help appropriate situations. It does so, I have argued, by assembling images of the political community through implicit reference to gender. Both in their peculiar embodiment as speakers and in the arguments themselves, politicians articulate aspects of the nation by inflecting gender with other ideas – of class or ethnicity, for example. Whether it is as a defensive protector of racial purity (Powell), an aggressive promoter of market freedom (Thatcher) or an inclusive, meritocratic modernizer (Blair), a gendered rhetoric is never simply about being either a man or woman, or even just masculine or feminine, but requires a combination of various elements at once.

Summary

I have argued that gender relates to rhetoric not merely as something to be spoken about but, moreover, as something through which speech and communication itself works. That is to say, gender is not simply a topic of debate, but also a means to persuade. Who it is that speaks, how they speak and what they speak about are all determined in some way as questions of gender. Because rhetoric refers to the 'situated' character of speech, it necessarily points us to the embodiment of voice and argument – the material locus of gender – through which situations are appropriated. This is an unavoidably political dimension, not least because the field of gender concerns relations of power and strategy. As I have argued, the work of feminism has been crucial in drawing attention to, exploring and contesting the ways in which women have had their bodies removed from spaces of deliberation and their voices and experiences diminished in favour of those of men. Gender, then, is not only a rhetorical means to persuade; it is at the same time a set of unequal relations of power that sets limits to the who, what and how of persuasion.

Equally, however, debates in gender theory remind us that the terms of gender are unstable categories open to all sorts of variation and combination. More than just a perspective to explore women's oppression, gender analysis permits us to see the ambivalence of both masculinity and femininity, their unevenness and their interrelated character. This is of particular significance in the realm of rhetoric, where hard-and-fast distinctions such as male/female are important as platforms from which to persuade but are also open to displacement and refashioning. The example of speeches on British nationality was thus used to explore the different inflections displayed by a gendered rhetoric.

Afterword

In this book I have offered a broad examination of the ways in which rhetoric is manifest in politics. In these final remarks I summarize some of the major claims I have made along the way, which might stimulate the reader's further reflection upon – and exploration of – practices of persuasion. Perhaps it will help to begin modestly, underlining what the book has and has *not* sought to do: it has offered an account of the historical background to rhetorical political enquiry, but not a detailed analysis of the development of rhetoric and its relevance to all political thinkers and rhetoricians; it has noted the key classifications and techniques of ancient rhetorical instruction, but not comprehensively surveyed all the devices that can be found; it has set out a way to apply these techniques to contemporary politics, but there are many variations and methods by which this application can be made and I have avoided an explicitly 'normative' approach; and it has looked at some key areas in which rhetorical enquiry can be illuminating, but a wide variety of relevant themes and issues could also have been included (such as the rhetoric of war, the rhetoric of dissent, policy rhetoric, right-wing rhetoric and so on). Rhetoric is not a narrowly circumscribed body of ideas to be summarized in one go or mobilized with one method alone. It is a prodigious and open-ended source for investigating practices of persuasion. Where this book undoubtedly falls short there are, thankfully, many others (as well as specialist journals) that can fill in the details, take alternative lines of enquiry and come to different conclusions. Such is the way with arguments.

My overriding concern has been to introduce the way politics can be thought of in relation to rhetoric, not exhaustively to demonstrate its many actual or potential permutations. Doubtless, scholars both of rhetoric and of politics will find inexplicable gaps or missing references. But what has been important to me is, above all, to set about thinking of politics as an activity that is itself unavoidably, intrinsically rhetorical. Where there are disputes, disagreements, uncertainties, choices or decisions, then politics stops being a routine process of management or administration and, instead, presents its citizens with opportunities to formulate, express, contest or legitimate shared judgements. At such moments, I have claimed, politics becomes a matter of inventively recasting principles to fit the circumstances and addressing audiences in order to rebuild certainty. This is what rhetoric is for: it is a practical form of guidance to assist the process of making persuasive arguments for judgements that cannot make themselves. It does not always succeed but, in politics, success will be impossible without it. The collection of accumulated techniques and instructions known as rhetoric constitutes a peculiar form of knowledge. It is neither systematic nor founded upon precise scientific grounds. Its boundaries with other disciplines are porous and its content varies markedly with the traditions and contexts in which it is practised. In short, like politics generally, rhetoric is more 'art' than science, dependent upon the creative capacity of its practitioners than on theoretical knowledge as such. Rhetoric is not something that can ever be exhaustively described in one volume.

But if rhetorical persuasion constitutes an art rather than a science, that does not mean we cannot think about it theoretically. Indeed, it is precisely because it is difficult to classify according to absolute rules that we need to reflect upon what guides our application of it. In this book I have appealed to a number of guiding principles to conceptualize the relation of rhetoric to politics. Let me sketch them here and show how they have informed the discussion in the preceding chapters.

Politics and the political

My opening argument was that rhetoric undertakes a mediating role between the routine activities of politics and the confrontation with basic principles that characterizes the dimension of 'the political' (see Chapter 1). In all the arguments, claims and counterclaims of routine politics, issues of principle are regularly confronted and evaded, affirmed or recast. Effective rhetoric works both sides of this division at once, drawing us towards some principles but bending or obscuring others. It is never easy to be absolutely certain which principles are at stake, or to what degree. The distinction between politics and the political is a guide to questioning, not a way of answering once and for all. Rhetoric is never defined by one or the other but operates at the boundary between them, alerting us to fundamental principles (our rights and freedoms, who belongs and who doesn't, right and wrong, life and death) while taking others for granted or downplaying their contentious nature. To regard persuasion as a political practice means asking how and with what success rhetorical action mediates what is certain and what is controversial. Modern citizens find themselves constantly facing matters of controversy as their rights clash or as states and other powers limit their freedoms. Although it has been downgraded as a political art in modern times, rhetoric is vital to the ways in which a common life among citizens is fashioned and represented (see Chapters 2 and 3). Here it is difficult to avoid clashes of principle and demands that some issues should have priority over others.

Space and time

I have argued that political rhetoric has an important role to play in orienting us towards issues. It does this by imagining space and time in specific ways – that is, by defining our situation in order to position us as audiences towards problems and dilemmas (see Chapters 4 and 5). Rhetoric, I have underscored, describes the 'situated' character of speech. It takes place at specific moments, adopting what meanings are available and appropriate in order to speak to audiences that are present there and then and to guide them through a situation. I have argued that to apply rhetorical categories to the analysis of politics is to focus on this situatedness and to ask how particular situations are 'appropriated' through speech (see Chapter 6). That is not to deny that speech can have unintended consequences or that the meaning of speeches transforms over time. Nor does it mean that speech has only one original meaning which we can grasp by close analysis of the context or intentions of the speaker. On the contrary, all meaning is polyvalent and co-existing accents can always be noted and different meanings found. Nonetheless, the best way to start thinking about that possibility is to highlight the way that rhetoric serves to prioritize certain orientations over others. I set out a general method to begin doing this in Chapter 6; the question of how situations are rhetorically appropriated was also central to Chapters 7 (on democracy), 8 (on the media) and 9 (on gender).

Language as action

Finally, I have insisted on the importance of thinking of rhetoric as a way to understand how language 'acts'. That is to say, although rhetoric inevitably draws attention to *what* we say, its focus is not on words as discreet containers of meaning but more on their movement in relation to situations. Rhetorical analysis in politics is not simply a species of literary studies or linguistics, although it shares much with those disciplines. When we look at rhetoric we are examining a process of intervention, not only a textual object. We must certainly read speeches and examine the words, phrases and meanings they gather into arguments. But, conceived as arguments, these are ways of acting upon the world, upon other subjects, and upon ourselves. This is what in Chapter 6 I called their 'projectile' character – meanings that come at us and try to rearrange the way we perceive or feel things. What matters here, as Chapters 7 and 8 noted in particular, is how this movement unfolds – for example, as affects articulated in networks of emotions and feelings or as ways of recruiting us as audiences willing to view the world through media. Often, when we are persuaded – however briefly – it is because we are 'moved' to reason in a particular way about some issue. Sometimes the most obscene or improbable ideas can seem acceptable because of the way we have been positioned rhetorically. Rhetoric can't do without language, but it is not reducible just to the qualities of a text. Perhaps it is better conceived as a 'practice' or a 'performance' – that is, as a discursive activity that gathers meaning and distributes it in a specific way. As we saw in Chapter 9, this gathering is as much about bodies as it is about ideas or words.

With these guiding principles in mind, I have endeavoured to prompt a rhetorical appreciation of politics that might subsequently be taken in all sorts of possible directions and applied to areas that I have not covered here. Undoubtedly, one virtue of politics is that it produces a never-ending stream of arguments and controversies for rhetoricians to explore. A book of this kind, then, should be conceived as only one step in an enquiry that entails asking that most political of questions: how are we persuaded?

Bibliography

Ahmed, S. 2004. 'Affective Economies', *Social Text*, 79, vol. 22, no. 2: 117–39.
Allen, R.C. 1992. 'Audience-Oriented Criticism and Television', in R.C. Allen (ed), *Channels of Discourse Reassembled: Television and Contemporary Criticism*, 2nd edn. London: Routledge, 101–37.
Amossy, R. 2001. '*Ethos* at the Crossroads of Disciplines: Rhetoric, Pragmatics, Sociology', *Poetics Today*, vol. 22, no. 1: 1–23.
Amossy, R. 2005. 'The Argumentative *Dimension* of Discourse', in F.H. van Eemeren and P. Houtlosser (eds), *Practices of Argumentation*. Amsterdam: John Benjamins, 87–98.
Anderson, B. 2006. *Imagined Communities: Reflections on the Origin and Spread of Nationalism*, revised edn. London: Verso.
Ankersmit, F.R., 1996. *Aesthetic Politics: Political Philosophy Beyond Fact and Value*. Stanford, CA: Stanford University Press.
Arendt, H. 1959. *The Human Condition: A Study of the Central Dilemmas Facing Modern Man*. New York: Doubleday Anchor.
Arendt, H. 2000. *The Portable Hannah Arendt*. P. Baehr (ed). London: Penguin.
Aristotle. 1988. *The Politics*. S. Everson (ed). Cambridge: Cambridge University Press.
Aristotle. 1991. *The Art of Rhetoric*. H. Lawson-Tancred (trans). London: Penguin.
Aronovitch, H. 1997. 'The Political Importance of Analogical Argument', *Political Studies*, vol. 45: 78–92.
Atkins, J. 2011. *Justifying New Labour Policy*. Basingstoke: Palgrave Macmillan.
Atkins, J. 2013. 'A Renewed Social Democracy for an "Age of Internationalism": An Interpretivist Account of New Labour's Foreign Policy', *British Journal of Politics and International Relations*, Special Issue on 'Interpreting British Foreign Policy', forthcoming.
Atkins, J. and Finlayson, A. 2013. '"… A 40-Year-Old Black Man Made the Point to Me": Everyday Knowledge and the Performance of Leadership in Contemporary British Politics', *Political Studies*, vol. 61, no. 1: 161–77.
Atkinson, M. 2004. *Lend Me Your Ears: All You Need to Know About Making Speeches and Presentations*. London: Vermilion.
Austin, J.L. 1962. *How to Do Things with Words*. Oxford: Oxford University Press.
Balibar, E. 2002. *Politics and the Other Scene*. London: Verso.
Balibar, E. 2004. *We, The People of Europe: Reflections on Transnational Citizenship*. Princeton, NJ: Princeton University Press.
Ball, T. 1995. *Reappraising Political Theory: Revisionist Studies in the History of Political Thought*. Oxford: Clarendon.

Bastow, S. and Martin, J. 2003. *Third Way Discourse: European Ideologies in the Twentieth Century*. Edinburgh: Edinburgh University Press.

BBC News. 2009. 'Angry Scenes Face Griffin at BBC'. Available from: http://news.bbc.co.uk/1/hi/8321157.stm [accessed 17 April 2012].

Bell, A. and Garrett, P (eds). 1998. *Approaches to Media Discourse*. Oxford: Blackwell.

Bellamy, R. 1992. *Liberalism and Modern Society: An Historical Argument*. Cambridge: Polity.

Bellamy, R. 2008. *Citizenship: A Very Short Introduction*. Oxford: Oxford University Press.

Berger, A.A. 2005. *Media Analysis Techniques*, 2nd edn. London: Sage.

Bernard-Donals, M. and Glejzer, R. (eds). 1998. *Rhetoric in an Anti-Foundational World: Language, Culture and Pedagogy*. London: Yale University Press.

Bernstein, R.J. 1976. *The Restructuring of Social and Political Theory*. London: Methuen.

Bevir, M. and Rhodes, R.A.W. 2003. *Interpreting British Governance*. London: Routledge.

Billig, M. 1991. *Ideology and Opinions: Studies in Rhetorical Psychology*. London: Sage.

Billig, M. 1996. *Arguing and Thinking: A Rhetorical Approach to Social Psychology*, 2nd edn. Cambridge: Cambridge University Press.

Bitzer, L.F. 1968. 'The Rhetorical Situation', *Philosophy and Rhetoric*, vol. 1, no. 1: 1–14.

BJPIR. 2012. 'Celebrity + Politics: Reflections on Popular Culture and Political Representation', Special Section of *British Journal of Politics and International Relations*, vol. 14, no. 3: 345–422.

Black, E. 1978. *Rhetorical Criticism: A Study in Method*. Wisconsin: University of Wisconsin Press.

Black, E. 1999. 'The Second Persona', in J.L. Lucaites, C.M. Condit and S. Caudill (eds), *Contemporary Rhetorical Theory: A Reader*. London: Guilford Press, 331–40.

Black, M. 1962. *Models and Metaphors: Studies in Language and Philosophy*. Ithaca: Cornell University Press.

Blair, T. 1997a. 'A Beacon to the World', in B. MacArthur (ed). 1999, *The Penguin Book of Twentieth-Century Speeches*. London: Penguin, 511–18.

Blair, T. 1997b. Tribute to Diana, August 31, annotated copy of text in Montgomery, M. 1999. 'Speaking Sincerely: Public Reactions to the Death of Diana', *Language and Literature*, vol. 8, no. 1: 6–9.

Bleiker, R. 2009. *Aesthetics and World Politics*. Basingstoke: Palgrave.

Blyth, M.M. 1997. '"Any More Bright Ideas?" The Ideational Turn of Comparative Political Economy', *Comparative Politics*, vol. 29, no. 1: 229–50.

Bourdieu, P. 1990. *The Logic of Practice*. R. Nice (trans.). Cambridge: Polity.

Brecher, B., Devenney, M. and Winter, A. (eds). 2010. *Discourses and Practices of Terrorism*. London: Routledge.

Brenner, N. 2004. *New State Spaces: Urban Governance and the Rescaling of Statehood*. Oxford: Oxford University Press.

Brody, M. 1993. *Manly Writing: Gender, Rhetoric, and the Rise of Composition*. Carbondale and Edwardsville: Southern Illinois University Press.

Bronner, S.E. 2011. *Critical Theory: A Very Short Introduction*. Oxford: Oxford University Press.

Brooks, P. and Gewirtz, P. (eds). 1996. *Law's Stories: Narrative and Rhetoric in the Law*. New Haven: Yale University Press.

Brummett, B. 2011. *Rhetoric in Popular Culture*, 3rd edn. London: Sage.

Burke, K. 1969. *A Rhetoric of Motives*. Berkeley: University of California Press.
Burke, R.J. 1982. 'Politics as Rhetoric', *Ethics*, vol. 93, no. 1: 45–55.
Burke, R.J. 1984. 'A Rhetorical Conception of Rationality', *Informal Logic*, vol. 6, no. 3: 17–25.
Butler, D. and Stokes, D. 1969. *Political Change in Britain: Forces Shaping Electoral Choice*. London: Macmillan.
Butler, J. 1997. *Excitable Speech: A Politics of the Performative*. London: Routledge.
Butler, J. 1999. *Gender Trouble: Feminism and the Subversion of Identity*, 2nd edn. London: Routledge.
Butler, J. 2004. *Precarious Life: The Powers of Mourning and Violence*. London: Verso.
Butsch, R. (ed). 2007. *Media and Public Spheres*. Basingstoke: Palgrave.
Calhoun, C. (ed). 1992. *Habermas and the Public Sphere*. Cambridge, MA: MIT Press.
Cameron, D. 2006. 'Theorising the Female Voice in Public Contexts', in J. Baxter (ed), *Speaking Out: The Female Voice in Public Contexts*. Basingstoke: Palgrave Macmillan, 3–20.
Campbell, K.K. and Jamieson, K.H. 2008. *Presidents Creating the Presidency: Deeds Done in Words*, 2nd edn. Chicago: University of Chicago Press.
Carstensen, M.B. 2011. 'Ideas are Not as Stable as Political Scientists Want Them To Be: A Theory of Incremental Ideational Change', *Political Studies*, vol. 59, no. 3: 596–615.
Carter, M. (1988) 'Stasis and Kairos: Principles of Social Construction in Classical Rhetoric', *Rhetoric Review*, vol. 7, no. 1: 97–112.
Carver, T. 1996. *Gender is Not a Synonym for Women*. London: Lynne Rienner.
Carver, T. and Pikalo, J. (eds). 2008. *Political Language and Metaphor: Interpreting and Changing the World*. London: Routledge.
Cato. 2010. *Guilty Men* [originally published in 1940]. London: Faber and Faber.
Cavarero, A. 2005. *For More than One Voice: Toward a Philosophy of Vocal Expression*. P.A. Kottman (trans). Stanford, CA: Stanford University Press.
Cavell, M. 2006. *Becoming a Subject: Reflections in Philosophy and Psychoanalysis*. Oxford: Oxford University Press.
Chambers, S. and Costain, A. (eds). 2000. *Deliberation, Democracy, and the Media*. Lanham, MD: Rowman and Littlefield.
Chambers, S.A. 2003. *Untimely Politics*. Edinburgh: Edinburgh University Press.
Charteris-Black, J. 2005. *Politicians and Rhetoric: The Persuasive Power of Metaphor*. Basingstoke: Palgrave.
Chodorow, N.J. 1989. *Feminism and Psychoanalytic Theory*. London: Yale University Press.
Churchill, W. 1940. 'Blood, Toil, Tears and Sweat', in B. MacArthur (ed). 1999, *The Penguin Book of Twentieth-Century Speeches*. London: Penguin, 187–88.
Cicero, M.T. 1949a. *On Invention*, in *Cicero II*. H.M. Hubbell (trans) and J. Henderson (ed). Cambridge, MA: Harvard University Press.
Cicero, M.T. 1949b. *The Best Kind of Orator*, in *Cicero II*. H.M. Hubbell (trans) and J. Henderson (ed). Cambridge, MA: Harvard University Press.
Cicero, M.T. 1962. *Orator*, in *Cicero V*, revised edn. G. L. Hendrickson and H.M. Hubbell (trans) and J. Henderson (ed). Cambridge, MA: Harvard University Press.
Cicero, M.T. 2001. *On the Ideal Orator*. J.M. May and J. Wisse (trans). Oxford: Oxford University Press.
Clark, T. 2009. 'Towards a Poetics of Contemporary Public Language: The Poetic Formula in Focus', *Journal of the Australasian Universities Modern Languages Association*, no. 111: 103–29.

Clark, T. 2011. 'Speech, Script, and Performance: Towards a Public Poetics of the Political Speechwriter's Role', *PRism*, vol. 8, no. 1. Available from: http://www.prismjournal.org/fileadmin/8_1/Clark.pdf [accessed 4 March 2012].
Clarke, H.D., Sanders, D., Stewart, M.C. and Whiteley, P.F. 2004. *Political Choice in Britain*. Oxford: Oxford University Press.
Cockcroft, R. and Cockcroft, S. 2005. *Persuading People: An Introduction to Rhetoric*, 2nd edn. Basingstoke: Palgrave.
Conley, T.M. 1990. *Rhetoric in the European Tradition*. Chicago: Chicago University Press.
Connell, R.W. 1987. *Gender and Power: Society, the Person and Sexual Politics*. Cambridge: Polity.
Connell, R.W. 2005. *Masculinities*, 2nd edn. Cambridge: Polity.
Connolly, J. 2007. *The State of Speech: Rhetoric and Political Thought in Ancient Rome*. Princeton, NJ: Princeton University Press.
Connolly, J. 2009. 'The Politics of Rhetorical Education', in E. Gunderson (ed), *The Cambridge Companion to Ancient Rhetoric*. Cambridge: Cambridge University Press, 126–44.
Connolly, W.E., 2002a. *Neuropolitics: Thinking, Culture, Speed*. London: University of Minnesota Press.
Connolly, W.E. 2002b. *The Augustinian Imperative: A Reflection on the Politics of Morality*. Lanham, MD: Rowman & Littlefield.
Consigny, S. 1974. 'Rhetoric and Its Situations', *Philosophy & Rhetoric*, vol. 7, no. 3 (Summer): 175–86.
Constant, B. 1988. 'The Liberty of the Ancients Compared with that of the Moderns', in B. Fontana (ed), *Constant: Political Writings*, Cambridge: Cambridge University Press, 308–28.
Corbett, E.P.J. and Connors, R. 1999. *Classical Rhetoric for the Modern Student*. Oxford: Oxford University Press.
Corbin, C. (ed). 1998. *Rhetoric in Postmodern America: Conversations with Michael Calvin McGee*. New York: The Guilford Press.
Corner, J. 1998. *Studying Media: Problems of Theory and Method*. Edinburgh: Edinburgh University Press.
Corner, J. and Rosenthal, A. 2005. *New Challenges for Documentary*, 2nd edn. Manchester: Manchester University Press.
Couldry, N. and McCarthy, A. (eds). 2004. *Mediaspace: Place, Scale and Culture in a Media Age*. London: Routledge.
Couldry, N., Livingstone, S. and Markham, T. 2010. *Media Consumption and Public Engagement: Beyond the Presumption of Engagement*, 2nd edn. Basingstoke: Palgrave.
Craib, I. 2001. *Psychoanalysis: A Critical Introduction*. Cambridge: Polity.
Dahlgren, P. (ed). 2009. *Media and Political Engagement: Citizens, Communication and Democracy*. Cambridge: Cambridge University Press.
Dallek, R. 2003. *John F. Kennedy: An Unfinished Life 1917–1963*. London: Penguin.
Daly, G. 1999. 'Ideology and its Paradoxes: Dimensions of Fantasy and Enjoyment', *Journal of Political Ideologies*, vol. 4, no. 2: 219–38.
Damasio, A. 1994. *Descartes' Error: Emotion, Reason and the Human Brain*. London: Vintage.
Damasio, A. 1999. *The Feeling of What Happens: Body, Emotion and the Making of Consciousness*. London: Vintage.

Bibliography

Davies, J.K. 1993. *Democracy and Classical Greece*, 2nd edn. London: Fontana.
Davis, A. 2007. *The Mediation of Power: A Critical Introduction*. London: Routledge.
Davis, A. 2010. *Political Communications and Social Theory*. London: Routledge.
Dawkins, R. 2006. *The God Delusion*. London: Transworld.
Dean, J. 2002. *Publicity's Secret: How Technoculture Capitalizes on Democracy*. London: Cornell University Press.
Derrida, J. 1976. *Of Grammatology*. G.C. Spivak (trans). Baltimore: Johns Hopkins University Press.
Derrida, J. 1978. *Writing and Difference*. A. Bass (trans). London: Routledge.
Derrida, J. 1988. *Limited Inc*. Evanston, IL: Northwestern University Press.
Dillon, J. and Gergel, T.L. (eds). 2003. *The Greek Sophists*. London: Penguin.
Donk, W. van der, Loader, B.D., Nixon, P.G. and Rucht, D. (eds). 2004. *Cyberprotest: New Media, Citizens and Social Movements*. London: Routledge.
Downs, A. 1957. *An Economic Theory of Democracy*. New York: Harper and Rowe.
Driver, S. and Martell, L. 1998. *New Labour: Politics After Thatcherism*. Cambridge: Polity.
Dryzek, J.S. 2000. *Deliberative Democracy and Beyond: Liberals, Critics, Contestations*. Oxford: Oxford University Press.
Dryzek, J.S. 2010. 'Rhetoric in Democracy: A Systemic Appreciation', *Political Theory*, vol. 38, no. 3: 319–39.
Dudnik, S., Hagemann, K. and Tosh, J. (eds). 2004. *Masculinties in Politics and War: Gendering Modern History*. Manchester: Manchester University Press.
Dugan, J. 2009. 'Rhetoric and the Roman Republic', in E. Gunderson (ed), *The Cambridge Companion to Ancient Rhetoric*. Cambridge: Cambridge University Press, 178–93.
Edelman, M. 1971. *Politics as Symbolic Action: Mass Arousal and Quiescence*. New York: Academic Press.
Edelman, M. 1988. *Constructing the Political Spectacle*. London: University of Chicago Press.
Elstub, S. 2010. 'The Third Generation of Deliberative Democracy', *Political Studies Review*, vol. 8, no. 3: 291–307.
Esposito, R. 2008. *Bíos. Biopolitics and Philosophy*. T. Campbell (trans). London: University of Minnesota Press.
Fabbrini, S. 2012. 'The Rise and Fall of Silvio Berlusconi: Personalization of Politics and its Limits'. *Comparative European Politics*, advanced online publication, doi:10.1057/cep.2012.18.
Fairclough, I. and Fairclough, N. 2012. *Political Discourse Analysis: A Method for Advanced Students*. London: Routledge.
Fairclough, N. 1993. *Discourse and Social Change*, 2nd edn. Cambridge: Polity.
Fairclough, N. 1995. *Media Discourse*. London: Hodder.
Fairclough, N. 2000. *New Labour, New Language?* London: Routledge.
Finlayson, A. 2003. *Making Sense of New Labour*. London: Lawrence & Wishart.
Finlayson, A. 2004. 'Political Science, Political Ideas and Rhetoric', *Economy and Society*, vol. 33, no. 4: 528–49.
Finlayson, A. 2007. 'From Beliefs to Arguments: Interpretive Methodology and Rhetorical Political Analysis', *British Journal of Politics and International Relations*, vol. 9, no. 4: 545–63.
Finlayson, A. 2012. 'Rhetoric and the Political Theory of Ideologies', *Political Studies*, vol. 60, no. 4: 751–67.

Finlayson, A. and Martin, J. 1997. 'Political Studies and Cultural Studies', *Politics*, vol. 17, no. 3: 175–81.
Finlayson, A. and Martin, J. 2008. '"It Ain't What You Say ...": British Political Studies and the Analysis of Speech and Rhetoric', *British Politics*, vol. 3: 445–64.
Fish, S. 1989. *Doing What Comes Naturally: Change, Rhetoric, and the Practice of Theory in Literary and Legal Studies*. Oxford: Clarendon.
Fish, S. 1994. *There's No Such Thing as Free Speech ... And It's a Good Thing Too*. Oxford: Oxford University Press.
Fishkin, J.S. 2009. *When the People Speak: Deliberative Democracy and Public Consultation*. Oxford: Oxford University Press.
Foucault, M. 1972. *The Archeology of Knowledge*. A.M. Sheridan Smith (trans). London: Routledge.
Foucault, M. 1977. *Discipline and Punish: The Birth of the Prison*. A. Sheridan (trans). New York: Vintage.
Foucault, M. 1980. *Power/Knowledge: Selected Interviews and Other Writings 1972–1977*. C. Gordon (ed). London: Harvester Wheatsheaf.
Foucault, M. 1997. *Ethics: Essential Works of Foucault 1954–1984, vol. 1*. P. Rabinow (ed). London: Penguin.
Frank, J.D. and Frank, J.B. 1991. *Persuasion and Healing: A Comparative Study of Psychotherapy*. Baltimore: Johns Hopkins University Press.
Freeden, M. 1996. *Ideologies and Political Theory: A Conceptual Approach*. Oxford: Clarendon.
Freedman, A. and Medway, P. (eds). 1994. *Genre and the New Rhetoric*. London: Routledge.
Freud, S., 1991. *Civilization, Society and Religion: Group Psychology, Civilization and Its Discontents and Other Works*. London: Penguin.
Freud, S., 2005. *Mourning and Melancholia*. In Freud, S., *On Murder, Mourning and Melancholia*. A. Phillips (ed). London: Penguin, 201–18.
Friedan, B. 1963. *The Feminine Mystique*. London: Penguin.
Frosh, S. 2011. *Feelings*. London: Routledge.
Gamble, A. 1988. *The Free Economy and the Strong State: The Politics of Thatcherism*. Basingstoke: Macmillan.
Garnham, N. 1992. 'The Media and the Public Sphere', in C. Calhoun (ed), *Habermas and the Public Sphere*. London: MIT Press, 359–76.
Garsten, B. 2006. *Saving Persuasion: A Defense of Rhetoric and Judgement*. Cambridge, MA: Harvard University Press.
Gerbaudo, P. 2012. *Tweets and the Streets: Social Media and Contemporary Activism*. London: Pluto.
Gilligan, C. 1982. *In A Different Voice: Psychological Theory and Women's Development*. London: Harvard University Press.
Ginsborg, P. 2005. *Silvio Berlusconi: Television, Power and Patrimony*, 2nd edn. London: Verso.
Glasgow University Media Group. 1995. *The Glasgow Media Group Reader, Vol. 1: News Content, Language and Visuals*. London: Routledge.
Gofas, A. and Hay, C. (eds). 2010. *The Role of Ideas in Political Analysis: A Portrait of Contemporary Debates*. London: Routledge.
Goodin, R.E. 2008. *Innovating Democracy: Democratic Theory and Practice After the Deliberative Turn*. Oxford: Oxford University Press.

176 Bibliography

Goodrich, P. 1987. *Legal Discourse: Studies in Linguistics, Rhetoric and Legal Analysis*. London: Macmillan.

Gramsci, A. 1971. *Selections from the Prison Notebooks*. Q. Hoare and G. Nowell-Smith (eds). London: Lawrence and Wishart.

Grassi, E. 1980. *Rhetoric as Philosophy*. Carbondale: Southern Illinois University Press.

Grassi, E. 1983. *Heidegger and the Question of Renaissance Humanism: Four Studies*. New York: Centre for Medieval and Renaissance Texts and Studies.

Graubard, S. 2009. *The Presidents: The Transformation of the American Presidency from Theodore Roosevelt to Barack Obama*, 2nd edn. London: Penguin.

Gray, J. 2000. *Two Faces of Liberalism*. Cambridge: Polity.

Gross, D.M. 2006. *The Secret History of Emotion: From Aristotle's Rhetoric to Modern Brain Science*. London: University of Chicago Press.

Gunderson, E. (ed). 2009. *The Cambridge Companion to Ancient Rhetoric*. Cambridge: Cambridge University Press.

Gutmann, A. and Thompson, D. 1996. *Democracy and Disagreement*. Cambridge, MA: Harvard University Press.

Habermas, J. 1987. *The Philosophical Discourse of Modernity*. F. Lawrence (trans). Cambridge: Polity.

Habermas, J. 1989. *The Structural Transformation of the Public Sphere: An Enquiry into a Category of Bourgeois Society*. T. Burger (trans). Cambridge, MA: MIT Press.

Habermas, J. 1996a. 'Three Normative Models of Democracy', in S. Benhabib (ed), *Democracy and Difference: Contesting the Boundaries of the Political*. Princeton, NJ: Princeton University Press, 21–30.

Habermas, J. 1996b. *The Habermas Reader*. W. Outhwaite (ed). Cambridge: Polity.

Habinek, T. 2005. *Ancient Rhetoric and Oratory*. Oxford: Blackwell.

Hall, S. 1988. *The Hard Road to Renewal: Thatcherism and the Crisis of the Left*. London: Verso.

Hamelink, C. 2007. 'The Professionalisation of Political Communication: Democracy at Stake', in R. Negrine, P. Mancini, C. Holtz-Bacha and S. Papathassopoulos (eds.), *The Professionalisation of Political Communication*. Bristol: Intellect, 179–88.

Hartley, J. 1992. *The Politics of Pictures: The Creation of the Public in the Age of Popular Media*. London: Routledge.

Hay, C. 1996. *Re-Stating Social and Political Change*. Buckingham: Open University Press.

Hay, C. 2002. *Political Analysis: A Critical Introduction*. Basingstoke: Palgrave.

Heater, D. 1990. *Citizenship: The Civic Ideal in World History, Politics and Education*. London: Longman.

Herman, E.S. and Chomsky, N. 1995. *Manufacturing Consent: The Political Economy of the Mass Media*. London: Vintage.

Herrick, J.A. 2005. *The History and Theory of Rhetoric: An Introduction*, 3rd edn. Boston: Pearson, Allyn and Bacon.

Higgins, M. 2008. *Media and Their Publics*. New York: Open University Press.

Hill, C.A. and Helmers, M. (eds). 2004. *Defining Visual Rhetorics*. London: Routledge.

Hindman, M. 2008. *The Myth of Digital Democracy*. Princeton, NJ: Princeton University Press.

Hobbes, T. 1991. *Leviathan*. R. Tuck (ed). Cambridge: Cambridge University Press.

Hobsbawm, J. (ed). 2006. *Where the Truth Lies: Trust and Morality in PR and Journalism*. London: Atlantic.

Hoffman, J. 2001. *Gender and Sovereignty: Feminism, the State and International Relations*. Basingstoke: Palgrave Macmillan.
Hoffman, M.F. and Ford, D.J. 2010. *Organizational Rhetoric: Situations and Strategies*. London: Sage.
Homer, 2003. *The Odyssey*. E.V. Rieu (trans). London: Penguin.
Hooper, C. 2001. *Manly States: Masculinities, International Relations and Gender Politics*. New York: Columbia University Press.
Howarth, D. 2000. *Discourse*. Buckingham: Open University Press.
Howarth, D. and Torfing, J. (eds). 2004. *Discourse Theory in European Politics: Identity, Policy and Governance*. Basingstoke: Palgrave Macmillan.
Howarth, D., Norval, A. and Stavrakakis, Y. (eds). 2000. *Discourse Theory and Political Analysis: Identities, Hegemonies and Social Change*. Manchester: Manchester University Press.
Howson, A. 2005. *Embodying Gender*. London: Sage.
Hume, D. 1987. *Essays. Moral, Political and Literary*. Indianapolis: Liberty Fund.
Isin, E.F. 2002. *Being Political: Genealogies of Citizenship*. Minneapolis, MN: University of Minnesota Press.
Isin, E.F. 2008. 'Theorizing Acts of Citizenship', in E. F. Isin and G. M. Nielsen (eds), *Acts of Citizenship*. London: Zed Books, 15–33.
Isin, E.F. 2009. 'Citizenship in Flux: The Figure of the Activist Citizen', *Subjectivity*, vol. 29: 367–88.
Jamieson, K.H. 1988. *Eloquence in an Electronic Age: the Transformation of Political Speechmaking*. Oxford: Oxford University Press.
Jessop, B. 1990. *State Theory: Putting Capitalist States in Their Place*. Cambridge: Polity.
Jessop, B. 2001. 'Institutional (Re)turns and the Strategic-relational Approach', *Environment and Planning A*, vol. 33, no. 7: 1213–35.
Jessop, B. 2002. *The Future of the Capitalist State*. Cambridge: Polity.
Jowett, G.S. and O'Donnell, V. 2006. *Propaganda and Persuasion*, 4th edn. London: Sage.
Kapust, D. 2011. 'Cicero on Decorum and the Morality of Rhetoric', *European Journal of Political Theory*, vol. 10, no. 1: 92–112.
Karpf, A. 2006. *The Human Voice: The Story of a Remarkable Talent*. London: Bloomsbury.
Keane, J. 1991. *The Media and Democracy*. Cambridge: Polity.
Kellner, D. 1995. *Media Culture: Cultural Studies, Identity and Politics Between the Modern and the Post-Modern*. London: Routledge.
Kellner, D. 2005. *Media Spectacle and the Crisis of Democracy: Terrorism, War and Election Battles*. Boulder, CO: Paradigm.
Kennedy, G.A. 1994. *A New History of Classical Rhetoric*. Princeton, NJ: Princeton University Press.
Kennedy, J.F. 1961. 'The Torch has been Passed to a New Generation', in B. MacArthur (ed), 1999. *The Penguin Book of Twentieth-Century Speeches*. London: Penguin, 297–301.
Kinnock, N. 1983. 'I Warn You', in B. MacArthur (ed), 1999. *The Penguin Book of Twentieth-Century Speeches*. London: Penguin, 439–41.
Kostelnick, C. and Hassett, M. 2003. *Shaping Information: The Rhetoric of Visual Conventions*. Carbondale: Southern Illinois University Press.

Kozloff, S. 1992. 'Narrative Theory and Television', in Allen, R.C. (ed), *Channels of Discourse Reassembled: Television and Contemporary Criticism*, 2nd edn. London: Routledge, 67–100.

Kymlicka, W. 2002. *Contemporary Political Philosophy: An Introduction*. Oxford: Oxford University Press.

Laclau, E. 1996. *Emancipation(s)*. London: Verso.

Laclau, E. and Mouffe, C. 2001. *Hegemony and Socialist Strategy: Towards a Radical Democratic Politics*, 2nd edn. London: Verso.

Lakoff, G. 2002. *Moral Politics: How Liberals and Conservatives Think*, 2nd edn. London: University of Chicago Press.

Lakoff, G. 2008. *The Political Mind: Why You Can't Understand 21st-Century American Politics with an 18th-Century Brain*. New York: Viking.

Lakoff, G. and Johnson, M. 2003. *Metaphors We Live By*. Chicago and London: University of Chicago Press.

Lancaster, S. 2010. *Speech Writing: The Expert Guide*. London: Robert Hale.

Landes, J.B. 1988. *Women and the Public Sphere in the Age of the French Revolution*. London: Cornell University Press.

Lanham, R.A. 1976. *The Motives of Eloquence: Literary Rhetoric in the Renaissance*. London: Yale University Press.

Lanham, R.A. 1991. *A Handlist of Rhetorical Terms*, 2nd edn. Berkeley, LA: University of California Press.

Lawson-Tancred, H. 1991. 'Introduction' to Aristotle. 1991. *The Art of Rhetoric*. H. Lawson-Tancred (trans). London: Penguin.

Lees-Marshment, J. 2008. *Political Marketing and British Political Parties*, 2nd edn. Manchester: Manchester University Press.

Lees-Marshment, J. 2009. *Political Marketing: Principles and Applications*. London: Routledge.

Lefort, C. 1988. *Democracy and Political Theory*. D. Macey (trans). Cambridge: Polity.

Leith, S. 2011. *You Talkin' To Me? Rhetoric From Aristotle to Obama*. London: Profile.

Lewis, J., Wahl-Jorgensen, K. and Inthorn, S. 2004. 'Images of Citizenship on Television News: Constructing a Passive Public', *Journalism Studies*, vol. 5, no. 2: 153–64.

Litosseliti, L. 2006. 'Constructing Gender in Public Arguments: The Female Voice as Emotional Voice', in J. Baxter (ed), *Speaking Out: The Female Voice in Public Contexts*. Basingstoke: Palgrave Macmillan, 40–58.

Little, A. and Lloyd, M. (eds). 2009. *The Politics of Radical Democracy*. Edinburgh: Edinburgh University Press.

Lloyd, M. 1999. 'Performativity, Parody, Politics', *Theory, Culture and Society*, vol. 16, no. 2: 195–213.

Lyotard, J. -F. 1984. *The Postmodern Condition: A Report on Knowledge*. G. Bennington and B. Massumi (trans). Manchester: Manchester University Press.

MacArthur, B. (ed). 1999. *The Penguin Book of Twentieth-Century Speeches*. London: Penguin.

McCloskey, D. 1998. *The Rhetoric of Economics*, 2nd edn. Madison, WI: University of Wisconsin Press.

Machiavelli, N. 1988. *The Prince*. Q. Skinner and R. Price (eds), Cambridge: Cambridge University Press.

McLean, I. 2001. *Rational Choice and British Politics: An Analysis of Rhetoric and Manipulation from Peel to Blair*. Oxford: Oxford University Press.

Macmillan, H. 1960. 'The Wind of Change', in B. McArthur (ed), 1999, *The Penguin Book of Twentieth-Century Speeches*. London: Penguin, 286–91.
Marchart, O. 2007. *Post-Foundational Political Thought: Political Difference in Nancy, Lefort, Badiou and Laclau*. Edinburgh: Edinburgh University Press.
Marcus, G.E. 2002. *The Sentimental Citizen: Emotion in Democratic Politics*. Pennsylvania: Pennsylvania University Press.
Marshall, T.H. and Bottomore, T. 1987. *Citizenship and Social Class*. London: Pluto.
Martin, J. 2010. 'A Radical Freedom? Gianni Vattimo's "Emancipatory Nihilism"', *Contemporary Political Theory*, vol. 9, no. 3: 325–44.
Marx, K. 1994. 'On the Jewish Question', in J. O'Malley (ed), *Karl Marx: Early Political Writings*. Cambridge: Cambridge University Press, 28–56.
Massumi, B. 1995. 'The Autonomy of Affect', *Cultural Critique*, vol. 31, Fall: 83–109.
Matheson, D. 2005. *Media Discourses: Analysing Media Texts*. Maidenhead: Open University Press.
May, T. 2008. *The Political Thought of Jacques Rancière*. Edinburgh: Edinburgh University Press.
Meyer, M. 1994. *Rhetoric, Language and Reason*. Pennsylvania: Pennsylvania State University Press.
Meyer, S. 1982. 'The John F. Kennedy Inauguration Speech: Function and Importance of its "Address System"', *Rhetoric Society Quarterly*, vol. 12, no. 4: 239–50.
Meyer, T. 2002. *Media Democracy: How the Media Colonize Politics*. Cambridge: Polity.
Miles, H. 2005. *Al-Jazeera: How Arab TV News Challenged the World*. London: Abacus.
Mills, S. 2003. *Gender and Politeness*. Cambridge: Cambridge University Press.
Montgomery, M. 1999. 'Speaking Sincerely: Public Reactions to the Death of Diana', *Language and Literature*, vol. 8, no. 1: 5–33.
Morrell, K. 2006. 'Aphorisms and Leaders' Rhetoric: A New Analytical Approach', *Leadership*, vol. 2, no. 3: 367–82.
Mouffe, C. (ed). 1992. *Dimensions of Radical Democracy: Pluralism, Citizenship, Community*. London: Verso.
Mouffe, C. 1993. *The Return of the Political*. London: Verso.
Mouffe, C. 2000. *The Democratic Paradox*. London: Verso.
Mouffe, C. 2005. *On the Political*. London: Routledge.
Musolff, A. 2004. *Metaphor and Political Discourse: Analogical Reasoning in Debates About Europe*. Palgrave: Macmillan.
Myers, F. 2000. 'Harold Macmillan's "Winds of Change" Speech: A Case Study in the Rhetoric of Policy Change', *Rhetoric & Public Affairs*, vol. 3, no. 4: 555–75.
Negrine, R., 2007. 'Professionalisation in the British Electoral and Political Context', in R. Negrine, P. Mancini, C. Holtz-Bacha and S. Papathanassopoulos (eds), *The Professionalisation of Political Communication*. Bristol: Intellect, 47–62.
Negrine, R., Mancini, P., Holtz-Bacha, C. and Papathanassopoulos, S. (eds). 2007. *The Professionalisation of Political Communication*. Bristol: Intellect.
Nelson, J.S. 1998. *Tropes of Politics: Science, Theory, Rhetoric, Action*. Madison: University of Wisconsin Press.
Neuman, W.R., Just, M.R. and Crigler, A.N. 1992. *Common Knowledge: News and the Construction of Political Meaning*. London: University of Chicago Press.
Nicholson, L. 1999. *The Play of Reason: From the Modern to the Postmodern*. Buckingham: Open University Press.
Norval, A.J. 2007. *Aversive Democracy: Inheritance and Originality in the Democratic Tradition*. Cambridge: Cambridge University Press.

Nunn, H. 2002. *Thatcher, Politics and Fantasy: The Political Culture of Gender and Nation*. London: Lawrence and Wishart.
Nusselder, A. 2013. 'Twitter and the Personalization of Politics', *Psychoanalysis, Culture and Society*, vol. 18, no. 1: 91–100.
Ober, J. 1991. *Mass and Elite in Democratic Athens: Rhetoric, Ideology and the Power of the People*. Princeton, NJ: Princeton University Press.
Olmsted, W. 2006. *Rhetoric: An Historical Introduction*. Oxford: Blackwell.
Olson, K. 2011. 'Legitimate Speech and Hegemonic Idiom: The Limits of Deliberative Democracy in the Diversity of Its Voices', *Political Studies*, vol. 59, no. 3: 527–46.
Ong, W.J. 1982. *Orality and Literacy: The Technologizing of the Word*. London: Routledge.
Opt, S.K. and Gring, M.A. 2009. *The Rhetoric of Social Intervention: An Introduction*. London: Sage.
Palonen, K. 2005. 'Political Theorizing as a Dimension of Political Life', *European Journal of Political Theory*, vol. 4, no. 4: 351–66.
Palonen, K. 2008. 'Political Times and the Rhetoric of Democratization', in K. Palonen, T. Pulkkinen and J. M. Rosales (eds), *Ashgate Research Companion to the Politics of Democratization: Concepts and Histories*. Aldershot: Ashgate, 371–88.
Parkinson, J. 2003. 'Legitimacy Problems in Deliberative Democracy', *Political Studies*, vol. 51, no. 1: 180–96.
Parkinson, J. 2006. *Deliberating in the Real World: Problems of Legitimacy in Deliberative Democracy*. Oxford: Oxford University Press.
Pateman, C. 1988. *The Sexual Contract*. Cambridge: Polity.
Perelman, C. and Olbrechts-Tyteca, L. 1969. *The New Rhetoric: A Treatise on Argumentation*. Indiana: University of Notre Dame.
Phillips, K.R. 1996. 'The Spaces of Public Dissension: Reconsidering the Public Sphere', *Communication Monographs*, vol. 63 (September): 231–48.
Phillips, K.R. 2006. 'Rhetorical Maneuvers: Subjectivity, Power, and Resistance', *Philosophy and Rhetoric*, vol. 39, no. 4: 310–32.
Pirie, M. 2006. *How to Win Every Argument: The Use and Abuse of Logic*. London: Continuum.
Plato. 1987. *The Republic*. D. Lee (trans). London: Penguin.
Plato. 2005. *Phaedrus*. C. Rowe (trans). London: Penguin.
Plato. 2010. *Gorgias*, in *Gorgias, Menexenus, Protagora*. M. Schofield (ed) and T. Griffith (trans). Cambridge: Cambridge University Press.
Popper, K.R. 1966. *The Open Society and Its Enemies. Vol I The Spell of Plato*. Princeton, NJ: Princeton University Press.
Postman, N. 2005. *Amusing Ourselves to Death: Public Discourse in the Age of Showbusiness*, New edn. London: Penguin.
Poulakos, T. 1997. *Speaking for the Polis: Isocrates' Rhetorical Education*. Columbia, South Carolina: University of South Carolina Press.
Powell, E. 1968. 'I Seem to See "the River Tiber Foaming With Much Blood"', in B. MacArthur (ed), 1999. *The Penguin Book of Twentieth-Century Speeches*. London: Penguin, 383–92.
Poynton, C. and Lee, A. 2011. 'Affect-ing discourse: towards an embodied discourse analytics', *Social Semiotics*, vol. 21, no. 5: 633–44.
Prokhovnik, R. 2002. *Rational Woman: A Feminist Critique of Dichotomy*, 2nd edn. Manchester: Manchester University Press.
Protevi, J. 2009. *Political Affect: Connecting the Social and the Somatic*. Minneapolis: University of Minnesota Press.

Quintilian. 2002. *The Orator's Education*, 5 vols. D. Russell (trans). Cambridge, MA: Harvard University Press.
Rancière, J. 1999. *Dis-agreement: Politics and Philosophy*. J. Rose (trans). Minnesota: University of Minnesota Press.
Rawls, J. 1999. *A Theory of Justice*. Rev. edn. Cambridge, MA: Harvard University Press.
Rawls, J. 2005. *Political Liberalism*. New York: Columbia University Press.
Redfield, M. 2009. *The Rhetoric of Terror: Reflections on 9/11 and the War on Terror*. New York: Fordham University Press.
Reynolds, J.F. (ed). 1993. *Rhetorical Memory and Delivery: Classical Concepts for Contemporary Composition and Communication*. London: Routledge.
Richards, J. 2008. *Rhetoric*. London: Routledge.
Riker, W.H. 1996. *The Strategy of Rhetoric: Campaigning for the American Constitution*. Yale: Yale University Press.
Rorty, R. 1989. *Contingency, Irony, and Solidarity*. Cambridge: Cambridge University Press.
Rorty, R. 1999. *Philosophy and Social Hope*. London: Penguin.
Rousseau, J.-J. 1968. *The Social Contract*. M. Cranston (ed). London: Penguin.
Rowland, R.C. 2002. *Analyzing Rhetoric: A Handbook for the Informed Citizen in a New Millennium*, 2nd edn. Dubuque, Iowa: Kendall/Hunt.
Rustin, M. 2009. 'The Missing Dimension: Emotions in the Social Sciences', in S.D. Sclater, D.W. Jones, H. Price and C. Yates (eds), *Emotion: New Psychosocial Perspectives*. Basingstoke: Palgrave Macmillan, 19–35.
Rutherford, J. 1997. *Forever England: Reflections on Masculinity and Empire*. London: Lawrence & Wishart.
Safire, W. (ed). 2004. *Lend Me Your Ears: Great Speeches in History*. London: Norton.
Saward, M. 2010. *The Representative Claim*. Oxford: Oxford University Press.
Scannell, P. 1996. *Radio, Television and Modern Life*. Oxford: Blackwell.
Schmidt, V.A. 2008. 'Discursive Institutionalism: The Explanatory Power of Ideas', *Annual Review of Political Science*, vol. 11, no. 1: 303–26.
Schmidt, V.A. 2010. 'Taking Ideas and Discourse Seriously: Explaining Change Through Discursive Institutionalism as the Fourth "New Institutionalism"', *European Political Science Review*, vol. 2, no. 1: 1–25.
Schumpeter, J.A. 1954. *Capitalism, Socialism and Democracy*. London: Allen and Unwin.
Scott, R.L. 1997. 'Cold War and Rhetoric: Conceptually and Critically', in M.J. Medhurst, R.L. Ivie, P. Wander and R.L. Scott (eds), *Cold War Rhetoric: Strategy, Metaphor and Ideology*. Michigan: Michigan State University Press, 19–28.
Sellnow, D.D. 2010. *The Rhetorical Power of Popular Culture: Considering Mediated Texts*. London: Sage.
Shaw, S. 2006. 'Governed by the Rules: The Female Voice in Parliamentary Debates', in J. Baxter (ed), *Speaking Out: The Female Voice in Public Contexts*. Basingstoke: Palgrave Macmillan, 81–101.
Shirlow, P. and McGovern, M. 1998. 'Language, Discourse and Dialogue: Sinn Fein and the Irish Peace Process', *Political Geography*, vol. 17, no. 2: 171–86.
Skinner, Q. 1978. *The Foundations of Modern Political Thought, Vol. 1: The Renaissance*. Cambridge: Cambridge University Press.
Skinner, Q. 1989. 'The State' in T. Ball, J. Farr and R.L. Hanson (eds), *Political Innovation and Conceptual Change*. Cambridge: Cambridge University Press, 90–131.
Skinner, Q. 2002a. *Visions of Politics, Vol. I Regarding Method*. Cambridge: Cambridge University Press.

Bibliography

Skinner, Q. 2002b. *Visions of Politics, Vol. II Renaissance Virtues*. Cambridge: Cambridge University Press.

Skinner, Q. 2002c. *Visions of Politics, Vol. III Hobbes and Civil Science*. Cambridge: Cambridge University Press.

de Sousa, R. 1987. *The Rationality of Emotion*. Cambridge, MA: MIT Press.

Sparks, C. and Tulloch, J. (eds). 2000. *Tabloid Tales: Global Debates Over Media Standards*. Oxford: Rowman & Littlefield.

Spence, S. 2007. *Figuratively Speaking: Rhetoric and Culture from Quintilian to the Twin Towers*. London: Duckworth.

Squires, J. 1999. *Gender in Political Theory*. Cambridge: Polity.

Street, J. 2001. *Mass Media, Politics and Democracy*. Basingstoke: Palgrave Macmillan.

Street, J. 2003. 'The Celebrity Politician: Political Style and Popular Culture', in D. Pels and J. Corner (eds), *Media and the Restyling of Politics: Consumerism, Celebrity and Cynicism*. London: Sage, 85–91.

Street, J. 2004. 'Celebrity Politicians: Popular Culture and Political Representation', *British Journal of Politics and International Relations*, vol. 6: 435–52.

Talbot, M. 2007. *Media Discourse: Representation and Interaction*. Edinburgh; Edinburgh University Press.

Talbot, M. 2010. *Language and Gender*, 2nd edn. Cambridge: Polity.

Taylor, C. 1985a. *Human Agency and Language: Philosophical Papers 1*. Cambridge: Cambridge University Press.

Taylor, C. 1985b. *Philosophy and the Human Sciences: Philosophical Papers 2*. Cambridge: Cambridge University Press.

Taylor, P.M. 1998. *War and the Media: Propaganda and Persuasion in the Gulf War*, 2nd edn. Manchester: Manchester University Press.

Thatcher, M. 1975. 'Let Me Give You My Vision', in B. MacArthur (ed). 1999. *The Penguin Book of Twentieth-Century Speeches*. London: Penguin, 409–13.

Thatcher, M. 1982. 'The Falklands Factor', in B. MacArthur (ed). 1999. *The Penguin Book of Twentieth-Century Speeches*. London: Penguin, 434–36.

Thatcher, M. 1988. 'The Frontiers of the State', in B. MacArthur (ed). 1999. *The Penguin Book of Twentieth-Century Speeches*. London: Penguin, 464–68.

Thomas, C.G. and Webb, E.K. 1994. 'From Orality to Rhetoric: An Intellectual Transformation', in I. Worthington (ed), *Persuasion: Greek Rhetoric in Action*. London: Routledge, 3–25.

Thompson, J.B. 1995. *The Media and Modernity: A Social Theory of the Media*. Cambridge: Polity.

Thompson, J.B. 2000. *Political Scandal: Power and Visibility in the Media Age*. Cambridge: Polity.

Thrift, N. 2007. *Non-Representational Theory: Space, Politics, Affect*. London: Routledge.

Thucydides. 1954. *The Peloponnesian War*. R. Warner (trans). London: Penguin.

Thussu, D.K. and Freedman, D. (eds). 2003. *War and the Media: Reporting Conflict 24/7*. London: Sage.

Tindale, C.W. 2004. *Rhetorical Argumentation: Principles of Theory and Practice*. London: Sage.

Tofel, R.J. 2005. *Sounding the Trumpet: The Making of John F. Kennedy's Inaugural Address*. Chicago: Ivan R. Dee.

Toulmin, S.E. 2003. *The Uses of Argument*, updated edn. Cambridge: Cambridge University Press.

Tulis, J.K. 1987. *The Rhetorical Presidency*. Princeton, NJ: Princeton University Press.
Turnbull, N. 2007. 'Problematology and Contingency in the Social Sciences', *Revue Internationale de Philosophie*, vol. 61, no. 4: 451–72.
Turner, G. 2011. *What's Become of Cultural Studies?* London: Sage.
Uhlmann, A.J. and Uhlmann, J.R. 2005. 'Embodiment Below Discourse: The Internalized Domination of the Masculine Perspective', *Women's Studies International Forum*, vol. 28: 93–103.
Vattimo, G. 2004. *Nihilism and Emancipation: Ethics, Politics and Law*. New York: Columbia University Press.
Vatz, R.E. 1973. 'The Myth of the Rhetorical Situation', *Philosophy and Rhetoric*, vol. 6, no. 3: 154–61.
Vickers, B. 1988. *In Defence of Rhetoric*. Oxford: Clarendon.
Wahl-Jorgensen, K. 2001. 'Letters to the Editor as a Forum for Public Deliberation: Modes of Publicity and Democratic Debate', *Critical Studies in Media Communication*, vol. 18, no. 3: 303–20.
Walker, M. 1993. *The Cold War and the Making of the Modern World*. London: Vintage.
Warner, M. 2002. 'Publics and Counter Publics', *Quarterly Journal of Speech*, vol. 88, no. 4: 413–25.
Warren, M. 2002. 'Deliberative Democracy', in A. Carter and G. Stokes (eds), *Democratic Theory Today: Challenges for the 21st Century*. Cambridge: Polity, 173–202.
Weiler, M. 1993. 'Ideology, Rhetoric and Argument', *Informal Logic*, vol. 15, no. 1: 15–28.
Westen, D. 2007. *The Political Brain: The Role of Emotion in Deciding the Fate of the Nation*. New York: Public Affairs.
Weston, A. 2000. *A Rulebook for Arguments*, 3rd edn. Indianapolis, IN: Hackett.
Whelehan, I. 1995. *Modern Feminist Thought: From the Second Wave to 'Post-Feminism'*. Edinburgh: Edinburgh University Press.
Williams, C. 2010. 'Affective Processes Without a Subject: Rethinking the Relation between Subjectivity and Affect with Spinoza', *Subjectivity*, vol. 3, no. 3: 245–62.
Wodak, R. 2011. *The Discourse of Politics in Action*, 2nd edn. Basingstoke: Palgrave.
Wollstonecraft, M. 2008. *A Vindication of the Rights of Woman* and *A Vindication of the Rights of Men*. Oxford: Oxford University Press.
Worman, N. 2009. 'Fighting Words: Status, Stature, and Verbal Contest in Archaic Poetry', in E. Gunderson (ed), *The Cambridge Companion to Ancient Rhetoric*. Cambridge: Cambridge University Press, 27–42.
Worthington, I. (ed). 1994. *Persuasion: Greek Rhetoric in Action*. London: Routledge.
Yack, B. 2006. 'Rhetoric and Public Reasoning: An Aristotelian Understanding of Political Deliberation', *Political Theory*, vol. 34, no. 4: 417–38.
Young, I.M. 2000. *Inclusion and Democracy*. Oxford: Oxford University Press.
Young, I.M. 2005. *On Female Bodily Experience. "Throwing Like a Girl" and Other Essays*. Oxford: Oxford University Press.
Yuval-Davis, N. 1997. *Gender and Nation*. London: Sage.
Žižek, S. 1989. *The Sublime Object of Ideology*. London: Verso.
Žižek, S. 2008a. *Violence: Six Sideways Reflections*. London: Profile.
Žižek, S. 2008b. *For They Know Not What They Do: Enjoyment as a Political Factor*, 2nd edn. London: Verso.

Index

Ahmed, S. 119
Al-Jazeera 144
Al Qaeda 144
Allen, R.C. 137–8
Amossy, R. 58, 71
anadiplosis 76
analogy 78–9, 80
anaphora 75
anastrophe 76
Anderson, B. 132
anecdote 77, 134, 162
Ankersmit, F. 41–2, 44, 47, 136
antimetabole 76; in JFK speech 104–5
antithesis 76
aphorism 61, 74, 79, 104
appeal: to ethos 57–8, 63–4, 68, 71, 72, 83, 93, 103, 111, 122, 128, 136, 141, 143, 147, 165; to logos 57–62, 68, 93, 103, 111, 128, 143, 147; to pathos 57–8, 63, 64–5, 68, 71, 72, 83, 93, 111, 122, 128, 136, 143, 147
Arab Spring 5–6, 145, 146
Arendt, H. 35, 38
argument: *see* discovery (*inventio*)
Aristotle 12, 15–16, 26, 52, 53, 59, 88, 93, 148; on citizenship 35; on emotions 113; on rhetoric 21–4; on syllogism and enthymeme 60–1
arrangement (*dispositio*) 13, 51, 52, 65–9, 70, 87, 103; in TV news 139–40, 142
asyndeton 76
Atkinson, M. 77
Austin, J.L. 10, 85

Ball, T. 28
BBC (British Broadcasting Corporation) 107, 129
Beaverbrook, Lord W.M.A. 129
behaviouralism 90–1

Berlusconi, S. 135–6
Bernstein, C. 128
Bevin, A. 84
Bevir, M. 92, 93
Bhutto, B. 150
Billig, M. 92–3
Bitzer, L.F. 95, 139
Blair, T. (UK Prime Minister) 57, 76, 85, 100; on Britishness 164–6; on Diana, Princess of Wales 122
body 84–5, 94, 121, 123, 148–66, 169
Brody, M 150
Brown, G. 74
Burke, K. 3, 4, 6, 57
Burke, R.J. 45
Bush, G.H.W. (US President) 75
Bush, G.W. (US President) 72, 80, 93, 112
Butler, J.: on mourning 118–19; on performativity 85–7

capitalism 37, 46, 98, 146
catachresis 82
Cavarero, A. 20
Cavell, M. 117–18
celebrity 87, 128, 135–6, 147
Chamberlain, N. 6–7
Chambers, S. 10
Chodorow, N. 157, 158
Churchill, W. 3, 74, 84, 94, 164; 'Blood, Toil' speech 75, 77
Cicero, M.T. 26, 34, 148; on delivery 83; on eloquent speech 64–5; on rhetoric 24–5; on status theory 56; war speeches 6–7, 86;
citizens: ancient 15, 16–18, 33, 34–6, 39–40, 50, 149–50; and Aristotle 22–3, 24, 148; and Cicero 25, 34; and contemporary political philosophy 43–50; and deliberation 13, 44–5, 46–7, 49, 108–10, 113, 124, 133;

and feminism 154–60; and gender 149–54; and Hobbes 27, 28; and media 128, 130–6, 144–6; and Plato 20; and Renaissance politics 25–6, 28; and representation 33–4, 38–43; and Rousseau 29–31; and the political 5, 33, 41, 42, 50; modern 13, 33–4, 36–8, 40–1, 50, 82, 150; rhetoric as tool for 12
cliché 74
Clinton, B. (US President) 122
Clinton, H. 85
Cold War 101–3, 105, 129
common sense 62, 73, 74, 98, 120
communitarianism 43
conclusion (*peroratio*) 66, 68–9
confirmatio 66, 67–8, 69; *see also* proof
Connolly, W.E. 116–17, 121, 124
consensus: and democratic theory 113, 120, 125; and liberalism 45; and rhetorical dispute 6, 24, 79, 107; media manufactured 129; post-war British 162, 163; rational 46–7
Conservative Party (UK) 80–1, 91, 136, 162, 163, 164
Consigny, S. 95–6
Constant, B. 37
Corax 16
critical theory 43, 45–7, 49–50; *see also* Habermas

Damasio, A. 114
Darwin, C. 59–60
Dawkins, R. 59–60
Dean, J. 146
Declaration of Independence (US) 112
decorum 55, 100, 103
De Gaulle, C. 99
deliberation: and Aristotle 23–4, 113, 148; and citizen participation 13, 38; and contract theory 26–7, 28, 30, 31; and democracy 108–13, 124–5; and discourse ethics 47, 49–50; and emotion 114–16, 124–6; and gender 148, 156, 166; and logos 58, 62; and media 130, 132, 133, 136, 142, 143, 146; and occasions of speech 52–3, 54, 85; and Plato 20; and Renaissance politics 26; and spaces of dialogue 54, 89, 166; and the political 41; and thinking 92
delivery (*pronuntiato*) 9, 13, 51, 52, 65, 70, 71, 83–7, 93, 100, 101, 103, 122; and gender 153; in TV news 141–2

democracy 3, 13, 21, 39, 72, 82, 84, 88, 107–26, 146, 169; and gender 150–2; aggregative model of 109; deliberative theory of 13, 47, 108–13, 124–5, 133; in ancient Greece 15–18, 40; radical theory of 49, 117, 120; rhetorical 124–5
Democratic Party (US) 116, 134
Demosthenes 16
Derrida, J. 48
Descartes, R. 114
dialectical analysis 89, 97–9, 106
Diana, Princess of Wales 122
discourse: concept of 11–12; embodied 153, 160; ethics 46–7, 110; Foucault's theory of 11, 48; moral 46; media 127, 137–43, 147; rhetorical approach to 11–12, 91–4, 100
discovery (*inventio*) 13, 51, 52, 57–65, 68, 70, 73, 87; in TV news 138–9, 142
Downs, A. 89–90
Dryzek, J. 111, 112

Eisenhower, D.D. 102
emotion 65, 72, 83; 107–26, 169; and deliberative democracy 111–13, 121; and gender 148; and neuroscience 114–17; and psychoanalysis 117–20; *see also* appeal to pathos
empty signifiers 82
Enlightenment 150
enthymeme 60–1, 98; *see also* Aristotle
epanalepsis 76
epistrophe 75–6, 76–7
epithet 74, 134, 163
European Union 79, 164
exigence 95, 96, 99, 100; in JFK's speech 102; in TV news 139

Facebook 145
Falkland Islands 164
family: and ethos 63; and gender 157; and nation 160, 161, 163, 164, 165; as an analogy 9; as a metaphor in US politics 116, 154; as a symbol 122, 153; debates on 82, 159
fantasy 119, 122, 153, 163
feminism 149, 154–60, 166
figures of speech 75–83, 93, 160; *see also* metaphor
Finlayson, A. 92–3
Foot, M. 84
Foucault, M. 11, 48, 123
Freeden, M. 41
Freud, S. 117

186 *Index*

Garibaldi, G. 74
Garsten, B. 30–1, 32, 124
gender 11, 12, 14, 45, 85–7, 148–166, 169; and sex 151, 155
genres of arrangement 69
genres of speech 52–5, 100, 142–3; *see also* occasions of speech
Gettysburg Address 74
Ghandi, I. 150
Gilligan, C. 157–8
Goebbels, J. 129
Goodin, B. 109
Gorgias 16, 19
Gramsci, A. 7, 62
Greece (ancient) 8, 15, 34–5, 40, 53, 82
Griffin, N. 107, 120
Guttman, A. 110

Habermas, J.: on discourse ethics 45–7, 50, 110, 111; on the public sphere 133
Hartley, J. 131
hate speech 121
Hay, C. 98
Higgins, M. 129, 142
Hitler, A. 6, 78, 84
Hobbes, T. 16, 31, 32, 45, 80; on rhetoric 26–9, 81
Homer 150
Hume, D. 37, 38
hyperbole 81, 132

ideas 10, 89–94, 98, 106
ideology 10–11, 12, 40–1, 58–9, 92–3, 106, 119, 137, 161, 163
immigration 81, 107, 162
inaugural address (US) 53, 69; JFK's 76, 89, 101–2, 103, 105, 106
inductive and deductive reasoning 59
International Court of Justice 54
introduction (*exordium*) 66
invention (*inventio*): *see* discovery
Iraq war 54, 57, 166
irony 81, 84
Isocrates 16, 18, 34
issue, the 13, 35, 52, 55–7, 62, 66, 70, 81, 83, 88, 96, 98, 130; *see also* stasis

Jamieson, K.H. 132–3
Jessop, B. 98
Jesus 76
Johnson, B. 136
Julius Caesar 76

kairos 35–6, 52, 95; *see also* time
Keating, P. 74
Kennedy, J.F. (US President) 76, 85, 89; inaugural speech analysis 101–6
King, Rev. M.L. 3, 93, 112
Kinnock, N. 77
Khruschev, N. 105
Kozloff, S. 140

Labour Party (UK) 77, 81, 91, 134, 164–5; *see also* New Labour
Laclau, E. 39, 82
Lakoff, G. 116, 124, 154
language: and affective unconscious 116; and gender 154–5; and human nature 28; and media 140–1; and politicians 134; and postmodernism 47–50; and rhetoric 9–10, 12, 93–4, 124, 169; and style (*elocutio*) 72–83, 140; and violence 6; constructivist idea of 9; denotative and connotative aspects 73, 75; instrumental idea of 72–3
Lefort, C. 39
Levenson Enquiry 128
lexicon 65
liberalism 10, 28, 40, 43–5, 49, 75, 114; and feminism 152, 155–6; and modern citizenship 36–8
Lincoln, A. (US President) 74, 76–7, 94
linguistics 11, 93–4, 106, 169
Locke, J. 43
Lyotard, J.-F. 47

Machiavelli, N. 38, 88
Macmillan, H. 97
Marcus, G.E. 114–16, 120, 124
Marx, K. 36, 40
Marxism 43
media (mass) 13–14, 83, 87, 118, 127–47, 169; new 144–6; social 145–6
memory (*memoria*) 13, 51, 52
Merkel, A. 150
metaphor 27–8, 77–81, 116, 141, 154, 160, 162, 165
metonymy 79, 80
Meyer, T. 139, 140
Mill, J.S. 43
Mouffe, C. 120, 121, 124, 125
Mussolini, B. 84

narration (*narratio*) 66, 67, 69; in TV news 138–40
nation 11, 14, 31, 41, 80, 97, 98, 118–19, 122, 132, 149, 160–6

Nazis 6, 129
neuroscience 13, 65, 108, 113, 114–17, 118, 120, 121, 123, 125
New Labour 164–6; *see also* Labour Party (UK)
Nixon, R. (US President) 85, 102, 128
Northern Ireland Peace Process 82, 101, 110, 112
Norval, A. 125

Obama, B. (US President) 72, 121, 134, 136
occasions of speech 52–5, 56, 84–5, 94, 100
Occupy protests 146

Palestine–Israel conflict 79
Palonen, K. 8
paradiastole 81–2
parallelism 76
parts of speech: *see* arrangement
pathos 31
performativity 85–7
Pericles 17
platitude 74
Plato 12, 15, 16, 23, 24, 29, 32, 40, 45, 88; on rhetoric 18–21
political marketing 121, 123, 134–5, 147
political science 1, 13, 89; interpretive approach 89, 91–2
political, dimension of the 2, 4, 9, 21; and democracy 124, 125; and gender 86, 148, 151, 152–3, 160; and modern society 33, 34, 38, 41, 45, 50; and politics 3–7, 13, 15, 34, 51, 88, 107, 113, 168; and rhetorical delivery 86
Popper, K. 20
postmodernism 43, 47–50
Powell, E. 162, 166
power: and deliberation 113; and discourse 11; and gender 154–60; and rhetoric 2, 3–4, 7, 19, 128, 130; and sovereignty 26–9, 152; and modern state 38–40, 152; vs domination 48, 123–4
private: and gender 148, 149, 151–2, 157–8; and General Will in Rousseau 29–30; and the media 128–31, 142, 145; in ancient and modern citizenship 33, 35–8, 40, 42, 43–44, 50; realm 13; *see also* public
proof 67, 71; *see also* appeal
propaganda 3, 111, 121, 123, 129
Protagoras 16–17

psychoanalysis 13, 117–20, 121, 125
psychology: 8; cognitive 91, 92; women's 157
public: realm 128, 129–31, 136, 142, 143–7; sphere 131–6, 148–9, 151–3, 156, 157
puzzle–solution format 77

Queen Victoria 161
Quintilian 25, 34, 150

race 11, 45, 107, 158, 162, 166
Radio Free America 129
Rancière, J. 20, 24, 82
rational choice theory 89–90, 91
Rawls, J. 44–5, 46
Reagan, N. 72
Reagan, R. (US President) 72
refutation (*refutio*) 66, 68, 69
Renaissance 150
rhetoric: aesthetic dimension of 41–3; -al question 77, 141; -al situation 88, 94–7, 99, 105, 106, 121, 127, 128, 137, 153, 154, 169; and education 34; and gender 13, 85–7; and ideology 40–1; and other disciplines 7–8; and representation 34, 38–43; and sovereignty 26; canons of 13, 87, 138; ceremonial (*epideictic*) 23, 52–3, 54; counterpublic 143–6; definition of 2, 168–9; deliberative (political) 23, 53–4; forensic (legal) 23, 53; humanist 25–6; schemes 75–7, 82; tropes 75, 77–83; versus 'truth' 3, 12, 22, 31
Rhodes, R. 92, 93
Rome 8, 34–5; republic 24–5, 29
Rorty, R. 43
Rousseau 12, 16, 26, 148; on rhetoric 29–31
Rutherford, J. 161, 162

Sarkozy, N. 136
Schmidt, V. 92, 93
Schumpeter, J. 90
Skinner, Q. 38, 67, 81
simile 78
situation: *see* rhetorical situation
Socrates 18–19
sophists 15; and Aristotle 22; and Plato 18, 20; and rhetoric 16–18
soundbite 73–4, 87
sovereignty 4, 6, 16, 26–31, 36, 38, 74, 81, 152, 164

space: and time 9, 10, 12, 14, 35–6, 41, 52, 94–5, 98, 99, 106, 121, 123, 132, 168–9; in JFK speech 104–5; in TV news 137–8
Squires, J. 151, 155, 156
stance 56
stasis 35–6, 52, 95; *see also* status; *see also* space
state (modern) 26, 31, 36–7, 38, 40, 43, 50, 98, 152, 168; British 160–1, 163–4; *see also* sovereignty
State of the Union Address (US) 54
status 35–6, 42, 56–7; *see also* stasis
strategy 88, 94–9, 115, 128, 134, 142, 143; affective 120–4; feminist 155–60
Street, J. 135, 136
structure and agency 89, 97–99; *see also* dialectical analysis
style (*elocutio*) 13, 51, 52, 65, 70, 71, 72–83, 87; in JFK speech 103–4; in TV news 140–1, 142
syllogism 60–1; *see also* Aristotle
synecdoche 79–80, 80–81

Talbot, M. 138
Thatcher, M. (UK Prime Minister) 74–5, 77, 150; and Britishness 163–4, 166; and delivery 84, 151; and metaphor 79; and the epithet 74
Thatcherism 163
Thompson, D. 110
Thucydides 17

time: and space 9, 10, 12, 14, 35–6, 41, 52, 94–5, 98, 99, 106, 121, 123, 132, 168–9; in JFK speech 104–5
Tisias 16
tone 65
topics (*topoi*) 61, 96, 103
Toulmin, S. 61–2
tricolon 76–7
Twitter 145

universal and particular 10, 39–41, 43, 45, 49, 50, 145

Vatz, R.E. 95
Vickers, B. 17
violence 5–6, 108, 152
voice 84–5, 94; and gender 149–50, 166; in TV news 141

Warner, M. 131, 143
Warren, M. 109, 110
Westen, D. 116
Wollstonecraft, M. 156
Woodward, B. 128

Yack, B. 113
Young, I.M. 111–12
Youtube 145

Žižek, S. 6, 119